P9-AQA-314

AN ANTHROPOLOGICAL ANALYSIS OF FOOD-GETTING TECHNOLOGY

WENDELL H. OSWALT

With the assistance of

GLORIA MANN

and

LEONN SATTERTHWAIT

Illustrated by

PATRICK FINNERTY

A WILEY-INTERSCIENCE PUBLICATION

JOHN WILEY & SONS, New York · London · Sydney · Toronto

Also by Wendell H. Oswalt

Mission of Change in Alaska
Napaskiak: An Alaskan Eskimo Community
This Land Was Theirs
Alaskan Eskimos
Understanding Our Culture
Other Peoples, Other Customs
Habitat and Technology

Library of Congress Cataloging in Publication Data:

Oswalt, Wendell H
    An anthropological analysis of food-getting technology.

    "A Wiley-Interscience publication."
    Bibliography: p.
    Includes index.

    1. Technological complexity. 2. Hunting, Primitive.
3. Agriculture, Primitive. I. Title. II. Title:
Food-getting technology.

GN407.085   301.2'1   76-17640
ISBN 0-471-65729-8

Printed in the United States of America

10 9 8 7 6 5 4 3 2 1

PREFACE

Technology, material culture, and artifacts are unexciting words, yet the ideas for which they stand are of immeasurable importance in the lives of all peoples—in the past, in the present, and presumably in any future that we may conceive. These key words most often evoke thoughts about the mundane or the highly technical. From another perspective technological achievements may be seen as responsible for many of our ills, and yet it is reasonable to assume that today's technology is underdeveloped in terms of our future needs and desires. Where we have been, what we are, and where we may be going are at least partially embodied in those things that we make and call artifacts.

Technology casts such a long shadow over all we do that we cannot begin to imagine living without its products. The ability of people to fashion materials into standardized forms has made it possible for human populations to occupy nearly all of the earth as well as to probe beneath and beyond its surface. The elaboration of skills and the expansion of knowledge required to produce artifacts are undeniably among the most remarkable of all human developments even though we may deplore some of the productions. Distrust of our material heritage exists, at least in part, because we seldom—if ever—attempt to understand how our artifacts came to be what they are or what future forms and purposes they may assume. An orderly approach to the things that people have made would serve us well, for only then could we begin to appreciate what technology has done for us, as well as to us, within the sweep of time. It would be unfair for me to imply that I can offer a key to what the future holds, but I do hope to impart greater understanding about the future of technology through an analysis of past achievements.

This book is an anthropological analysis of technology from its hypothesized beginnings. One primary goal is to offer a means for measuring the complexity of manufactures made by *any* people, which in turn makes it theoretically possible to assess and compare changes in material culture through *all* of human time. Why involve ourselves with such concerns? Let me state the reasons in brief.

All people use objects that they have made. Thus the production of artifacts characterizes every human society and serves as a crucial means of distinguishing people from nearly all other creatures.

Of all the information about the pasts of people we have far more data about technology than about any other quality of their culture. Thus, in any attempt to plot changing human lifeways through time, technology serves as a most useful guide.

It is accepted as beyond reputable dispute that changes in manufactures are cumulative on a long-range and broad-scale basis. Thus for the study of evolution in culture, technology is the most amenable dimension.

All the things that we make today are based on knowledge derived from past achievements. Thus we will not, in fact cannot, produce anything in the immediate future that is not derived from an existing part of our present technological knowledge. It is the technology of the remote and recent past that in a very real sense has led to the artifacts that we now make, and past achievements serve as the essential substratum for the inventions of tomorrow.

Whether we like it or not, technology is increasing in importance on a day-to-day basis. We might rejoice in this because it indicates growing human control over the natural world. If, however, one considers this disturbing, one might be well advised to at least "know the enemy."

All people make objects in order to obtain food. Thus what we eat and how we acquire it are dependent on our technology. The availability of eatables more than anything else establishes the standard of living for a society, and as a result the artifacts devoted to food production may be considered the most critical manufactures in any people's inventory.

In sum the thrust of this book is as follows: All people make things in order to live as humans, and the forms produced have changed through time in an orderly manner. It is worthwhile to analyze these changes so that we may better comprehend the nature of our material past, present, and future.

WENDELL H. OSWALT

University of California
Los Angeles
March 1976

ACKNOWLEDGMENTS

I am very grateful to Jane C. Goodale, Leopold Pospisil, and Thayer Scudder for information based on their field studies. Detailed information about modern planting equipment was kindly made available by Alvin F. Aggen, Marion Amescua, and Bill Schreiner. The frontispiece is adapted from illustrations provided by the Pitt Rivers Museum, Oxford, England.

Special recognition is due to Leonn Satterthwait for his original and insightful contributions to understanding the ecological adaptations of food-getting technology. Once again I am exceedingly grateful to Helen Taylor Oswalt as a helpful critic and copy editor.

W. H. O.

CONTENTS

028816

FIGURES

TABLES

▲▲▲▲▲▲▲▲

AN
ANTHROPOLOGICAL
ANALYSIS
OF FOOD-GETTING
TECHNOLOGY

INTRODUCTION

The central goal of this book is an assessment of technological complexity offered within an integrated framework. As the ideas of one chapter lead to those of the next, there are few opportunities to offer asides and background information, especially since I have a distaste for footnotes. Yet it is desirable, perhaps even essential, to set forth in brief the base from which this study has emerged. Thus the pages to follow are introductory in a strict sense. Since technology is the topic of central concern, my first goal is to set forth a concept of culture which emphasizes the things that people make. My second purpose is to summarize briefly the anthropological background from which my approach to the study of material culture has arisen. A third purpose is to identify the data base around which the core chapters are developed.

The anthropological concept of "culture" has existed for about 130 years and is widely accepted. Yet the term has been defined in so many diverse ways that I must state precisely how it will be used in this study. Most definitions emphasize that culture involves learned, shared behavior, and the specifics sometimes are cited. The classic definition by Edward B. Tylor (1871, 1) serves as an example: "Culture or Civilization ... is that complex whole which includes knowledge, belief, art, morals, law, custom, and any other capabilities

1

and habits acquired by man as a member of society." Other definitions stress the historical dimensions, normative rules, organization, or symbolic nature of culture. Anyone interested in a far greater understanding of the ways in which culture has been defined should consult the books by Roy Wagner (1975) or Alfred L. Kroeber and Clyde Kluckhohn (1963) that are devoted to the subject.

In this book the theoretical position and definition of culture set forth by Cornelius Osgood are accepted (1951; *see also* Osgood, 1940, 25–9; 1958, 21–2; 1959, 13–9). He emphasized that sociocultural anthropologists are concerned with empirical (perceived) and nonempirical (conceived) data about different peoples; thus the subject matter of anthropology derives from both the sciences and the arts. Empirical data may be validated, but that pertaining to the arts may not, which poses a very real epistemological problem when information about exotic societies is assembled. Manufactures such as boats, hairnets, and knives may be seen and described by one or more observers, and these accounts are subject to verification by others. Osgood suggests that perceivable qualities be termed *percepta*. Museums are filled with percepta called artifacts; they are static, at equilibrium, and may be grouped under the broader heading of material culture. Percepta also include speech and actions that are social in nature; words and sentences, a mother-in-law taboo, a gesture expressing fearfulness, or a man's typical behavior toward a son are examples. Here we have vocal or visible action by individuals, and the occurrence may be verified, although not in the same way as that of material forms since the situations and responses of social percepta never reoccur in an identical manner. Social and material percepta are joined when people make and use artifacts, and this combination is termed *techniculture*. In addition to the social and material percepta of a people there occur *concepta*, or ideas as objects of thought. Included are religion without its social involvements or equipment; philosophy and mythology; thoughts about beauty, evil, good, and truth; speculation about people and the universe, and any other ideas of a similar nature. Concepta are expressed as social percepta through words. Concepta encompass the humanistic realm of thought which cannot be verified by empirical means but requires logical validation. Thus culture is comprised of percepta and concepta, nothing more nor less.

In terms of a formal definition, "Culture consists of all ideas of the manufactures, behavior, and ideas of the aggregate of human beings which have been directly observed or communicated to one's mind and of which one is conscious" (Osgood, 1951, 208). Repetition of the word "ideas" in this definition is critical to Osgood's meaning. The first use of *ideas* refers to the observer's or ego's concept of the manufactures and behavior he perceives; the second refers to the informant's ideas. Thus a clear distinction is drawn between what the anthropologist interprets a culture to be and the ideas of the people involved. An "aggregate of human beings" is the carrying unit or social milieu, and one is distinguished from another when its lifeway is significantly different. The words "which have been directly observed or communicated" refer to that which is seen or expressed by word or action and convey the requirement that culture must be learned or acquired. "One's mind" refers to the mind of the recorder or observer, and "of which one is conscious" conveys the quality of personal awareness. Above all, Osgood felt that an ethnographer should attempt to determine the ideas of informants and convey these as accurately as possible.

This definition of culture seems superior to all others because it balances the empirical and nonempirical qualities of human life-styles. It stresses that culture is more than anything else a mental construct on the part of the observer and thus exists in one's mind as an approach to what is conceived and perceived. Culture is reflected in thoughts, behavior, and things in equal but clearly distinct terms. Osgood is not alone in stressing "ideas" as the most critical quality of culture. Clark Wissler (1916, 197) wrote that "a culture is a definite association complex of ideas." Kluckhohn and William H. Kelly (1945, 97) characterized culture as "a summation of all the ideas for standardized types of behavior." One other definition in the same vein, by Walter W. Taylor (1948, 109–10), deserves inclusion. "By culture as a descriptive concept, I mean all those mental constructs or ideas which have been learned or created after birth by an individual. . . . The term *idea* includes such categories as attitudes, meanings, sentiments, feelings, values, goals, purposes, interests, knowledge, beliefs, relationships, [and] associations."

The thrust behind the definitions offered by Wissler, Osgood, Taylor, and Kluckhohn and Kelly is that culture is a configuration of ideas in the minds of performers conveyed to the minds of observers. This concept of culture contrasts with the materialist's view that cultural forms are external to anyone's mind. Specialists in the study of material culture as well as many other anthropologists often are content with the materialist's approach. An arrowhead dug from the ground, a boat drawn up on a beach, a ceremony performed, or a childrearing practice all are manifestations of culture to the materialist. Even those ceremonies of a people that have been unseen by observers are to materialists a part of their culture, and the same is true of artifacts yet unfound in a ruin. Other anthropologists maintain that we cannot know that which we must presume.

In sum, manufactures comprise *material culture*, and an *artifact* is a specific in this context. Behavior is considered *social culture*, and its artifactual analogue is a *sociofact*. Ideas are *mental culture*, with each intangible specific an *ideofact*. These then are the dimensions of culture and the "facts" on which it is based.

▲▲▲

As cabinets of curiosities in libraries gave way to showcases in museums, the organization of large and varied collections of artifacts for display became a major concern. One difficulty was that curators had no realistic ideas about the comparative ages of most antiquities, and often they could not identify the makers. It first became apparent to Scandinavian scholars that they must probe behind written history, through archaeology, to plot chronological developments. At this point in time evolutionary studies of technology began to emerge. Christian J. Thomsen (1788–1865), the first curator of what was to become the Danish National Museum, conceived a series of exhibits designed to mirror technological stages in Danish prehistory. In 1818–20 he arranged displays to represent what he thought to be successive prehistoric ages. The key to the classification was the materials used to make implements and weapons. He reasoned that the sequence was from stone to bronze and then to productions in iron. Although the idea of three stages of technological growth had prevailed earlier among Greek scholars, Thomsen appears to have been the first to apply it to the organization of artifacts, and his display sequence soon became widely accepted. Thomsen's developmental approach to material culture predates the contributions of Charles Darwin to biological evolution, Edward B. Tylor's study of progressive changes in religious life, and the evolutionary framework, identified by ethnical periods, advanced by Lewis H. Morgan. However neither Thomsen nor his immediate successors conceived of the classification in strictly evolutionary terms. For example, the presence in Denmark of artifacts made from bronze and later iron, showing an abrupt change in the use of materials, was attributed to invaders, not to local developments (Daniel, 1950, 38–54; Hermansen, 1941).

After the achievements of Thomsen and others have been acknowledged, attention next is called to a study by an English military officer, Augustus Henry Lane Fox (1827–1900), who by royal license changed his last name to Pitt-Rivers in 1880. Reasonably early in his career he was involved in experimental efforts to develop more effective service rifles, and he became impressed by the difference between short-term technological changes of no lasting

ur (1863–1939), curator of the Pitt Rivers Museum at Oxford from
is death, was among the most active supporters of the evolutionary
conceived by Lane Fox. The analysis of musical bows by Balfour
ifies the methodology. After studying ethnographic examples, he
that the musical bow developed from hunting bows, which occasion-
ed as musical instruments, and he found that in fact this practice
among some peoples. From this form emerged specialized musical
at later were held over a resonant chamber, such as a hollow gourd.
ext step was to attach a bow to a gourd, and still later multiple bows were
d to a single gourd. Such advances eventually led to the emergence of the
. In broad outline the Lane Fox approach to technological evolution was
pted by such notable anthropologists as Edward B. Tylor (1871, v. 1, 13–4,
9) in England and Otis T. Mason (1895) in the United States. These men,
e Balfour, were actually more interested in the cultural history of particular
rms than in perfecting an all-encompassing analytical framework for plotting
technological evolution. The method in its fullest development was applied
to changes in art styles, as typified by a book-length work on the subject by
Alfred C. Haddon (1895).

A basic presumption underlying the Lane Fox assessment of technological
change was that forms evolved as increasing numbers of *ideas* were being concentrated in the manufacture of an artifact type. New ideas most often were
attributed to accidents, such as a different quality of material or some un-
planned variability affecting production, but they also might have been
borrowed from another people or based on an amalgamation of concepts from
different peoples. It was recognized further that in widely separated areas similar
forms could have developed independently of one another (Lane Fox, 1906, 96,
139–40, 153). A second very explicit assumption was that all manufactures, rude
as well as complicated, represented a continuity with productions in the past.
The artifacts made by savage and barbaric peoples were thought to exemplify
arrested technological progress, and therefore studying these forms should
make it possible "to trace the succession of ideas" (Lane Fox, 1906, 3).

Tylor (1871, v. 1, 64–5) used the word *survival* as a generic term for an old
form lasting into modern times. A survival is the continuance of a custom
after the conditions that gave rise to it no longer prevail. Tylor cited numerous
examples, such as the bow and arrow becoming a child's toy, methods of
divination being used as modern games of chance, and proverbs, sayings, or
sneezing formulas continuing but with their original meaning lost. He noted
that an old woman who uses a hand loom long after the introduction of the
flying shuttle is "not a century behind her times, but she is a case of survival"

consequence and those that prove
deals primarily with the range and
rifles. Among the variables considered
and groove, and the quality of cartridg
slight changes in bullet design were critica.
of rifles. After noting that these steps led to
to arrange his extensive ethnographic collecti
to be developmental sequences. According t
Lane Fox was "the first man to study the mate
evolutionary fashion."

At the time Lane Fox (1875) was detailing an evolu
his collection, the theory of biological evolution al.
established. Diverse efforts were being made to apply
developments in terms of "progressive" changes from sin
from homogeneous to heterogeneous. His primary goal
"The object of an anthropological collection [is] to trace out,
only evidence available, the sequence of ideas by which mankir
from the condition of the lower animals to that in which we fi
present time, and by this means to provide really reliable materials
sophy of progress" (Lane Fox, 1875, 300). His classification was bas
hypothesis that the manufactures for primitive peoples reflected, in a
way, the productions of primeval men. He reasoned that natural forms
as prototypes for artifacts and that ideas embodied in the structure of art.
increased in complexity through time. Exhibits of artifacts from around
world were arranged primarily according to their form and use; bows, club,
and spears were grouped to illustrate developmental sequences from simpler
to more advanced forms. Subgroupings were arranged on the basis of geographical regions, and the diffusion of types was taken into consideration
whenever possible. Artifacts approaching the shapes of natural objects were
judged as the simplest, oldest, and most generalized. They evolved by gradual
and slight modifications into specialized, more recent, and complex forms.
His most rudimentary types were described as products of savage and barbaric
societies and the most complex forms as artifacts of technologically advanced
peoples. He felt that simpler forms represented technological continuity from
earlier times and that the manufactures of modern primitive peoples could,
in a general way, be used to reconstruct the technological pasts of societies
that are now more developed.

A small group of ethnographers accepted the approach of Lane Fox as a
valid means for establishing broad evolutionary sequences in technology.

6

Henry Balfo
1893 until h
taxonomy
(1899) typ
reasoned
ally ser
existed
bows t
The n
joine
harp
acc
58
li
f

(Tylor, 1871, v. 1, 15). While instances of survivals may not be significant in many contexts, they are extremely helpful in tracing evolutionary and historical changes. Tylor (1871, v. 1, 28) wrote, "The thesis which I venture to sustain, within limits, is simply this, that the savage state in some measure represents an early condition of mankind, out of which the higher culture has gradually been developed or evolved." Tylor (1871, v. 1, 58) cited the analysis of primitive weapons by Lane Fox to support his thesis with reference to technological change and briefly mentioned other examples, but he was most interested in demonstrating the emergence of religious systems through the study of survivals.

In an earlier work Tylor (1865, 236–59) had attempted to plot the development of fire-making devices from elementary to elaborate types by considering design and type distributions. He felt that it was reasonable to begin the series with the fire plow, which consists of a blunted stick rapidly run back and forth in the groove of another piece of wood. Next came the hand-propelled fire drill, which is a shaft of wood spun between the palms so that one end is rotated rapidly against a fireboard. It was succeeded by the strap drill made by wrapping a cord around a shaft, downward pressure being applied from a bearing at the upper end of the shaft; pulling one end of the cord and then the other caused sparks to be produced on a fireboard. A still more advanced form was produced by replacing the cord with a small bow, which provided a more efficient means for rotating the drill shaft. This sequence of artifacts for making fire, from the fire plow to the bow drill, was one of Tylor's most carefully plotted illustrations of technological evolution. When, as in his study of religion, diverse survivals were considered within a coherent analytical framework, we have the "comparative method" in ethnology. It is based on the proposition that the lifeways of contemporary aboriginal peoples resemble, to a greater or lesser degree, those of peoples from times long past and that the oldest customs or forms are the simplest.

The notable evolutionary classification conceived by Lewis H. Morgan (1818–81) was designed to trace diverse aspects of sociocultural change from the beginnings of human time. He employed the comparative method and plotted a sequence of developments leading from Savagery, to Barbarism, to Civilization. These "ethnical periods" and lesser stages were separated by a series of precise markers that included changes in family life, kinship terminologies, sociopolitical organization, and technology. Particular forms, such as the bow and arrow, iron tools, and pottery, were singled out as indicators of technological progress (Morgan, 1877, 3–18). It soon became apparent, however, that most of the markers identified were not as useful as Morgan had supposed. Yet this fact only partially detracts from the boldness of Morgan's integrated system for plotting sociocultural developments.

Ethnographic collections at the U.S. National Museum were arranged for exhibit with the aim of illustrating technological progress in an evolutionary manner. The individual most responsible for the plan was Otis T. Mason (1838–1908), who became curator of ethnology at the museum in 1884. Mason was the author of numerous detailed studies about particular artifact types, such as basketry, harpoons, and throwing-boards. His forte was classification, which is best presented in his book *The Origins of Invention* (1895). Whether discussing fire-making devices, tools, or weapons of war, he began by describing those forms that were most elementary or natural: fire generated by the friction of sticks, shells used for knives, or warfare as duels with or without weapons. Next were artifacts that were slight modifications of natural forms; then came more elaborate compound productions. At this point his evolutionary arrangements began to break down because of diversification of design and materials. The ordering became intuitive and impressionistic because there were no guiding principles for the consistent assessment of increasing technological complexity. Mason did not attempt a grand design for evolutionary changes in the manner of Lane Fox or Morgan.

As 1900 approached, studies concerning aboriginal technology on a generalizing, temporal basis declined abruptly in importance, especially in the United States. An evolutionary perspective was rejected by the most influential anthropologist, Franz Boas (1858–1942). In a well-known article published in 1896 he argued for detailed, parallel studies of different peoples within localized areas; conclusions were to be drawn after careful point by point consideration of data within a limited comparative framework. He was at least in part reacting against the grand designs of the evolutionists. The "historical method" emerged, to remain the dominant approach to ethnological studies until the 1930s. Under the direct or indirect influence of Boas, historical particularists assembled a great deal of ethnographic information about the manufactures of tribal peoples. The analysis of technology on a broad basis was not considered worthwhile, but surprisingly few detailed interpretive studies of limited scope were attempted. When the English anthropologist Alfred C. Haddon (1855–1940) published his *History of Anthropology* in 1910, only two of the 154 pages were devoted to technology. The pertinent pages dealt mainly with the contributions of Lane Fox and Mason and the evolution of art styles, a topic of special interest to Haddon.

The analysis of aboriginal material culture on a broadly integrative yet particularistic scale rarely has been attempted during this century. The rather vague and impressionistic classification of Lane Fox was pursued by Balfour but only with reference to particular forms; he never attempted a grand plan in the manner of Lane Fox. It was another Englishman, Herbert S. Harrison (1873–1958), a curator at the Horniman Museum, who most resolutely sought to establish an evolutionary framework based on the detailed analysis of particular forms in the study of material culture. In his most definitive statement Harrison (1930) attempted to adapt a biological model to the changes in material culture. He used such terms as primary, numerical, free, and cross "mutations" to cope with the minutiae of technological changes. The classification by Harrison represents a systematic effort to plot technological evolution by conceiving of all technological innovations within a single framework. He reasoned that people are unimaginative creatures and that truly independent inventions are rare. He admitted fully that he too was rather unimaginative and credited Lane Fox as being the first to realize the critical importance of small changes in the development of technological forms.

In one sense the *only* evolutionary classification for material culture to emphasize particulars within a grand design began and ended with the efforts of Lane Fox Pitt-Rivers. He alone analyzed diverse aboriginal artifacts from around the world and classified them into formal clusters according to an evolutionary system.

Archaeologists in general long have concerned themselves with technological changes through time, but because of the limitations of their data base, successes in their efforts to plot technological evolution have been less than glowing. The name of V. Gordon Childe stands out as singularly important in terms of sustaining an interest in and stressing the role of orderly changes in technology. We also must give lasting credit to Leslie A. White for his efforts to impress on forgetful generations of anthropologists that sociocultural evolution demands a dominant position in anthropological studies.

If technological evolution is to be measured effectively, we must build on the base provided by Lane Fox. It is his stress on *ideas*, particulars, order and progress, continuity in the development of types, and the use of ethnographic analogies that make his approach so compelling. Yet certain fundamental questions that were glossed over or ignored in his approach must be resolved. We first must establish precisely what is to be measured and then set forth a means for measurement. We must pay careful attention to particulars but never allow them to envelop us. We are obligated to be highly inductive without ever losing sight of our deductive purpose. We are compelled to seek the broadest and most meaningful stance by conceiving units for analysis that may be applied not only to the oldest manufactures of peoples but to those being made today and to be invented tomorrow.

After a specific conceptual approach to the study of technology has been introduced in the three chapters comprising Part 1, the data base is set forth in Parts 2 and 3. It consists of 1175 items of material culture used by the members of thirty-six select societies. In Part 2 each form is classified according to the most important way in which it was utilized to obtain food. The purpose is to identify structural styles of forms in terms of their number of parts. Part 3 is an analysis of the material inventories of the peoples sampled by geographical region and subsistence focus. Here the forms are evaluated and compared, and the inventories are ranked in terms of their overall complexity.

The information in Parts 2 and 3 is based exclusively on ethnographic reports for thirty-six societies that, in ideal terms, were using only aboriginal forms when described. The basic criterion for including a people was whether their material culture, and the ways in which forms were used, had been reported in adequate detail in a published account. Thus the sample is highly selective and nonrandom since completeness of the required information was the primary basis for inclusion. Two selected people may have lived near one another and shared close cultural ties or they may have had no historically recognized cultural bonds and been at opposite ends of the earth; other peoples represent points between these extremes. People were chosen secondarily on the basis of their technoeconomic adaptations. Representation was sought among gatherers, fishermen, and hunters as well as cultivators of root and cereal crops. People who were primarily pastoral were avoided, but animal husbandry did play an important part in the economies of some farmers considered. Finally, and of far less importance, selection was made on the basis of major geographical regions. Four peoples were selected to represent each major technoeconomic focus in each of the five principal geographical regions. Within a particular cluster, such as desert area foragers, the first group entered is the one with the lowest average number of parts per food-getting form, followed by peoples with increasingly higher averages. Those chosen and their relative positions are as follow:

Desert areas

Foragers

Surprise Valley Paiute, northwestern United States
Aranda, central Australia
Naron Bushmen, southern Africa
Owens Valley Paiute, western United States

Farmers

Pima, southwestern United States
Walapai, southwestern United States
Hopi, southwestern United States
Yuma, southwestern United States

Tropical areas

Foragers

Tiwi, northern Australia
Ingura, northern Australia
Chenchu, eastern India
Andamanese, Sea of Bengal

Root crop farmers

Jivaro, Ecuador
Trukese, Caroline Islands
Pukapuka, Pacific Ocean atoll
Kapauku, western New Guinea

Cereal crop farmers

Sema Naga, Assam and Burma
Akamba, Kenya
Tanala, Malagasy Republic
Gwembe Tonga, Zambia

Temperate areas

Foragers

Tasmanians, Tasmania
Klamath, northwestern United States
Yakutat Tlingit, southeastern Alaska
Twana, northwestern United States

Farmers

  Huron, western Ontario, Canada
  Aymara, southern Peru
  Ojibwa, northern Minnesota and adjacent southern Canada
  Lepcha, Sikkim

Subarctic areas

Foragers

  Caribou Eskimos, central Canada
  Nabesna, central Alaska
  Anvik-Shageluk Ingalik, western Alaska
  Tanaina, south-central Alaska

Arctic areas

Foragers

  Copper Eskimos, northwestern Canada
  Iglulik, central Canada
  Tareumiut, northern Alaska
  Angmagsalik, East Greenland

In terms of geographical representation, all four people in a cluster are sometimes drawn from a limited area. The most extreme case of proximity and relatedness is that of the desert farmers, all of whom lived in the southwestern United States. Their selection was more purposeful than fortuitous. In the search for desert farmers very few peoples were located who had well-described aboriginal technologies. Therefore it was decided to concentrate on those from one region. By restricting the sample to a limited area, it was hoped that the variability of food-getting forms on a localized basis could be gauged. Only Eskimos represent the arctic, and their populations were rather closely related in spite of the distances that separated them. Likewise three of the four groups of subarctic foragers were Athapaskans from Alaska, which partially, but only partially, was dictated by the availability of relevant data on their technologies. Additional peoples sampled also lived relatively near one another, such as the Huron and Ojibwa in North America; they were chosen in part because few aboriginal peoples who were temperate area farmers were described reasonably well. In essence *all* inventories are separate units since each people involved must have provided food effectively for its members and have had an economically adaptive inventory of material forms.

The original sample included forty-six peoples whose food-getting forms were analyzed, but this number was reduced to thirty-six after a preliminary evaluation of each. The discarded inventories, and the basis for their exclusions, are as follow: Seri and Polar Eskimos were eliminated because the adequacy of the aboriginal baseline data seemed questionable; the Yaqui were set aside because so many forms they used were of European derivation; the Pitapita and Yahgan were discarded because they had been included in a preliminary statement about technology (Oswalt, 1973), and they could be replaced by other peoples for whom the information was good and who were from similar geographical regions; the Chugach and Menomini data obviously were incomplete; the Naskapi were not included because the pertinent information was not available in time for inclusion in the sample; finally, information about the technology of the Siriono and Yagua is superior, but their slight dependence on domestic root crops made their economies unlike other root crop cultivators in the sample.

PART 1

▲▲▲▲▲▲▲

A TECHNOSYSTEM

▲▲▲▲▲▲▲▲

CHAPTER 1

NATUREFACTS
AND ARTIFACTS

The technological basis for much that is human is beyond dispute, and the ability of people to make highly diverse things clearly distinguishes them from all other creatures. Apparently it was in 1760 that Benjamin Franklin, with insight and parsimony, characterized man as "a tool-making animal" (Boswell, 1887, v. 3, 245), and this description remains eminently acceptable today. The dependence of people on the things that they make and use unifies all mankind, and material objects clearly are essential as an ongoing basis for human life. It is difficult if not impossible to envision all the technological forms that people have been making for millions of years, yet each patterned form is a human creation designed to serve a human purpose. My goal is to organize the products of technology into a system and to establish its order within well-defined parameters. An evolutionary perspective is implicit, but the primary purpose is to set forth a method of measurement designed to gauge technological complexity within a single framework for the manufactures of all peoples.

If the human condition began to emerge as our predecessors became the

makers of tools, we must somehow probe the background of this beginning
and at least speculatively consider what near-people were doing that might
have led to the origins of technology. Let us first consider the idea of a naturefact.

The word *naturefact* was coined to distinguish a cluster of forms that often
has been either ignored or defined so narrowly that its importance went
unappreciated (Oswalt, 1973, 14–7). Yet naturefacts serve as the logical basis
from which all man-made productions may have originated. Some forms that
I call naturefacts others have termed "improvised hand weapons," "ready-to-
hand tools and weapons" (Oakley, 1954, 12, 22), "nature-made objects ... as
rude implements" (Nelson, 1932, 111–2), or "instant tools" (Gould, 1969, 82).
Early in human times, when these forms presumably were of greatest importance, people are said to have been "tool-using" as opposed to "tool-making"
in a later period (Oakley, 1954, 14). It is helpful to form a more exact conception
of the objects that may represent the prototypes for all manufactures.

Naturefacts are natural forms, used in place or withdrawn from a habitat, that are used without
prior modification by creatures. Configurations in nature employed by species without
being moved or modified in any manner are *intact naturefacts.* To hide behind a
rock and wait for game to pass is to "use" the rock as a blind, whether the
hunter is a lion or a man. When wolves or men drive animals into a cul-de-sac,
this natural feature becomes a game trap. When a leopard stores a dead animal
in a tree to provide a later meal, the tree becomes a food cache. Driving game
off cliffs or into bogs is a similar usage. When a chimpanzee strikes a nutshell
against a tree trunk to break the shell, the tree trunk serves as an intact naturefact. The same was true when an aboriginal Modoc woman in the northwestern
United States leaned against the end of a projecting log to apply pressure on
her abdomen and thereby induce an abortion (Ray, 1963, 101). In a very real
sense any natural configuration employed to a species' advantage becomes an
intact naturefact. When cormorants nest along the ledges of cliffs or bears
hibernate in caves, these natural features serve a similar function. Behavior of
a different order is involved when loose objects are picked up and used. This
appears to be the most elementary step in "tool" usage, and these forms are
termed *free naturefacts.* Examples include rocks and stones employed as missiles,
sticks used as clubs, or stones serving as hammers. Free naturefacts are "natural
tools and weapons."

In the definition of naturefact the word *creatures* suffices to isolate the users
and was introduced to accommodate any animal employing a natural object.
It is far more important to identify naturefacts on the basis of their form,
natural qualities, and unnatural use than to be overly concerned with which

species used them. Henceforth only free naturefacts will be considered because they serve as the most direct anatomical extensions of creatures. They enable animals to perform tasks that are difficult or impossible to accomplish with teeth or beaks and hands or paws. The objects manipulated by contemporary nonhumans often serve in food getting, as the examples to follow illustrate. Black-breasted buzzards of interior Australia fly low over nesting emus to frighten them away. Then the buzzard picks up a stone or clump of earth, circles above the nest again, and drops the missile on the eggs (Chisholm, 1954, 381–2). An Egyptian vulture in Tanzania may pick up a stone with its beak, stand next to a nest of ostrich eggs, and hurl the stone repeatedly in an attempt to break an egg (van Lawick-Goodall, 1968b). A southern sea otter along the central coast of California may swim to the surface holding a stone and place the stone on its chest to use as an anvil for breaking open an abalone shell (Fisher, 1939; Hall and Schaller, 1964). Among primates chimpanzees are known to use a variety of naturefacts to obtain food. In Liberia they have been seen cracking oil palm nuts between two stones (Beatty, 1951, 118); in west Africa chimpanzees may poke a presumably natural twig into a bee's nest and then lick the adhering honey from it (Merfield and Miller, 1956, 45); and in Tanzania they bang edibles having hard shells against rocks or tree trunks. Here too they probe natural sticks into termite or ant nests and then withdraw the sticks to obtain the insects attached to them (van Lawick-Goodall, 1968a, 185, 204–6).

Apart from food-getting activities the use of naturefacts by nonhuman primates has been observed most often during agonistic displays, and among animals in the wild the greatest variability has been reported for chimpanzees. For instance, those in Tanzania throw pebbles, stones, and rocks weighing over five pounds, as well as sticks that appear to have been picked up from the ground (van Lawick-Goodall, 1968a, 203, 305). In the Congo chimpanzees have been seen brandishing and throwing sticks at a presumed enemy, a stuffed leopard. They also may use an intact naturefact in these displays. Flexible trees were whipped back and forth by the trunk toward an enemy at very close range, and similar behavior has been noted among chimpanzees in Tanzania, who swayed saplings or branches to strike at objects that they feared. A group of wild chimpanzees in a large enclosure in Guinea beat at a stuffed leopard with large wooden clubs that apparently had been picked up from the ground (Kortlandt, 1967, 216–7, 220; van Lawick-Goodall, 1968a, 204). Naturefacts seldom are used in other contexts by chimpanzees, but examples are recorded. After heavy rains individuals seeking to dry themselves rub their backs and shoulders against trees, and sticks sometimes are picked up to probe at unfamiliar or potentially dangerous objects (van Lawick-Goodall, 1968a, 202, 206–7).

The uses of naturefacts by chimpanzees may have little if any bearing on the development of technology among humans, yet a number of notations seem pertinent. In terms of diet and familiarity with plants, wild chimpanzees usually eat diverse plant products. Animals in the Gombe Stream Reserve of Tanzania were seen eating 37 types of fruits, 21 leaves or leaf buds, 6 blossoms, 4 seeds, 3 stems, and 2 barks, for a total of 63 different plant edibles. They spent from six to seven hours a day feeding, and nearly all food was obtained when they were in trees (Goodall, 1965, 440). These observations illustrate that chimpanzees were accustomed to handling plants for hours on end and were aware of the different qualities of natural forms as a result of their feeding behavior. Given the intelligence and curiosity of chimpanzees in general, the frequency with which those in the wild handled different natural forms, and their use of at least seven naturefacts with different qualities (leaves, grass, twigs, small sticks, large sticks, stones, and rocks), it might be asked why they did not use extrasomatic forms to a greater extent. Phyllis Jay Dolhinow and Naomi Bishop (1972, 323) suggest that chimpanzees failed to develop manipulative skills because they did not practice their use of naturefacts. In a summary statement about the use of sticks and stones and similar forms by wild primates, Adriaan Kortlandt and M. Kooij (1963, 80) noted that the nonagonistic use of forms has been reported far less than their use in agonistic behavior: "Nothing more convincingly demonstrates that the technological age on earth started with the emergence of weapons rather than gadgets."

Whether or not a "naturefact stage" prevailed in the development of human technology is not known. Furthermore it is unlikely that evidence for usages such as those recorded among chimpanzees ever will be revealed at sites where emerging human populations lived. Even if sticks and stones were found it probably could not be demonstrated that they were used as naturefacts. One means for gaining a better, or at least a different, understanding of technologic origins is to consider the naturefacts used by aboriginal peoples in the recent past. This approach cannot reveal anything directly about the origins of material culture, but it can offer insight into possibilities and even probabilities.

All aboriginal peoples in early historic times obviously made artifacts that were used in the direct procurement of food. Occasionally, or perhaps most often, a naturefact was an on-the-spot substitute for an artifact. In other instances it appears that certain forms of naturefacts were employed habitually, which suggests that they may have been used in a similar manner long ago.

Examples of free naturefacts employed in the direct procurement of terrestrial species are listed in Table 1-1. In a search of ethnographic sources relatively

Table 1–1 Examples of free naturefacts used by aboriginal peoples to harvest food on land

Form	Use	People	Source
Stick	Kill immature animals that have been run down	Kung Bushmen	Lee, 1966, 131
Stick	Honey removal	Ingura	Tindale, 1925–8, 82
Stone	Missile for birds		*Ibid.*, 80
Stone	Break into ant nest to obtain larvae	Princess Charlotte Bay area, Australia	Roth, 1901, 16
Stick	Remove cactus fruit	Seri	McGee, 1898, 206
Club	Kill peccaries	Siriono	Holmberg, 1950, 25
Stone	Batter down tree for leaves; kill birds or snakes	Tasmanians	Robinson, 1966, 188, 310, 557
Stick	Dig roots or birds from underground nests; remove platypus from burrow		*Ibid.*, 273, 543-4; Roth, 1890, 110
Stick	Kill a sleeping lizard	Tiwi	Goodale, 1957, 32
Stick	Dig roots and tubers	Trukese	LeBar, 1964, 92
Rock	Batter a beached, sleeping seal	Yahgan	Gusinde, 1961, 219
Shell	Scrape sap from tree		*Ibid.*, 301

few different forms are reported. When thinking about what the first naturefacts might have been, we must exclude the forms that aboriginal peoples used to procure food resources from water since plants and animals do not appear to have been taken from aquatic settings on a habitual basis until rather recent times. Most of the forms listed in this table were used to harvest food resources that were relatively fixed in physical terms, such as plants or honey from a bee's nest. Then too the animal species obtained with free naturefacts, such as the platypus and birds, are not dangerous. In the case of the Yahgan, a man might batter a sleeping beached seal with a rock if he did not have a club at hand. In these contexts most naturefacts were employed against species incapable of effective escape, for whatever reason. Furthermore, and possibly of greater importance, the animals taken usually were stunned or battered to death. *The highly desirable piercing and cutting qualities of weapons appear to occur only rarely in nature.* This suggests the possibility that man may not have been an efficient hunter, especially of large game animals, until artifactual weapons were produced. According to the quotation cited, Kortlandt and Kooij reason that it was agonistic weapons that launched man on his career as a technologist. It seems more likely, however, that instruments rather than weapons were the first highly adaptive forms, exclusive of "gadgets," employed by people. In this context an instrument is a form used to obtain a harmless edible that is incapable of effective escape, whereas a weapon is used to obtain an edible species that is capable of effective movement and may or may not be physically dangerous. Most free naturefacts are forms representing a "preweaponry stage."

Table 1–2   Examples of free naturefacts used by aboriginal peoples for purposes other than for the direct harvest of edible species

Form	Use	People	Source
Tools			
Clam shell	Knife, scraper	Andamanese	Radcliffe-Brown, 1948, 447
Pebble	Hammerstone		*Ibid.,* 500
Pumice	Skin scraper	Angmagsalik	Thalbitzer, 1914, 21, 504
Sharp stone	Scraper, knife		*Ibid.,* 21
Shell	Fat scraper		*Ibid.,* 504
Stick	Remove tendons from game	Aranda	Spencer and Gillen, 1927, v. 1, 18–9
Stone + stone + stone	Bone suspended between two stones, struck with third to remove marrow	Cree	Zierhut, 1967, 35
Pebble	Smooth wood	Ingura	Tindale, 1925–8, 95
Stone + stone	Remove shell of fruit		*Ibid.,* 76
Stone	Process skins	Modoc	Ray, 1963, 191
Shell	Smooth pottery	Siriono	Holmberg, 1950, 14
Stick + stick	Remove hot pots from fire		Ryden, 1941, 94
Stick	Loosen seeds in a gourd		Holmberg, 1950, 13
Rough stone	Grind paint	Tlingit	De Laguna, 1972, 416
Cobblestone	Hammer		*Ibid.,* 415
Basalt slab	Grind	Trukese	LeBar, 1964, 10
Basalt fragment	Peck		*Ibid.,* 10
Branch coral	File		*Ibid.,* 163, 181
Shell	Hair cutter	Yahgan	Gusinde, 1961, 82
Shell + shell	Tweezers		*Ibid.,* 82
Ceremonial object			
Stick or stone	Prayer offering	Modoc	Ray, 1963, 23
Stone	Puberty ritual	Tlingit	De Laguna, 1972, 521
Container			
Shell	Paint holder	Yahgan	Gusinde, 1961, 93
Weapon			
Rock	Throw during quarrels or kill wounded enemy	Modoc	Ray, 1963, 15, 142

Examples of free naturefacts used by aboriginal peoples for purposes other than providing food are listed in Table 1-2. Additional instances could be included, but most would be variations on the items cited. When one considers all the seemingly useful natural forms, the list is notably short. By implication free naturefacts had relatively limited use potential in technohistory. If there is one notable cluster, it is "natural tools," which in itself is significant since it indicates that free naturefacts were most useful in altering other forms. They could serve people well after they had begun to make things, but not as usable objects in themselves.

In sum, naturefacts are a unique cluster of natural objects used by creatures to supplement or extend their anatomical capabilities, and they are the most elementary extrasomatic forms. The patterning of their use anticipates the patterning in artifact usage, especially among humans. In food getting, naturefacts served as instruments rather than as effective weapons because they normally do not pierce and cut. Thus emerging man may not have been an efficient hunter of large game. The most significant conclusion is that while free naturefacts were of limited effectiveness, their use provided the manipulative experience on which artifact production may reasonably have been based.

The word *artefact*, or in American usage *artifact*, was coined by Samuel T. Coleridge in 1821 (Burchfield, 1972, v. 1, 128). The word first was used to refer to an inkstand (Coleridge, 1821, 256), and in 1834 Coleridge (1838, v. 3, 347) applied the term to poison shaped as a lump of sugar. The inkstand and lump of sugar obviously were complete forms. It appears that the first use of artifact in an anthropological context was by Daniel G. Brinton (1890, 75, fn.) when he referred to "the presence of artefacts and shells from the Pacific in old graves on the Atlantic coast."

A modern dictionary definition of artifact is "a usually simple object (as a tool or ornament) showing human workmanship or modification as distinguished from a natural object" (*Webster's Third New International Dictionary*, 1961, 124). If the word *simple* were deleted, this definition would be acceptable to many anthropologists. For example, David L. Clarke (1968, 186) defines an artifact as "any object modified by a set of humanly imposed attributes," and for Mischa Titiev (1963, 632) an artifact is "any object that is consciously manufactured for human use." More all-encompassing definitions include the one by John J. Honigmann (1959, 11), who defines an artifact as "any man-made characteristic of the environment," while for Robert C. Dunnell (1971, 117) it is "anything which exhibits any physical attributes that can be assumed to be the results of human activity." The latter definitions would cover worked antler and bone, or a garbage heap, these being by-products of manufacturing and other human activities. My preferred definition stresses finished forms and their uses: *An artifact is the end product resulting from the modification of a physical mass in order to fulfill a useful purpose.* In this definition the term *human* is avoided to acknowledge that other species on occasion make things to be used.

Among the most elementary artifacts are those that are literally twisted, torn, or broken free from their natural contexts—representing modification of a physical mass—and then used. The act of removal requires a different measure of purposefulness than that which leads to simply picking up and using an object, and therefore these forms are denoted as artifacts rather than free naturefacts. When a branch is broken from a tree or a handful of grass is torn from a clump to serve some nonfood purpose, a natural configuration is changed in a definite and unnatural manner. These forms are artifacts because there is purposeful modification of the natural forms.

Given the naturefact-artifact dichotomy for extrasomatic forms employed by species, there are predictably objects that do not fit neatly into either category. For example, some spiders spin a single thread with a sticky ball of silk at the lower end. The spider uses its legs to cast this "weapon" at nearby insects in the manner of a bola (Kaston, 1965, 351–2). In some ways the thread and ball combination is a naturefact, but because its creation is different from normal spinning it might be considered an artifact. Slight modifications of utilized natural forms also are reported for nonhuman primates and aboriginal foragers. When a chimpanzee bends branches at the forks of a tree to make a nest, it does not detach the branches from their natural context, but it does modify a raw material in a patterned manner as in artifact production (van Lawick-Goodall, 1968a, 196–200). The Siriono of Bolivia occasionally marked their trails by bending back a twig or leaf (Holmberg, 1950, 23, 42); each time they did so they modified a natural form ever so slightly, but with purpose and patterning. Furthermore it is reported that an aboriginal Australian man in northern Queensland sometimes threw a section of a naturally hollow log into a water hole. Returning to the spot a few hours later, he would lift the log to the surface at an angle, using one hand to cover the lower end. As he allowed the water in the log to trickle through his fingers, he trapped the fish and other eatable species inside (Roth, 1901, 21). In this instance the log is a free naturefact removed from its context and used, but throwing the log into the water hole and retrieving it later is a step beyond simple natural utility. Each of these examples represents a change in form beyond what is considered natural, and thus each is considered an artifact.

Naturefacts and artifacts sometimes blend, but for most items of material culture in ethnographic collections categorical naturefact-artifact distinctions may be made readily. Some paleoethnographic finds are difficult to categorize, but once people began to make more than slight modifications on natural materials, the identification of artifacts became unambiguous. Clothing, housing, tools, utensils, vehicles, and weapons all are classes of artifacts. Some commentators find it useful to distinguish between portable man-made forms, which they term artifacts, and others that are fixed and are called "structures" or "features." The latter would include ditches, graves, hearths, trails, and mines (e.g., Chard, 1975, 23). For my purposes this distinction usually is not drawn. Any modified and utilized form is an artifact, be it a wood splinter toothpick, a pin, or a skyscraper. I also would include cultivated fields, dams, and irrigation networks as artifacts because they are integrated, patterned, and purposeful modifications of the natural landscape.

People cannot claim to be the only makers of artifacts. Birds fashion nests and beavers build dams that are acceptable within the scope of our definition, if only because there is no other generic term that includes these manufactures. Very simple artifacts occasionally are manipulated by birds. Two species of wrens in Australia detach flower petals to use in courtship displays (Hindwood, 1948, 389–91), and a woodpecker-finch on the Galapagos Islands may remove a cactus spine to impale an insect located in a crack of a tree (Lack, 1961, 58–9). The production of simple artifacts by primates is rather common; spider monkeys in Panama break branches from trees and let them fall toward people (Carpenter, 1935, 173–4), while orangutans in Sarawak detach and then throw tree branches toward intruders (Schaller, 1961, 81–2). On occasion gorillas in the Congo twist branches or herbs free and hurl them (Schaller, 1963, 224–5).

As we might anticipate, the nonhuman species that uses the most diverse free naturefacts is also the one with the greatest propensity for making elementary artifacts, and this species is of course the chimpanzee. Observations by van Lawick-Goodall (1968a, 203–8, 305) in Tanzania include the following examples: handfuls of leaves are detached to rub or wipe foreign substances such as feces, sticky plant juices, or water from their bodies; lianas, stalks, stems, strips of bark, or twigs are detached, broken to the desired length, and stripped of leaves when necessary to probe ant or termite nests; sticks broken free are thrown in playful or aggressive acts. Kortlandt (1967, 216–7) reported that in agonistic situations chimpanzees sometimes break off small trees to throw or to brandish while charging an enemy.

We know very little about the beginnings of technology among people, especially if a "naturefact stage" of development is considered a distinct possibility. Even if sites that contained only natural forms were found, it might not be possible to identify the objects recovered as clearly having been used by people. At best we might hope to find natural stones bearing marks produced by use in a context that suggests people were involved. Flaked stones once attributed to human workmanship and fittingly called "dawn stones," or eoliths, usually have been discredited and now are judged as having been fashioned by natural forces. The Cromer flakes and pre-Chellean stones from England and the Kafuan forms from Uganda appear to have been produced by nature rather than by people. Among the oldest lithic productions of uncontested human workmanship are core tools and choppers fashioned about 2.6 million years ago in Kenya (Isaac et al., 1971). Although this date may approximate the beginnings of stone tool manufacture, it is conceivable that artifacts made from perishable materials were fashioned in much earlier times.

Table 1–3 Examples of elementary artifacts used by aboriginal peoples in nonfood-getting activities

Form cluster	Use	People	Source
Body modification device			
Thorn	Septum piercer	Modoc	Ray, 1963, 177
Porcupine quill	Tattooing needle		*Ibid.*, 178
Stingray spine	Bloodletter	Siriono	Holmberg, 1950, 83
Rat tooth	Scarification		*Ibid.*, 69, 87
Leaf	Body cleaner		*Ibid.*, 75
Feather	Neonate septum piercer	Tlingit	De Laguna, 1972, 504
Tool			
Toothed fish mandible	Knife	Siriono	Holmberg, 1950, 14
Bone	Awl	Trukese	LeBar, 1964, 12
Twig with leaves	Broom	Yagua	Fejos, 1943, 59
Other			
Leaf	Drinking cup	Siriono	Holmberg, 1950, 37
Bone	Divination	Tlingit	De Laguna, 1972, 521

According to ethnographic reports, comparatively few elementary artifacts served to obtain edibles. It would seem that the sticks and club cited in Table 1-1 could have been elementary artifacts rather than free naturefacts and still would have been used the same way in food-getting activities. Aboriginal peoples also used very simple artifacts for purposes other than the direct harvest of edibles; examples appear in Table 1-3. The most notable characteristic of these forms is that most of them were used with reference to human bodies.

Thus far I have attempted to demonstrate that all the things *used* by creatures may be divided into two groups, naturefacts and artifacts. It is reasoned, given the experience of people in handling materials today, that to simply pick something up and use it to serve a purpose is more elementary in technological terms than it is to modify the object before use. Presumably the same has been true in the recent and more distant past in human experience. To bring a free naturefact into play all that is necessary—which is a great deal—is to realize that it may be employed to accomplish a desired end. To rip or tear something from its context for a particular purpose is a technological achievement of a greater order because the form purposefully is modified. The step beyond, that of carefully modifying the object to create an artifact, is what ordinarily would be called a technological change.

Naturefacts and artifacts alike are composed of materials and have physical form. It is banal to state, but important to acknowledge, that everything must be produced from something. By reviewing the gross properties of widely available natural materials we are better able to understand the characteristics of artifacts as they were produced through most of time. The physiological capacity of ancient or modern peoples to make things is not considered, simply because we know that artifacts were in fact produced. Discussion of the mental qualities required to fashion artifacts is avoided, and the same is true of probable changes in human thought processes through time. These topics are unexplored because so little substantive information is available or especially enlightening to our purpose. Instead, a retrospective view of possible artifact production, given the raw materials found in diverse habitats around the world, is offered.

Before contemplating a sample of natural materials, we review the kinds of objects that emerging humans, and their immediate forerunners, may have manipulated on a day-to-day basis. Presumably it was foods that were handled most intensively and for longer periods of time than any other cluster of natural forms. Clifford J. Jolly (1970, 21) suggests that in the development of the hominid line the "small-object-feeding" complex was crucial. The earliest recognized fossil hominid, dating from the Miocene to the early Pliocene, is *Ramapithecus* from northern India. *Ramapithecus* possibly fed on small, hard seeds given the habitat that it presumably occupied and its molars clearly adapted to grinding. In a summary of the eating habits of *Ramapithecus*, Elwyn L. Simons (1972, 274) wrote, "Presumably, the greater grinding efficiency and the larger, broader, and more durable cheek teeth indicate adaptation for a tougher, coarser diet—just the sort of diet that might more easily be found on the ground in the form of seeds, roots, and perhaps even raw meat and bones."

The *Australopithecus* bones found in Africa represent indirect descendants of *Ramapithecus* and direct ancestors of modern people. The diet of the australopithecines has not been established with certainty. Some commentators feel that vegetable foods were the primary staples for at least certain populations (e.g. Krantz, 1973, 162). Others favor a varied diet of plant and animal foods (e.g., Robinson, 1963; Campbell, 1966, 201–2), and still others have stressed that the species involved may have been more successful as hunters than generally is acknowledged (e.g., Birdsell, 1972, 262–5; Washburn and Lancaster, 1968, 214).

Although unanimity does not prevail about the diet of emerging humans, it is safe to infer that plant foods were important. If edibles included berries, fruits, leaves, nuts, and seeds, then diverse plants must have been fingered, bent, climbed, and held. Furthermore, if varied vegetable products were consumed, it is likely that they came from plants with many different physical qualities that people would come to understand. In sum, organic forms, especially plants, probably were investigated and manipulated more often and with greater intensity than inorganic forms because they provided food.

It usually is presumed that people acquired their human qualities in sectors of Africa where tropical forests gave way to open grasslands. In these and all other habitats known to have supported aboriginal populations, we find a broad range of materials with use potential in a technological sense. As an initial aid in the analysis of material culture, raw materials are classified according to their hardness because the more consolidated the material, the more difficult it is to work. When people used only anatomical means, their fingernails, hands, or teeth, to change the shape of materials, relatively hard materials were less likely to have been worked.

In a sense liquids are the "softest" natural substances, and comparatively few forms occur widely. The most obvious example is water, followed by such animal products as blood, milk, and urine (Table 1-4). Liquids alone had very little potential as discrete units in nonindustrial technologies, judging from their uses by early historic foragers. A few examples do exist, however, such as pouring water down the hole of a burrowing animal to drown it. Oil, saliva, or mucus could serve secondarily as a lubricant in the manufacture or use of an artifact. In a similar manner, among aboriginal hunters, plastics such as moist clay, plant resin, and various forms of wax usually were not fashioned into discrete entities without the composition of the material first being altered with the aid of an outside agent. For example, fire was used to change a moist clay vessel into hardened pottery. Some plastics were modified to serve as artifact binders or sealants, but these practices are not known to have great antiquity. In sum, liquids sometimes were employed in making or using artifacts, and processed plastics often served to join the parts of artifacts.

Table 1-4 Natural materials found in diverse habitats

Liquids	Plastics	Flexibles	Solids
Blood	Asphaltum	Bark	Antler, horn, and nails
Juices, plant	Clay, moist	Brush	Bone
Milk	Gum, resin, or sap	Creepers and vines	Copper, native
Mucus	Wax	Feathers	Dirt clods
Oil		Grasses	Shell
Saliva		Hair	Spines, plant
Urine		Intestines	Stone
Water		Leaves	Teeth and tusks
		Sinew	Wood, relatively rigid
		Skins	
		Wood, pliable	

The technologic potential for making objects of flexibles was greater than that for liquids or plastics, but in a generic sense the range of forms produced from flexibles alone appears to have been rather modest. If the small-object feeding complex had prevailed among the earliest people, containers would have been essential for transporting most foods. Carrying eatables from one place to another suggests campsites, thoughts about future meals, and sharing. Flexibles such as leaves and pieces of bark or sections of skins could have served as elementary containers. Sherwood L. Washburn and C. S. Lancaster (1968, 219) stress the significance of receptacles and label their innovation as "one of the most fundamental advances in human evolution."

In aboriginal societies the largest cluster of widely distributed forms made entirely from flexibles consisted of containers. Bark trays, grass baskets, folded leaves, and animal skins serve as examples. Flexibles were transformed by early historic foragers into clothing and footwear, which are in a sense containers for people. It is not assumed that the first humans produced a wide variety of artifacts from these materials—quite to the contrary. Most of the forms cited are known only in relatively recent contexts. Since comparatively few artifacts were made entirely from flexibles by historic foragers, we may presume that the range of similar manufactures in much earlier times was small.

A fourth major cluster of materials is solids, and it seems important that there is greater gradation among natural solids than in the other groups. Stone may range from extremely hard flint and jade to very soft sandstone and soapstone (steatite). In certain areas, such as in alluvial sectors of the Amazon River basin and portions of western Alaska, stone is absent, but most inhabitable regions of the earth contain numerous types of stone. Woods too have a variability in hardness which, while possibly not as great as in stone, is nonetheless broad. The contrast between the hardness of certain desert woods and soft pine is striking. Once again woodless areas exist, such as the core of the Barren Grounds in central Canada. Animals with antlers, horns, or tusks are dispersed widely, but they may be absent from major landmasses as was the case for Australia in aboriginal times. If the nature of the materials defined as solids is considered, it can be seen that their earliest uses for human purpose probably were as bashers, diggers, knives, and scrapers. One major conclusion about the qualities of solids is that many could serve effectively as cutters; furthermore they vary widely by area in terms of their form and hardness, especially when compared with flexibles.

This classification of materials according to their hardness is elementary, and numerous gradations exist within and between the four clusters. The distinctions drawn make it possible to begin differentiating between the materials that were widely available to people. This has been attempted in Table 1-4, and on the basis of what has been noted, the following inferences are reasonable.

Early humans may have fashioned artifacts first from flexibles and then from solids. If plants provided most of the food, we would expect the frequent handling of these flexibles to lead to their purposeful modification for human use before that of solids. In addition, forms may have been made from flexibles first because most solids are more difficult to alter from their natural state, especially in the absence of extrasomatic tools. The experience gained in modifying wood might have been a major step toward working other solids because wood ranges from highly flexible to very solid in a single configuration, such as a tree. Although flexibles serve admirably to fashion containers, reliable cutters could not be made until solids were processed. As combinations developed, flexibles and plastics came to be used mainly to join two or more relatively solid materials. Before compound artifacts could have been crafted from any combination of raw materials, it was necessary to have gained prior experience in processing each material separately and creating from it other, presumably simpler, forms. Finally, liquids served largely as means for modifying materials in other categories.

This brief inquiry into the nature of raw materials serves to illustrate that inhabitable environments have broadly similar basic technologic resources even though the quantities available may differ greatly. The limited potential of use for particular natural materials would tend to unify production achievements throughout the world, especially among early human populations and early historic foragers. Thus technology would appear to be one of the more homogeneous aspects of early cultures.

CHAPTER 2

MEASURING
TECHNOLOGICAL
COMPLEXITY

Technology may be defined as all the ways in which people produce artifacts, and the uncommon word *technography* is especially pertinent in light of the goals of this volume. It refers primarily to the description of artifacts made by particular peoples at specific times and places; thus technography is an aspect of ethnography, the broader description of peoples' lifeways. Generations of fieldworkers have written technographic accounts about aboriginal peoples as they came into contact with industrial societies. These researches are in the natural history tradition of data collection; the primary goals have been the recording of information about aboriginal life-styles and collection of examples of what was made. The net results are large collections of aboriginal artifacts in ethnographic museums and a great deal of information, including much on material culture, filling rows of volumes found in libraries. As the number of aboriginal groups declined, anthropological interest in technology began to lose much of its momentum. Most ethnographers have been reluctant to describe and analyze the technologies of peoples in the process of westernization, if only because imported manufactured goods often have replaced locally handcrafted artifacts within a relatively short span of time.

Contemporary anthropologists clearly slight technology far more often than they report and appraise it. Exceptions do exist, but they are uncommon. In the comparative or ethnological study of peoples, most American anthropologists have all but abandoned consideration of technology, as evidenced by the small number of published articles dealing with the topic. Even in ethnographic monographs, where we might expect reasonable detail on material culture, the subject may be ignored, given cursory review, or dealt with in an uneven manner. Archaeologists are the only researchers who currently describe and analyze the material productions of aboriginal peoples with care. They habitually devote attention to the structure of artifacts and strive to establish localized sequences in an effort to reconstruct cultural history. They also draw analogies between their finds and the forms made by aboriginal peoples. In addition, some archaeologists seek to isolate cultural process on the basis of material remains (e.g., Binford, 1968, 5–32). As worthwhile as all of these efforts are, the conclusions derived are quite limited in terms of technology as a whole. One obvious reason is that the paleoethnographic record is dependent on those materials that are well preserved. There seems to be little doubt that the vast majority of artifacts made by aboriginal peoples were fashioned from highly perishable organic materials.

Technology has yet to receive thoughtful evaluation as a central quality of culture among anthropologists. In the book *Man the Hunter*, edited by Richard B. Lee and Irven DeVore (1968), sixty-seven prominent anthropologists offered what often are insightful views about hunting populations, past and present. We would expect the index of a book such as this to reflect the volume's emphasis, which is indeed the case. We find 21 listings for "Technology," 4 for "Material culture," and 4 for "Artifacts." "Social organization" warrants 93 entries, and there are 54 listings for "Marriage." The naive, or perhaps not so naive, assumption would be that social organization and marriage are far more important in the lives of hunters than are their artifacts and material culture. When technology is discussed, it usually is presented as a secondary, or even tangential, quality in the lives of hunters, which is absurd. Of the commentaries about technology in *Man the Hunter*, only those by William S. Laughlin, Sherwood L. Washburn, and C. S. Lancaster are worthy of special note, and all of these individuals are primarily physical anthropologists, not ethnologists.

During the last forty years in particular ethnologists usually have described and then summarily dismissed the manufactures of aboriginal peoples as "well adapted but simple and essentially homogeneous." When comparative evaluations have been made about specific forms or clusters of forms, they usually have been designed to answer definite questions. The origins of particular types, the local development of specialized craft skills, and the independent invention of types as opposed to their spread or diffusion have attracted attention. As useful as these approaches unquestionably are for understanding technological developments, the result often is a list of comparisons in a rather narrow frame of reference. At the opposite extreme are evaluations of total inventories in ethnographic or paleoethnographic contexts with only the most gross distinctions drawn. Examples include studies of the Paleolithic, Mesolithic, and Neolithic stoneworking traditions and identification of a people as being in a Stone Age or an Iron Age. These divisions again are useful only in the broad sweep of technological differences. When more specific comparisons are made about the material culture of one people as opposed to another, we find that the judgments are impressionistic. The following statements are reasonably typical: "Aboriginal Australian and Bushman technologies are simple." "Eskimo technology is complex." "The Indians of the Northwest Coast of North America had a well-developed woodworking technology." "The Tasmanians had the simplest technology ever reported for an aboriginal people." These sentences in fact represent opinions and scholarly guesses that may or may not be valid; we simply do not know how much truth they contain because a reasoned basis for the conclusions is never presented.

I find this disinterest in technology to be perplexing in light of two widely accepted truisms: that material culture is an essential dimension of culture and that artifacts have evolved from a few, generalized simple forms to many specialized complex forms. If man is best characterized as a "tool-using animal" and if technology has changed by the evolutionary process, then why is it that anthropologists have not devoted more serious attention to the accretion of technological knowledge? I do not deny that developmental theories and grand designs have been offered about technology; I am thinking of the works of Lewis H. Morgan, Karl Marx, V. Gordon Childe, and Leslie A. White. Yet when I attempt to identify the most insightful commentator on technological evolution, I must look back to the English anthropologist Lane Fox Pitt-Rivers, who published his most definitive statement in 1875. As indicated in the Introduction, I find the effort by Lane Fox the most valuable of those mentioned because he sought to validate a deductive theory of cultural evolution by bringing to bear, in an inductive manner, empirical data, ethnographic artifacts.

The foregoing observations serve to place this book and its concepts into perspective. I obviously subscribe to the concept of technological evolution—with all that it implies—and recognize that the *comparative method*, broadly interpreted, is the most reasonable means to assess the complexity of material culture. Yet before any judgments can be rendered about technological complexity, I must establish the basis on which comparisons are to be drawn. *The primary purpose of this chapter is to identify the discrete structural units from which artifacts are made.* Since these units must be distinguishable on a cross-cultural basis, what I seek is a common denominator for all technological productions.

All artifacts, no matter where or when they were made, share three fundamental characteristics: each is fashioned from something, has physical form, and serves at least one purpose. We may begin by considering one-part, hand-crafted forms made from raw materials that occur in nature. It appears that nature's offerings always are diminished in physical size or mass in a patterned manner when artifacts with a single part are produced. Something always is taken away from a habitat to serve a human purpose. A chunk of flint from a quarry or a flint nodule from a streambed may be flaked in order to fashion a chopper. A section of a tree limb is cut free and sharpened at one end to make a digging stick, or a long rigid stick is pointed at one end to produce a spear. A bark tray, horn wedge, bamboo sliver knife, notched log ladder, and buckskin blanket all are fashioned from consolidated physical masses, and each finished form consists of one material. In these examples the reduction of a raw material from its natural state is clear in the production of an artifact. The same is true of forms that might not initially be considered products of reduction. For instance, fruit might be picked from a tree and thrown into a stream to lure fish that are then shot with arrows; the fruit is an artifact in this context. The same is true when a section of poisonous root is cut from a bush, pounded, and cast into a pool to kill fish. Artifact parts may be made according to the same principle of production, as the following instances reveal: slate is ground to make a lance blade; gum is removed from a tree to caulk a boat; a leather thong is cut from a skin to serve as a binder; branches are cut free to cover a pitfall; and a piece of wood is whittled into a whistle. Innumerable additional examples could be cited of solid and flexible raw materials that are found in nature and reduced to produce an artifact or its parts.

We must likewise recognize that to produce a structural unit, whether an artifact or an artifact part, distinct elements may be combined after their initial reduction from a mass. A cotton string may consist of hundreds of elements, individual cotton fibers, from a number of different plants. Hundreds or even thousands of physically distinct fibers may be embodied in a wool blanket, a sisal rope, or a fishnet made from twisted sinew lines. The same is true for the brush and poles in a game guide that is 1000 yards in length, the sticks in a granary, or the rocks in a weir. In each of these examples distinct elements are joined with similar ones in the production of an artifact. Fusion may be involved when clay, feathers, sand, and water are combined to make a clay pot or particles of copper and tin are smelted with charcoal to cast a bronze knife blade. To count the number of physically distinct elements comprising many artifacts is a seemingly impossible task, and even when it is possible to do so, it does not appear to be a very fruitful means for assessing technological accomplishments. For example, a two-foot length of cotton string with 100 twisted fibers could not by any reasonable standard be judged twice as complex as a similar foot-long piece of string with half as many fibers. The smallest physical parts or elements represent the minutiae of technology, and their numbers may be indeterminate. To recognize their existence and to realize that on an individual basis an element does not necessarily function as a separate entity are necessary steps before attempting to assess the structural units of artifacts.

Stressing materials when attempting to classify artifacts cross-culturally is unwise because of their diversity and uneven distribution on a worldwide basis. By way of example, we know that all people made and used knives having blades of such diverse materials as bamboo, flint, shell, or slate depending at least in part on where they lived. How these materials were converted into blades depended not only on their physical qualities but on the tools and skills of the craftsmen. Actually the *idea* of a blade as a structural entity is far more important than the particular material used to produce the blade. If no satisfactory material were available, there would be no blade, but when there was any material with the potential of conversion into blades, its specific qualities were not overly important. The same would be true for the chipped stone used as arrowpoints. Alternatively the points might have been made from chert, flint, or obsidian because of personal preference or the availability of these materials. When one material may serve as well as another for the same structural purpose in the same context, the material is ignored. The use of different materials in such instances presumably represents alternative means for achieving a given structural unit. In a like manner a binder might have been prepared from leather, plant fiber, or sinew, and represented by a braided line, single strip, or twisted cord. The importance of each binder is *not* in terms of the materials *or* the way in which they were joined. It is critical whether or not binders existed and the ways in which they were employed. Thus structure or form, not material or production technique, assumes the greatest importance in attempting to make broadscale comparisons of technology on a cross-cultural basis. In the inventories cited later, when materials are listed, the purpose is for descriptive clarity above all else.

Given the explicit emphasis on completed structural units it is essential to set aside the variables that stand between raw materials and the parts of finished artifacts. We recognize that a great deal of time and effort may be required to obtain raw materials or the converse may prevail, yet neither involvement is considered when evaluating a finished form. The same is true for all of the methods, tasks, techniques, and tools required in producing an artifact. It is recognized that in the production of handcrafted artifacts one person may have been skilled and another unskilled, but once again this variability is not considered. The relative degree of skill is of no real consequence as long as the completed structural unit served the purpose for which it was intended. In the same vein it is quite clear that some artifacts were made for day-to-day use, and others were employed on an infrequent, seasonal, or even annual basis. These differences in use directly influenced the utility span of an artifact and its parts, yet durability is not evaluated. No consideration is given to the amount of individual or cooperative effort that went into the processing of materials or the production of structural units. None of these variables is assessed since attention is centered on structural parts and their contributions to a completed configuration.

It is now time to concentrate on the structural characteristics of finished artifacts. The technological entity identified as a *technounit* is offered as the basic unit for analysis. In general terms technounits are all the different kinds of parts that make up an artifact. A more exacting definition is that *a technounit is an integrated, physically distinct, and unique structural configuration that contributes to the form of a finished artifact.* The concept of a technounit is such that it may be applied in the analysis of the structural characteristics for any naturefact or artifact. Thus it is isolated as a common denominator in analyzing any material culture. A technounit is physically distinct from all other technounits in a particular form. The uniqueness of each technounit is in terms of the structural contribution that it makes to a complete form. The concept may best be elaborated with examples.

A stone used as a hammerstone is a one-technounit naturefact, and the same is true for a stick picked up and used as a club or a clam shell retrieved from a beach and used as a knife. In each instance the natural form, as a physically integrated mass, embodies a single technounit. A sandstone slab for grinding slate blades, a pebble to smooth wood, a free piece of coral to file wood are further examples.

To detach a large leaf from a tree and use it as a container is to create a one-technounit artifact. A similar process is involved in the following examples: a sharp bone is removed from a dead animal and used as an awl, a thorn is twisted from a cactus plant to pierce a baby's septum, a branch is detached from a tree and used to remove spines from an edible cactus, and a stick is broken to size and bent double to pick cactus fruit. These forms are elementary artifacts because each is created by breaking, tearing, or wrenching a consolidated physical mass free from its natural context and then utilizing it as a finished form consisting of one technounit. Another way to produce elementary artifacts that comprise a single technounit is to combine essentially duplicative elements. A wad of leaves to clean one's body, a handful of sand to abrade a skin, and a bundle of grass used as a sponge are examples. In each instance similar elements are combined to form a technounit that is able to function alone.

The forms just cited are "manufactured" only in a very basic sense. Most one-technounit artifacts are created by making more definite changes of a distinctly technological nature. A branch is cut and sharpened to make a digging stick, a fish-killing club is carved from a piece of wood, a leaf is folded carefully onto itself to produce a container, the handle and blade of a hoe are carved from one piece of wood, a knife is flaked from a piece of chert, and so on. The structural differences among these forms may be slight or great, but in each instance the specific structural attributes are less important than the qualification as a technounit. For this taxonomy the most important fact is that each form represents a single technounit.

It is essential to note that according to the definition each technounit makes a unique structural contribution to a finished artifact. This means above all else that a technounit can be counted only once when assessing the parts of a form. For the bundle of grass used as a sponge the individual grass stalks are elements combined, and together they make a single contribution to the finished form. The same is true for the sand used to process a skin or a wad of leaves as a body wipe. Thus we may have few or many similar elements contributing to the creation of a single technounit. A like evaluation applies to all the poles in a weir, the rocks comprising a weir, the pieces of brush in a game guide, or the stones of a cairn. In our culture the same type of configurations occur: the cedar shakes of a roof, the studs in a wall, or the boards of a fence. In each instance the replicative elements make a unitary contribution to the structure of a form. A weir can include nine or 986 poles, the number being of no direct concern; the key realization in terms of a technounit is that the poles in combination create a unified structural unit. Thus we arrive at the concept of equivalents among elements or parts in their contribution to a finished form. Additional examples of equivalents include the balls of a bola; the prongs of a leister; the sticks of a guide fence to a snare; the ribs to the body of a canoe; the two, three, or four feather vanes on an arrow; and the binders holding the feather vanes to an arrow shaft.

In sum, *a structural unit may be produced by employing the reduction process to alter a consolidated mass. An equally effective means of creating a structural entity is by utilizing the conjunction process to combine like elements.* Either process may function to create a basic unit in technology.

Compound forms made from natural materials always have at least two technounits. Tools best illustrate the combination; a flaked flint knife blade set into a wooden handle, a bone awl fitted in a wood haft, a slate drill point wedged into an antler handle are examples. In each instance the blade or point represents one technounit and the handle a second. Other two-part forms include a snare line tied directly to a long pole, a wood flute with a separate mouthpiece, or a wood plank with a cord attached, its purpose being to level a plowed field. Once again each technounit contributes a different structural quality to the finished form.

Artifacts that consist of a single technounit were commonly made by aboriginal peoples; the same is true for forms with three parts but not for those with two parts. One reason may be that two parts often will not hold together in use without some form of binder. Thus binders often form the third part. A stone spearpoint, for example, rarely was attached directly to a shaft without a binder to hold the two together. A typical spear consists of a point, shaft, and point-shaft binder.

Once again it is necessary to emphasize that in the evaluation of technounits the specific physical qualities of a part or its substitute are not important if the purpose served was the same. Eskimos might make a number of spears to hunt caribou from kayaks. The points conceivably could be fashioned from either ground slate *or* chipped stone. The shaft might be thick *or* thin and produced from birch *or* spruce. The point-shaft binder could be a braided line fashioned from many elements *or* a sealskin thong. The same forms could be used also as whaling lances or bear spears. It is the structure of this form in terms of technounit numbers that is most significant. As technounits, the alternative points, shafts, or binders are considered one point, one shaft, and one binder since each, regardless of material, makes a single contribution to the finished artifact.

Handcrafted artifacts of like design and purpose may be expected to vary in size. A shaft for a caribou-killing spear may be comparatively long, short, or somewhere between, depending on the physical size of the maker and user.

Personal preference might lead one man to fashion large arrowheads for hunting deer and another to make small ones for the same purpose, but most men made arrowheads that fell between these extremes. As long as an artifact or its parts had the same general function, these distinctions in size are ignored. In sum, artifacts or their parts may range in size from big to little, thick to thin, or long to short along a continuum, but when they functioned in the same way and were similar in physical configuration, they are regarded as the same. Among food-getting artifacts size distinctions are most often recorded for forms identified as facilities, represented by deadfalls, nets, snares, and traps. This is predictable since they are more likely to be species specific than are implements such as clubs and spears. When there is a clear *discontinuity* in technounit sizes for use with different species, similarly designed forms must be regarded as distinctive. For instance, a long pole served to dislodge fruit from a tall cactus, and a short pole was used for knocking fruit from a relatively short cactus. These were made as different forms to serve different requirements and therefore are classified as separate forms. In like manner one standardized weed cutter was five feet in length, and another was always two feet long, with no gradations reported. Thus two different styles of weed cutters are identified.

It seemed most desirable to count all the different *kinds* of technounits reported in a particular inventory for a precise measure of the diversity of parts rather than to total the technounits per form. Since shafts, points, and especially binders recur in most inventories, it would seem reasonable to count each of them only once as a part. This procedure would ensure that similar technounits would be entered only once in an inventory total. However it was found that different kinds of technounits could not be totaled because no means can be conceived to separate like from similar technounits. It is not possible *always* to identify one technounit as different from another when analyzing separate artifacts. For example, when does a "shaft" become a "handle," or how may we consistently and logically distinguish "poles" from "sticks" and "posts" in strictly technological terms on a cross-cultural basis? Likewise are harpoon handlines and float lines the same or different? Are plant resin and congealed blood equivalents as binders? In fish traps are wood splints and willow withes for the trap body fully comparable or different? In each instance the degree of similarity or difference cannot be defined precisely. With these and other difficulties in mind, it was decided to concentrate on totals of all technounits per form even though quite similar or almost identical parts may occur from one artifact to the next. Arrows are a typical example. A people might have had six different uses for arrows and six forms that had similar and dissimilar technounits, yet all six arrows included shafts, shaft-head binders, vanes, and shaft-vane binders. The four technounits common to all the arrows total twenty-four technounits, which seems somewhat excessive. However the different purposes served by the clearly unique arrows are important to identify, and the fact that six different arrows were made is important enough to balance the size of the technounit totals. The same would be true of like poisons used in different contexts. In sum we note that it is essential to record the use of similar technounits in different artifact styles because it represents technological variability in form and use, not replication within a form.

The qualifications of a technounit have been described in sufficient detail to indicate how one may be distinguished from another. Additional constraints on the concept are set forth in the next chapter, in which food-getting forms become the special focus of attention. As thus far presented, technounits are offered as the building blocks of technology.

After measuring the structural complexity of finished forms, the next step is the consideration of the idea of complexity. The most pertinent dictionary definition of complex is "having many varied interrelated parts, patterns, or elements" (*Webster's Third New International Dictionary*, 1961, 465). For my purposes complexity may be identified at a number of different levels for the accomplishing of distinct purposes. We might simply count all the forms made or used by two different peoples such as the Tiwi of Australia and the Ingalik of western Alaska. When doing so we assume that the forms identified represent the integrated patterning of their material cultures. The people with the higher total would be identified as having the more complex technology. The comparison then could be expanded to include any other peoples around the world. This procedure would point up the diversity of forms above all else, but it could not indicate the number of different parts embodied in any form. One people might conceivably have made and used ten food-getting forms, with one part each. Another people could have produced ten such forms with an average of three parts each. Both people would have the same total if forms alone were considered. Thus, by simply counting all the different forms, one could establish a relatively crude measure of complexity.

A similar analysis may be performed for a more restricted patterning. The number of different harpoons made by East Greenland Eskimos could be totaled and compared with similar productions among the Eskimos at Point Barrow in Alaska. The net result would represent the degree of stylistic diversity; this approach could be expanded to include the same forms among other Eskimos for a broader, yet gross index to the formal variability involved in harpoons. The same procedure might be followed for these or other peoples with reference to other subsets in material inventories. Comparative totals for clothing, conveyances, structures, tools, and utensils could be determined readily after the limits of "types" were established. Once again the total number of different forms cannot be used to identify the technological differences represented within the individual forms. The opposite extreme would be to count each physically distinct element that comprises a form. In many instances the task seemingly would be impossible. All of the molecules of clay plus the grains of sand and feathers that add up to a clay pot, the leaves covering a pitfall, or the individual strands of hair in a belt would yield very high and rather meaningless totals with reference to the technological complexity involved. In sum, totaling all the different forms in a given set provides a general measure of complexity for that particular set and may be useful for certain studies, but totaling elements contained in most forms is quite unrealistic and unrewarding.

The concept of a technounit has been proposed as a unit of measure within technology that identifies the parts of artifacts without dropping to the element level. *The number of technounits that create a finished artifact is offered as a measure of an artifact's complexity.* This measure is quite acceptable in terms of complex as meaning "varied interrelated parts." On the basis of technounit numbers, diverse comparisons may be made for items of material culture. We might total all the technounits for the material culture of the Aranda in central Australia for comparison with a similar inventory of the Naron Bushmen in southern Africa. We could then determine which inventory included the greater number of technounits and which thereby could be judged as more complex. Similar evaluations could be made of material inventories for any other peoples for whom the data are adequate. The same procedure could be followed to assess the relative complexity of various awls made by the Ingalik of southwestern Alaska or the different forms of sealing harpoons among the Iglulik Eskimos in central Canada. Cross-cultural comparisons likewise are possible. We might total the number of technounits represented in digging sticks produced by the Chumash of California and compare this with the total number of technounits in similar forms produced by the Aymara of Peru, to establish comparative rankings.

To count all the forms in an inventory yields a gross assessment of total complexity. To total all technounits of an inventory provides a more precise statement of complexity. In most studies entire inventories are not likely to be evaluated in terms of technounits, if only because of the time and effort required. It is more likely that a sample will be selected with a particular problem in mind. Clusters of forms for possible attention include clothing, conveyances, fishing equipment, hunting weapons, structures, tools, traps, utensils, or items of personal adornment. Constellations of forms for study might be conceived differently, such as mechanical devices, bladed forms, or structures designed for storage. Whatever the subset for analysis, one must not attempt comparisons across subsets. A one-technounit bone needle is not fully comparable as a tool to a one-part wooden totem pole. Nor would it be legitimate to compare a one-technounit dugout canoe as a conveyance with a one-part antler wedge as a tool. Because of the immense variability in the universe defined as artifacts, we must isolate coherent groups of forms on an ecological, evolutionary, functional, historical, or structural basis and make comparisons between them to arrive at statements about relative technological complexity.

A summary statistic to represent all the different forms as well as all of their parts would serve us well in evaluating the overall complexity of an inventory. The best procedure seems to be to total the number of technounits involved and divide this figure by the total number of forms in order to establish a complexity index. *The average number of technounits per form is considered the most satisfactory measure of technological complexity.* Thus in any comparative study of technology we begin by identifying a particular problem or hypothesis to test. A cluster of material items is isolated, the forms are counted, their technounits totaled, and averages determined. This procedure makes it possible to specify the relative complexity of manufactures in substantive or comparative terms. We would be able to determine the relative complexity of Aranda and Bushman tools, Caribou and Copper Eskimo clothing, Ingalik and Klamath bows, or Yurok and Nabesna houses. We are also in a position to rank the complexity of forms used by peoples in the subarctic and temperate regions for procuring herd animals or for food storage. Comparisons such as these are just a few examples among many possibilities. It is the technounit concept as a measurable unit of technology that makes the evaluation of complexity possible in material culture.

CHAPTER 3

SUBSISTANTS AND
THEIR COMPLEXITY

Technounits, as the different kinds of parts in a finished artifact, have been introduced as building blocks in material culture. The technounits of a given form in an aboriginal technology usually may be established with relative ease. Yet to analyze all the forms made by diverse peoples in terms of technounits is a physical impossibility. Admittedly some foragers had few items of material culture, but most were far more prolific producers and users of things than one might expect. A number of examples are informative. The Tiwi of northern Australia (Basedow, 1913; Goodale, 1957, 1971; Hart and Pilling, 1960; Spencer, 1914) used about seventy-five different naturefacts and artifacts, depending on the definition of a "type." A comparable figure for the Siriono of Bolivia (Holmberg, 1950) is ninety, and for the Chenchu of India (Fürer-Haimendorf, 1943) it is about 100. Because of their limited inventories, it would be feasible to analyze all the forms involved in terms of technounits, but the practicality of studying everything made by most aboriginal populations is doubtful. The Yakutat area Tlingit of southeastern Alaska (De Laguna, 1972) form total is 179, and for the Trukese of Micronesia (LeBar, 1964) it is 215. The Anvik area Ingalik of western Alaska (Osgood, 1940, 1958) fashioned some 410 different forms. Even these latter peoples are not considered to possess especially developed technologies. Thus it is essential to identify a sample of forms that will represent a meaningful range of technologic achievements for any material culture. It is necessary that the sample represent technology as it fulfills essential human needs.

Food clearly is an essential human need, and therefore it is reasonable to select food-getting naturefacts and artifacts for studied consideration. A population cannot survive without the ability to provide a continuing food supply for its members. In the absence of food such basics as clothing, shelter, and psychic or physical security mean nothing. Food in the stomach is essential physiologically for all peoples everywhere. On a short-term basis water may very well be more important than food for sustaining life, and on a long-term basis vitamins and minerals are unquestionably critical. However it clearly is the effectiveness with which people obtain food on a day-to-day, year-to-year, and generational basis that not only channels but molds the texture of their lives. Stated simply, all ongoing societies must develop minimal means for obtaining food.

In terms of parsimony it would be helpful to have a technical term to identify the artifacts most directly and intimately involved with food as opposed to all other forms. We possess words that define segments along the spectrum, but none are adequate. Generic terms for artifacts used to obtain food include hunting weapons, fishing equipment, and farming implements. As useful as these and other words are in linking material culture with food procurement, none is adequate for my purposes. I must be able to specify the forms employed in food getting with enough precision to isolate them from all other naturefacts and artifacts in a consistent manner and on a cross-cultural basis. Thus I have coined a new word, *subsistant*, derived from *subsist*, "to support with provisions," and the suffix *-ant*, "the agent that performs a specific action or process." In general, subsistants are technological forms used to provide species with food. The word originally was applied to forms used by aboriginal foragers (Oswalt, 1973, 24–5) but now must accommodate the food-getting technologies of all past and present foragers and farmers. *A subsistant is an extrasomatic form that is removed from a natural context or manufactured and is applied directly to obtain food.* This definition is designed to include all of those things that clearly enable a predator to obtain its prey. Subsistants act directly either on species or on the resource base to procure edibles. In the process subsistants may influence the behavior of a species, modify its habitat, or protect it for later harvesting.

No matter how cleverly people may use their limbs or bodies to obtain food, the anatomical part is not a subsistant. To pick fruit, plant seeds, or collect shellfish by hand does not involve subsistants. Similarly the process of stomping on an ant's nest to induce the ants to crawl up one's legs and then picking them off by hand to eat involves only human anatomy. The same is true when an animal is run down and killed by hand or when honey is sucked from a flower. The potential for obtaining eatables by anatomical means is much the same for any human population.

A subsistant may be a natural object that served to obtain food. To throw a stone at a duck, to pick up a stick to kill a porcupine, and to batter down a small tree with a rock to obtain edible leaves are examples. A subsistant may occasionally be a natural substance, such as water poured down a hole to drown an edible rat. However most known subsistants are artifacts, not naturefacts. Among foragers (collectors, fishermen, and hunters) common artifacts that were used directly to obtain nourishment include bows and arrows, fishhooks, fruit-picking poles, gill nets, leisters, spears, and traps. Other subsistants that acted on wild species in a different manner but for a food-getting purpose include artifactual blinds, guides, fish lures, and torches to blind animals. In each instance the information or misinformation that is conveyed to the species directly facilitates its procurement. These subsistants affect the behavior of species above all else. Still other forms acted directly on the habitats of species; examples include a pick to chip a fishing hole in lake ice or an ax used to chop into a hollow log to retrieve an opossum. In general we find that most subsistants used by foragers acted directly on species in the manner of weapons and traps.

Among intensive farmers most subsistants served to modify the habitat of species and to protect them for eventual harvest. Thus there is a major functional difference between the forms employed by foragers and farmers. Examples include digging sticks to plant cuttings or seeds, harrows, hoes, plows, rakes, shovels to dig irrigation ditches, stone terraces for cultivating rice, and weed cutters. Domestic species raised in an artificial habitat such as a garden plot are protected by the use of fences, predator traps, scarecrows, or slings and missiles to frighten birds away. A comparatively narrow range of subsistants was employed by aboriginal farmers for harvesting. Included are digging sticks, knives, and sickles. Animal husbandry harvest subsistants include knives to kill species and binders to hold large animals in order to kill them. We also would include corrals, hobbles, lassos, tethers, and even a carrying bag for a piglet. Each of these artifacts implemented or facilitated the procurement of food and was a direct technological link between humans and their edible resources.

Among foragers a comparatively brief span of time separated the use of a subsistant and the actual harvest. Tubers were located and dug immediately. A speared animal was killed before it could escape. Any delay was of comparatively short duration. Nets, snares, and traps were set and checked within a few days. The use of subsistants in farming and in animal husbandry, however, often involved an extended time span between use and harvest. Thus there are two critical differences in use configurations. First, direct-action subsistants were more developed by foragers, whereas forms used to modify habitats were more developed among farmers. Second, the delay factor between use and harvest was brief for foragers but extended for farmers.

Many additional forms could have been included in an expanded definition of subsistants, yet it was decided to restrict the term as much as possible without ignoring any critical usages. The bow and arrow are subsistants, but ancillary forms such as quivers, sinew twisters, and wrist guards are not included. The highly developed support technology for harpoons among Eskimos is likewise set aside; excluded are harpoon rests, hunters' lamps, sealing stools, walls of snow to protect a hunter, and wound plugs. The same is true of conveyances such as boats, climbing ropes, and snowshoes. Each transports human predators to their prey, but then human hands or other forms are brought into play as the actual means of obtaining the edibles.

By definition a subsistant is an extrasomatic form either manufactured or removed from a natural context for use in obtaining food. Because of these qualifications, subsistants cannot be substances contributing to the growth of domestic plants or animals. We would not include the food for wild animals as a subsistant, and the same logic extends to feed and water for domestic animals as well as water and fertilizer for domestic plants.

People quite obviously manipulate their habitats in highly diverse ways in order to obtain food. Some forms that are technically included in the subsistant definition will be excluded in the analysis to follow. These are largely features created to foster the development of edibles. Furrows and planting mounds, drainage and irrigation ditches, and garden plots or fields are excluded. They make desired changes on the base, but they are not technological forms in and of themselves. The same is true when a fisherman chops a hole in ice. The hole is not considered to be a subsistant since it is not the form that takes the fish; the ice pick is the functioning subsistant. Likewise an ax is a subsistant when it is used to chop a hole in a log from which grubs are retrieved, but the hole as a modification on the grubs' habitat is ignored. To include the pit of a pitfall might seem to be an exception, but it is not. The pit is a device that directly obtains an animal.

In drawing the distinction between subsistants and nonsubsistants, it is inevitable that a decision about a particular form may be arbitrary. This is understandable given the tremendous diversity of manufactures directly or indirectly related to food getting and the desire to include only those forms actually used in a direct manner to supply food. Subsistants as technological forms cannot be natural forces such as fire as the "phenomenon of combustion," but a torch used to burn grassland and drive game is a subsistant in this context. A firebrand used to ignite fuel to smoke a squirrel from its hole or to burn over a garden plot before planting is a subsistant because it is applied directly to obtain food, and the same is true for water poured down a rat hole. Examples of questionable classification are forms that have a clear supernatural purpose but a doubtful practical use. For instance, a person may say a prayer over a small stick with feathers attached and place the "prayer stick" in a garden. Such a stick would not be considered a subsistant because it is not judged to make a clear contribution to the protection of the crop. Yet when a long pole with white dangles suspended from it is placed in a garden and a prayer is said over it, the artifact is judged a subsistant. The reason is that because of its size and structure the form no doubt served to frighten away predators.

Contrary to what might be expected, not all weapons or traps are included as subsistants. In terms of the definition, a particular form must have had an established food-getting purpose. Excluded would be ceremonial bows, sacred arrows, model traps made for practice, snares designed to strangle ghosts, or slings and missiles used exclusively by children as playthings. Occasionally it is difficult to determine from an ethnographic account whether a form served effectively in the procurement of food. The general procedure has been that if there is clear doubt a form should not be included.

One question of counting that emerges is whether to consider physically distinct forms that are used together as one or two subsistants. These are identified as linked forms, and examples include bows and arrows, game guides and surrounds, harpoons and throwing-boards, slings and missiles, and weirs and traps. Each form has been counted as a separate subsistant, but the linkage always is reported in the inventories either by an ampersand or a comment accompanying the form's description. Counting each such technological form is designed to give full recognition to the distinctiveness of its configuration of technounits. This is especially valuable when dealing with different styles of arrows used with one form of bow or when dealing with different harpoons used with one style of throwing-board.

Another question is how to evaluate those subsistants that function in the same manner but occur as a naturefact and also as an artifact. In these cases the forms are entered under both headings, and their respective technounits contribute to the inventory. The reason is the desire to identify total technological diversity in all established contexts for food getting.

If one form served two functions, as a subsistant and a nonsubsistant, it would be considered only in its subsistant context. Certain items of material culture served varied purposes, some of which had to do with the direct procurement of food. An adz may have been used primarily as a tool to craft wooden artifacts, but it also may have served to cut into a hollow log to retrieve honey, chop down a tree with edible leaves, or clear a garden plot. Likewise a spear or arrow could have served to kill either game or enemies, who were not eaten. *In examples such as these only the subsistant purposes are recorded.* Furthermore in the inventories any form has only one primary entry. Therefore if a subsistant was employed in different contexts, an effort is made to identify the most important use, and this is listed first, with alternative uses in parentheses. Thus the purpose of an ax as a subsistant might have been either to clear a garden plot in farming activities or to chop down wild trees for edible fruit in collecting activities. The ax would be listed under the more important heading according to use. If it cannot be determined which use was dominant, the placement becomes arbitrary.

The foregoing text should clarify the distinction between subsistants and nonsubsistants. If questions about the precise identification of food-getting forms linger, they probably can be resolved by referring to Chapters 4 through 7 and the Appendix, which list innumerable examples for societies around the world.

Before specific guidelines can be offered for evaluating subsistants in terms of their technounits, it is necessary to divide subsistants into two major clusters on the basis of their form and operation. Subsistants that retain the same physical form before and during their use are defined as *simple* or *nonmechanical*. A digging stick, fruit-picking pole, hoe, seed beater, and spear are examples. By contrast the parts of *complex* or *mechanical* subsistants change their relationship with one another when the form is used. A toggle-headed harpoon penetrates a seal's skin, and the head detaches from the foreshaft, remaining connected to the shaft by a stout line. As the seal attempts to escape, the head, line, and shaft change their relationship with one another as the shaft is pulled through the water. Thus at least two of the technounits, the head and line, are disarranged from their position as the harpoon is used. The same is true when a bear gnawing at bait moves a bait stick, dislodges a samson post, and releases a fall log that kills it. In the distinction between simple and complex subsistants any change of form by breakage is ignored.

The either–or distinction between simple and complex subsistants results in a number of partially or entirely arbitrary decisions. The most important is that when a single technounit moves unto itself the operation is defined as simple. For example, when the noose of a tether snare pulls tight around the neck of a hare, there is movement of only one part, the noose, unto itself. However a spring-pole snare is complex because the spring pole, a trigger, and the noose move when the form is in operation. Although the cover over a pitfall may break under the weight of an animal, the subsistant is identified as simple. Linked forms such as the bow and arrow, blowgun and dart, crossbow and arrow, sling and missile, spear and throwing-board are always judged as complex because one form changes its relationship to the other.

The simple–complex distinction provides another means of separating subsistants on the basis of their form and the manner in which they perform in technological terms. It also provides another index to the complexity of a material culture. People with more complex subsistants have larger technounit averages and thus manifest greater technological complexity.

The thesis being developed is that diverse aspects of complexity in material culture for one people or for many may be gauged in terms of their subsistants, the functioning of each in terms of its mechanics and purpose, and the technounit numbers of each. Procedural questions about what is and what is not identified as a subsistant have been considered. The next step is to detail the specific guidelines for evaluating subsistants and technounits as they are reported in ethnographic accounts.

1. *Distinguishing between subsistant forms.* After naturefacts and artifacts have been identified as subsistants, the first question is how to distinguish one formal configuration, or "type," from another. A cardinal guideline is that *one subsistant is distinct from another when differences are found in the configuration of structural units.* Thus technounits and the way in which they are put together serve to distinguish one subsistant from another. Gradations in size and material differences presumably represent alternatives that are contingent on craft skill, the availability of materials, or the user's physical size, and these are secondary to the basic structure of the form.

2. *Counting subsistants with more than one function.* A second cardinal guideline for evaluating subsistants is that *a subsistant employed in different contexts may be counted only once in an inventory.* A stick may have been used to dislodge fruit and secondarily

to dig tubers; it would be counted only once in a fruit-getting context with its secondary uses noted. The same throwing-board may have been used with a bird dart or a bladder dart for seals, but the throwing-board and its technounits are entered only once in an inventory. This guideline most often need not be considered because of the separate and distinct contexts for which most subsistants were made. However it is very important in evaluating technologies having an overlap in subsistant usages.

3. *Counting technounits. Any technounit may make only a single numerical contribution to a subsistant.* When all the parts of a subsistant are structurally different, this procedure is quite apparent. A spear might consist of a stone point, a wood shaft, and a thong as the point-shaft binder; the resulting artifact consists of three technounits. If the wooden shaft of a bow is tied directly to a sinew bowstring, the form consists of two technounits. When two or more physically distinct elements are nearly identical in the structural purpose that they serve, their technounit count is one. Examples include the balls of a bola, prongs of a leister, and teeth of a herring rake. This guideline also applies to the poles or rocks of a weir, stakes in a game guide, stones in an agricultural terrace, and so on. For a gill net the upper and lower backing lines, floats, and sinkers are each counted only once. The purpose is to stress the distinct qualities of the technounits comprising subsistants rather than to consider essentially replicative elements as equal in significance. *It is the number of different kinds of technounits comprising an artifact that commands attention.*

4. *Idiosyncratic versus established forms.* Every effort must be made to identify and include all the established forms for the time period represented by an ethnographic account. The prevailing subsistants at a given time, those habitually used in seasonal or day-to-day food-getting efforts, constitute the working subsistant inventory. An ethnographer may state that a form was known but was not used at the time the information was being collected. Judgments are required in these instances, and *archaic forms should not be included.* However, if the descriptions are of the aboriginal period but are recorded after a considerable span of historic contact, the forms that lingered in the memories of informants are included since they presumably prevailed during the late aboriginal period. For example, hunters in northern Canada generally used steel traps by the time their material cultures were recorded by ethnographers, but individuals could recall the details of deadfalls and snares, which had prevailed prior to intensive Euro-American contacts.

Unusual or opportunistic forms are not included because they were not standard. A man may sharpen a stick to use as a leister in obtaining a fish for supper on a particular day and never do so again. This production and usage obviously are a possible source of innovation, but the form did not prevail as a subsistant.

Far greater insight could be gained by knowing the relative number of digging sticks, spears, traps, and so on, used. We would then have a measure of a form's relative importance in terms of actual use. However these data are never, to my knowledge, reported in detail and rarely are even considered in ethnographic accounts. Therefore we are forced to consider each established subsistant as a single unit.

5. *Decorative technounits. All parts having only ornamental or supernatural import are excluded from the count of subsistant technounits.* Examples include red ocher paint on a weapon shaft to make it appear attractive, plugs or insets used in conjunction with decorative etched designs, orchid stem wrappings on arrows to make the arrows look more pleasing, and feathers hung from spear shafts for supernatural purposes. The reason for such exclusions is that they do not have an objective role in increasing the effectiveness of a form and in this sense they are nonfunctional. At the same time it must be recognized that certain technounits served subsistant functions and were secondarily decorative; these are counted as functioning technounits. Examples include the inset plugs for eyes and teeth suspended from the body of a lure to attract fish. Likewise grease and blood may be smeared on a bow shaft to strengthen the wood, although they may appear to be only decorative.

6. *Arbitrary evaluations.* When analyzing the material culture of highly diverse aboriginal peoples, one of the most important goals is to render consistent judgments about what is and what is not a subsistant and even whether a cluster of forms should be included in an inventory. Consistent *exclusions* are as follow: Intact naturefacts (e.g., a natural blind, a cliff over which to drive game) are never included because the extent of their employment probably has never been described fully in any ethnographic account. Features on the landscape created artificially for the purpose of producing crops are not considered; examples include drainage ditches, earth fill or vegetable matter as a base for planting, furrows, planting holes, and planting mounds. Artificial water holes for animals are excluded as are artifacts associated with watering and feeding plants or animals.

Many peoples used fire for subsistant purposes, but the technology for producing fire is not analyzed. When fire or smoke was applied directly for a subsistant purpose, a "torch" is entered in an inventory even though the actual form may have been a firebrand. In rare instances "fuel" is classified as a subsistant.

As with subsistants, it sometimes is not possible to make consistent judgments about technounits except on an arbitrary basis, as indicated by the following examples. _Nets_ were widely used to take fish, but accounts often do not include details about the design of a net. Therefore it was decided always to evaluate netting as one technounit since this frequently appears to have been the case. _Imported metal_ usually was used by aboriginal populations in a subsistant context by the time we have reasonably complete ethnographic accounts. In somewhat earlier, or even much earlier, times stone usually had been the material used for the relevant technounit or form. A part made of brass, copper, or iron consistently has been evaluated as representing one technounit. The reason is that these imported materials customarily were processed by aboriginal peoples in the same manner as stone had been in earlier times. For consistency the same judgment has been made for _finished metal products_, such as hoe blades or arrowpoints received in trade, or iron already worked by a people. However very few of the populations sampled actually made their own metal products.

7. _The presumed existence of technounits or subsistants._ Given the uneven quality of descriptions about material culture in ethnographic accounts, it sometimes is necessary to assume the presence of a part or occasionally of an entire subsistant. In inventories the letter _A_ follows the entry for a technounit that is _assumed_ to have been present, _AA_ for _all assumed_. Ethnographies that require many assumptions cannot be analyzed effectively because the data are not comparable to those contained in more expansive accounts. At the same time the amount of detail required for analyzing subsistants necessitates making a few assumptions even when superior ethnographies are being consulted. While assumptions should not be excessive, it often is advantageous to make a small number to complete an inventory. Not infrequently a binder is unreported when the structure of a form would necessitate its existence, and it therefore must be assumed. A noose snare may be reported with no indication that it was attached to anything, but a bush or stone anchor justly may be assumed to have existed. Likewise a hunting knife may be described with no mention of a ferrule on the handle, but this part is indicated in an illustration of the knife and thus is assumed. Or if there exist references to an undescribed club used to kill animals, a club legitimately may be listed as assumed. The most tenuous assumptions are those made for the parts of traps when descrip-

tions are unclear or incomplete. The general procedure is to select the accounts that are most complete, make only conservative assumptions about presumed absences, and restrict the number of such assumptions to as few as possible. Thus there clearly is a subjective element in assessing the parts of some artifacts.

These guidelines make it possible to isolate and evaluate subsistants and their technounits in a rather exacting manner. If the guidelines are expanded or modified, every effort must be made to do so in a manner resulting in consistency for each evaluation. Because of the detail and accuracy that are required, it also is highly desirable to have at least two independent assessments of any inventory.

Given the manner in which technounits have been defined and the way in which complexity is being measured, we may ask whether there exist "useless" technounits in finished subsistants other than those with a decorative or supernatural purpose. If subsistants commonly included technounits that did not contribute to their food-getting purposes, then a little or a great deal of possible error would be inherent in the idea of using a technounit as a measure of technological complexity. As a general observation all subsistants must work effectively to feed people, and any needless parts are technologically extraneous. However a small number of technounits that appear to have been nondecorative, nonfunctional, and nonsupernatural have been identified on subsistants. One example is the chipped stone blade set into the handles of many throwing-boards from central Australia. The weight of the stone blade may have been important to counterbalance the spear held by the throwing-board, but it is conceivable that the blade served only as a knife in nonsubsistant contexts. I suspect also that some ingredients in poisons for spearpoints or arrowpoints served no effective purpose, and the same is true of certain medicines for curing illnesses among animals. In sum, however, it appears that very few subsistant technounits were without structural purpose in food-getting efforts.

In the remainder of this chapter examples of subsistants indicate how certain forms may have evolved and become more specialized. Hypothetical developments are cited since comparatively little is known about the chronological changes in most aboriginal forms. A second purpose is to illustrate that among aboriginal artifacts existing at the time of historic contact, those forms having the greater numbers of technounits were the more complex within any given cluster.

Of all the one-part subsistants it would appear that the natural stick must have been an important archetype. A stick as a naturefact could be long and thin or short and stout to serve various food-getting purposes quite effectively. Animals might be clubbed or perhaps speared, roots could be dug, or inaccessible fruits and nuts knocked free. By first concentrating on the basic natural stick for obtaining plant foods, we may plot hypothetical changes in terms of the concepts that have been introduced. A relatively short stick presumably could be used to dig up roots better than human hands and thereby was adaptive for food-getting activities. When a stick purposefully was pointed at one end, the product was an artifactual digging stick, which seemingly served its purpose better than those found in nature. Among most aboriginal peoples, foragers and farmers alike, this form was popular. Many foragers employed the one-part digging stick to dig up roots and tubers or to retrieve burrowing animals. Similar forms were used by farmers for like purposes as well as for planting cuttings or seeds and harvesting root crops. The basic design sometimes was amplified to create a spatula-shaped point at one end or points at each end. As important as these or any other modifications on a one-techno-unit digging stick may have been, they cannot be evaluated in the proposed measure of complexity because a single part is involved in each instance. This resulting loss of information is not only acceptable but desirable in the cross-cultural comparison of forms; the presumption is that the information represented by additional parts is of greater magnitude and significance in the broad-scale development of technology.

After comparing different styles of digging sticks reported in ethnographies (Fig. 3-1*a–e*), we begin to understand how more complex forms may have emerged by the addition of technounits and why some forms are more developed than others made at essentially the same time. If the artificially pointed, one-part digging stick is taken as the prototype (*a*), any form with two techno-units is more complex. Two-part forms include those made by the Chumash of California (Kroeber, 1925, 563, 935–6) and Bushmen in southern Africa, both of whom placed a stone ring around a stick (van Rippen, 1918, 76–9). Some Bushmen not only fitted a stone ring around a digging stick (*b*) but wedged a piece of wood between the ring and the shaft (*c*) to prevent the ring from slipping (Ratzel, 1896, v. 1, 88). A still more developed Bushman form (*d*) had a stone ring and also a point of horn lashed at one end of the shaft (Schapera, 1951, 141), resulting in a four-technounit form. Any number of people made digging sticks with separate points attached to shafts, but the Inca of Peru produced a still more elaborate form termed a foot-plow (*e*), which was used for planting as well as for harvesting potatoes. A pole was tipped with a

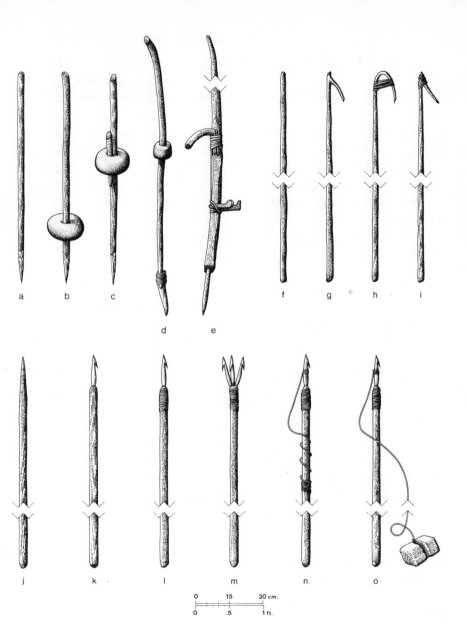

Figure 3-1 Digging sticks, fruit-picking poles, and weapons: (*a*) typical one-part digging stick; (*b–d*) Bushman digging sticks [(*d*) Courtesy of the British Museum; from Schapera, 1951]; (*e*) Inca foot-plow; (*f*) Chenchu pole to dislodge fruit; (*g*) Pitapita seed-removal hook; (*h*) Siriono fruit-picking pole; (*i*) Andamanese fruit-picking pole; (*j*) one-part shaft spear; (*k*) two-part spear; (*l*) three-part spear; (*m*) three-part leister; (*n*) four-part harpoon dart; (*o*) five-part harpoon dart.

wood or bronze point, and essentially modern forms had a double-pronged footrest as well as a handrest bound to the shaft, with a wedge placed between the handrest and the binder (Means, 1931, Figs. 222, 223; Rowe, 1946, 211; Figs. 23c, 24a, d).

The implication is that whenever a technounit is added to the one-piece digging stick, the resulting form is more developed. Apparently stone rings came to be included on Chumash and some Bushman sticks to provide greater thrust for digging in hard soil. The Inca form possibly emerged in response to intensive farming practices. Each of these digging sticks with its technounits is listed as follows:

Style		tu
A	1	digging stick (prototype)
B	2	+ stone ring (Bushman, Chumash)
C	3	+ + shaft-ring wedge (Bushman)
D	4	+ + horn point + shaft-point binder (Bushman)
E	6	shaft + wood point + wood handrest + wood footrest + rest-shaft binders + footrest-binder wedge (Inca)

Given the basic stick as Style A and the manner in which technological knowledge accretes today, it is inconceivable that Style A did not serve as the archetype from which styles B through E emerged. Likewise B must have preceded C. Considering the attributes of D, we have no way of knowing from these data whether the stone ring preceded, followed, or was added to the basic stick at the same time as the horn point and its binder. Neither is it possible to establish a temporal sequence for D and E from the information at hand. It might be that the two-technounit stone-ringed digging stick, Style B, originated after the six-technounit form represented by Style E. If so then any unilineal model for the one to six progression of digging stick technounits would be invalid, but a multilineal model could accommodate the differences. For the moment the primary point is that within a functional cluster the artifacts that have greater numbers of technounits are more evolved in technological terms. The chronology of such changes or the pattern of change may differ within or between areas, but the basic concept that an increased number of technounits means greater complexity remains consistent for fully aboriginal technologies.

As an aside it must be noted that the addition of doughnut-shaped stones to digging sticks made by the Chumash and Bushmen, with no intermediary distributional links, suggests that they conceived of the form without mutual contact. Thus we infer the independent invention of the stone-ringed digging stick in aboriginal California and southern Africa. In the context of the present study this fact is interesting but *not* important. The significant factor is that the number of technounits for the two different forms reflects the same degree of technological complexity.

Long poles for dislodging fruit, nuts, or seeds presumably are among the most elementary forms of natural sticks used as subsistants. By considering these in terms of technounit numbers as they were reported among different peoples at the time of historic contact, we again may gain a certain amount of insight into the sequence of possible developments (Fig. 3-1*f–i*). The Chenchu of India (Fürer-Haimendorf, 1943, 64) used long natural poles to dislodge fruit (*f*). The Pitapita of northern Australia (Roth, 1897, 92) used a hook-ended pole for obtaining seeds from trees; the form presumably was a one-technounit artifact, with the base of a branch serving as the hook (*g*). The two-technounit pole used by the Siriono of Bolivia to collect inaccessible fruit (Holmberg, 1950, 28) consisted of a palm midrib that was bent back at one end to form a hook that was held firm with a liana (*h*). The people on the Andaman Islands in the Sea of Bengal used a more complex pole to pick fruit (Man, 1883, 398; Radcliffe-Brown, 1948, 418, 476). It was as much as fifteen feet in length and consisted of three technounits (*i*): the hook, a pole, and a hook-pole binder. In terms of overall design and technounit number it is inferred that the natural stick used by the Chenchu represents the prototype. An artifactual hooked pole made from a single piece of wood is a logical progression. It was followed, in terms of technological developments, by compound forms, of which the Siriono style is simpler in terms of technounit number than the Andamanese fruit picker. It might be asserted that the Siriono hook is cleverer or more ingenious because it was made by bending one end of the pole back onto itself to form the hook. Nonetheless it is technologically simpler than the Andamanese hook because fewer technounits are represented.

We likewise may retrodict basic developments in the evolution of the harpoon dart and leister (fish spear) from the shaft spear on the basis of increasing technounit numbers (Fig. 3-1*j–o*). Again we begin with a natural stick that presumably was used as a multipurpose naturefact, usually to obtain plant foods but occasionally to kill or maim animals. When a relatively long, stout stick purposefully was sharpened to a point at one end, it became a shaft spear for use against animals (*j*). A separate barbed point might then have been attached to a shaft as a more effective piercing device (*k*), and a point-shaft binder might have been added at that time or soon thereafter (*l*). Thus we have reconstructed the emergence of a spear with three technounits: point + shaft + point-shaft binder. A refinement along one line would have been to add three barbed points of similar design to the end of a shaft to produce a leister (m). In a more direct line, the spear developed further when the base of the point (tang) was fitted loosely into the end of the shaft and a connecting line was attached to both parts (n). With this development a simple shaft spear was transformed into a harpoon dart. A still more involved form occurred when the line from the point was attached to a separate float (o).

The major steps in the evolution of the natural stick to the spear and then to the harpoon dart have only partial support from excavated recoveries because organic materials decay rapidly under most circumstances. Therefore this developmental sequence has been reconstructed by following the theoretical evolutionary model and considering the manner in which technological knowledge accumulates today. In these terms it appears inconceivable that the composite spear could have been invented before a form made from a single technounit prevailed or that a harpoon dart with a separate float could have originated before the form with a line attached only to the shaft.

The greatest failing of technographers and technologists concerned with changes in artifact form is that they have been engrossed, even charmed and enchanted, with the methods of working particular materials or with the tools and techniques of workmanship. To stress these particulars obscures recognition that as different kinds of parts are combined artifacts evolve into more effective forms. Admittedly counting parts or technounits is simplistic in many ways, but doing so yields a measurable assessment of artifact complexity.

PART 2

THE
SUBSISTANT
TAXONOMY

CHAPTER 4

INSTRUMENTS

Aboriginal peoples typically expended a great deal of energy in the quest for food. The round of seasonal activities always was organized in terms of food procurement, and ceremonies were held during periods of plenty. To obtain edibles on a routine basis required at a minimum the use of technological forms handled in a skillful manner and with prior knowledge concerning key characteristics of the species sought. Supernatural involvements often were centered on edible species, and if there was one aspect of a child's upbringing that remained important on a lifetime basis, it probably was teachings about food and the means to obtain it. Among foragers who did not store food, the search for something to eat occupied a portion of nearly every day of their active adult lives, and the preparation of meals was part of their daily routine. Because of the many different settings in which people lived and the variety of edibles that they consumed, highly diverse strategies were employed in subsistence pursuits. Yet each strategy focused on the key characteristics of the particular edible sought. In this chapter and the three that follow, the characteristics of edible species and the technological forms employed to deal with them are presented in combination.

People everywhere, as terrestrial beings in anatomical and habitual terms, have essentially the same capacity for agility, intelligence, and physical mobility. They usually move about by walking or running, less often by climbing or swimming, and they commonly manipulate objects by lifting, pulling, pushing, throwing, and thrusting. These are general observations about the ways in which humans may position themselves and act in their role as predators. *The theme of this chapter is that fixed or relatively stationary species that do not pose a threat to human well-being are the edibles most subject to predation with the most elementary subsistants.* The word *elementary* is defined largely in terms of the small number of technounits per form. Conversely, as set forth in the chapters that follow, those species of animals capable of greater physical mobility than people, and those that may pose a threat to human safety if pursued, are less subject to predation and therefore can be taken only with subsistants that are technologically more complex. In sum and in general, those edibles that are harmless to people and do not have the capacity for effective movement are the easiest to harvest with the simplest forms.

The word *instrument* identifies *hand-manipulated subsistants that customarily are used to impinge on masses incapable of significant motion and relatively harmless to people.* Instruments may be used against any species meeting these criteria, whether it be terrestrial or aquatic, plant or animal, wild or domestic. From paleoethnographic evidence it appears that people began to exploit aquatic food resources systematically about 12,000 years ago when Mesolithic peoples in northern Europe began to depend heavily on fish and shellfish as food (G. Clark, 1971, 92–8; J. G. D. Clark, 1948, 50). It also is probable that about 10,000 years ago the first species were domesticated for use as food (e.g., Chard, 1975, 216–20).

Of the 1175 subsistant total for the thirty-six peoples sampled, 210 forms have been identified as instruments. These are arranged in four tables (Tables 4-1 through 4-4) on the basis of whether they are naturefacts or artifacts and whether they obtained plant or animal species. The table subdivisions distinguish which instruments were used against wild or domestic species and whether they were used in terrestrial or aquatic contexts. Each instrument is listed in a table with its technounit number in parentheses. Its primary use is identified, and alternative designations are in parentheses. The order of presentation within each grouping is by people and geographical region, following the sequence described in the Introduction. In the tables for this and all the other chapters of Part 2, each form used by any people is listed only *once* and is reported in terms of known or presumed primary food-getting purposes. Specific references, alternative uses, and other subsistants that might be used at the same time are recorded in the inventories for particular peoples which comprise the Appendix.

The naturefact–artifact distinction is made to clarify the ways in which natural forms were used, the breadth of their distribution, and their technological characteristics. In the process we also are able to gain some indication of possible naturefact uses in times more remote. A dichotomy also is drawn between forms used to obtain wild as opposed to domestic species. Since wild species were exploited exclusively until comparatively recent times, this division enables us to establish whether instruments were perhaps more varied or technologically simpler for obtaining wild as opposed to domestic species.

To separate instruments used on land from those used in water is important because of the recentness of aquatic resource exploitations. For our purposes terrestrial species are defined as those that habitually were reaped on land and just above or below its surface, whereas aquatic species are associated directly with water. An instrument is employed on a habitual basis only if the species sought is not capable of effective motion and is not dangerous to human predators in a harvest context. Nourishment is obtained in terrestrial settings through the harvesting of domestic crops, fruits, nuts, seeds, and wild berries. Ants, grubs, and porcupines, which are essentially immobile, are taken on land, while roots and some burrowing animals found a short distance beneath the land surface may be taken with instruments. Beavers and seals, if customariyl killed on land, are terrestrial in the context of their harvest. Immobility applies to a sleeping bird knocked from its roost, a lethargic lizard killed with a stick while sunning itself, a hibernating bear stabbed to death, or normally mobile and dangerous animals that are incapacitated by trauma. Aquatic species taken with instruments include shellfish, an octopus removed from a hole in rocks, and any water plant or its product. Forms used through holes in ice take aquatic species, but if a species such as a polar bear normally is taken on the surface of ice, the context is considered terrestrial.

All of the instruments used by the peoples sampled are listed in Tables 4-1 through 4-4, arranged according to the criteria cited. The placement of a particular instrument is based on the most reasonable judgments in two independent evaluations. Since ethnographic sources seldom distinguish between natural forms and artifacts, the identification of some naturefacts may be in error. Furthermore ethnographers sometimes did not identify the primary use of an instrument as opposed to secondary uses, and this has led to some arbitrary decisions about the purposes served by certain forms. For economy of presentation forms that are similar in design and purpose are listed as one entry in any section of a table. Thus all digging sticks used to obtain wild plant products comprise a single entry, which is followed by the names of the groups using the form. If a digging stick served to obtain domestic plant products instead of wild, its entry would be within the domestic plant subdivision. In other words entries are based first on the general structural characteristics of a form, digging stick being separate from ax, and secondarily on the purpose it served, digging stick for wild plants being a separate form and therefore a separate entry from digging stick for domestic plants. The tables include forms and the people employing them. Technounit totals for each form precede the name of the people; two or more numbers within parentheses indicate forms of the same style. The discussion of the information in each table focuses on the most widely prevailing forms or on unusual ones in terms of their structural complexity.

Naturefacts Used to Obtain Plant Foods (Table 4-1) It hardly need be noted that aboriginal peoples were adept at harvesting many wild and domestic plant

Table 4-1   Naturefacts used as instruments primarily to obtain plant foods

Form (1 tu each) and function	People
A. *Wild plants on land*	
Seed (berry)-removal stick	Aranda, Walapai
Long stick, dislodge pinecones	S. V. Paiute
Pole, dislodge fruit	Walapai, Chenchu
Hammerstone to obtain mescal	Walapai
Forked stick, seed beater	Walapai
Tree-chopping stone, fell tree with edible leaves	Tasmanians
Digging stick	Tasmanians
B. *Domestic plants on land*	
Digging stick, root crops	Trukese
C. *Wild plants in water*	
None	
D. *Domestic plants in water*	
None	

products with their limbs and hands rather than by using extrasomatic forms. Natural instruments may be presumed to have served as elementary extensions of human arms to reach food products or as human hands in dislodging and digging for foods. We would expect that the naturefacts reported most often were employed on an opportunistic basis. However this possibility is difficult to document because of the incompleteness of most ethnographic accounts in this respect. In only one instance was a naturefact used with an artifact for obtaining plant foods; the Walapai used a hammerstone with a mescal chisel that was an artifact. Natural instruments most often were employed by people in desert and tropical settings, but even among them the total includes only seven examples. The diminutive size of the inventory indicates the degree to which aboriginal peoples had come to depend on artifacts.

Artifacts Used to Obtain Plant Foods (Table 4-2) A prevailing truism dictates that the forms made and used by aboriginal peoples to obtain plant foods are few in

Table 4-2 *Artifacts used as instruments primarily to obtain plant foods*

Form (1–6 tu) and function	People
A. *Wild plants on land*	
Digging stick	(2) S. V. Paiute, (1) Aranda, (1) Naron, (1) O. V. Paiute, (1) Tiwi, (1) Ingura, (3, 3) Chenchu, (1) Andamanese, (4) Klamath, (1) Tlingit, (1) Twana, (1) Lepcha, (1) Nabesna, (1) Ingalik
Racketlike seed beater	(6) S. V. Paiute, (4) O. V. Paiute, (2) Walapai, (3) Klamath
Fruit(nut)-dislodging pole	(3) O. V. Paiute, (3) Pima
Fruit-removal hook	(3) Walapai, (3) Andamanese
Irrigation ditch-clearing pole	(1) O. V. Paiute
One-piece tongs, collect cactus fruit	(1) Pima, (1) Walapai, (1) Hopi
Stick, remove thorns from prickly pear fruit	(1) Pima
Mescal chisel	(1) Walapai
Branch, brush spines from cactus fruit	(1) Walapai
Crooked stick, dislodge pinecones	(1) Walapai
Ax, chop tree for fruit (tap maple tree)	(2) Chenchu, (3) Ojibwa
Wood spile, tap maple tree sap	(1) Ojibwa
Seed-beating stick	(1) Klamath
Bone knife, remove edible inner bark from pine	(1) Klamath
B. *Domestic plants on land*	
Ax ("chopper," "machete"), clear plot	(3) Pima, (3) Jivaro, (4, 1) Kapauku, (2) Naga, (2, 2) Akamba, (5) Tanala, (2) Tonga, (3) Huron, (2) Lepcha
Hoe (spud), clear plot (plant, cultivate, weed)	(1) Pima, (2) Hopi, (2, 1) Naga, (2) Tonga, (3) Huron, (3) Aymara, (1, 1) Ojibwa, (2, 2) Lepcha

Table 4-2 (Continued)

Form (1–6 tu) and function	People
Shovel (spade), construct terraces (cultivate, harvest)	(1) Pima, (1,1) Kapauku, (1) Akamba, (2) Tanala, (4) Aymara
Digging stick, clear plot (plant, cultivate, harvest)	(1) Pima, (1) Walapai, (1) Hopi, (1) Yuma, (1) Jivaro, (1) Trukese, (1) Pukapuka, (1) Kapauku, (1) Akamba, (1) Tanala, (1) Huron, (1) Lepcha
Hand shovel (trowel)	(1) Walapai, (1) Hopi
Rake	(3) Hopi, (3) Naga
Weed cutter	(1) Hopi, (1) Yuma, (1) Kapauku
Knife, harvest (clear plot, cultivate, make plant cuttings)	(1) Yuma, (1) Jivaro, (1) Trukese, (1) Pukapuka, (1) Kapauku, (3) Naga, (3) Akamba, (3) Tonga, (3,3) Lepcha
Planting pole	(1) Jivaro, (1) Tanala
Breadfruit-picking pole	(3) Trukese
Land-clearing stick	(1) Trukese
Tree-felling blade	(3) Trukese
Coconut shell, excavate plot	(1) Pukapuka
Wood club, clod breaker	(1) Naga
Pole, clod breaker	(1) Akamba
Stone-headed clod crusher	(3,2) Aymara
Threshing stick	(1) Tonga
Plow	(6) Aymara, (6) Lepcha
Plow harness	(2, 1) Aymara
Sickle	(3) Aymara, (3) Lepcha
Root grubber	(1) Ojibwa
Wood lever, pry roots	(1) Ojibwa
Harrow	(5) Lepcha
Wood plank, level plowed ground	(2) Lepcha
C. *Wild plants in water*	
Water lily seed-collection basket	(3) Klamath
Sticks, harvest wild rice	(2) Ojibwa
D. *Domestic plants in water*	
Knife to harvest rice	(1) Tanala

number and technologically simple. These bits of conventional wisdom are supported by the data in the sample. On land only 14 styles of instruments served to obtain wild plant foods, and 24 styles were used with domestic species of plants. If we divide the number of different instruments noted into their technounit totals, we find that for forms used to obtain wild plants on land the average number of technounits is 1.8, and for domestic plants on land the average is 1.9. Thus the technological complexity of instruments used in these contexts is low and is essentially the same. This statement could not be verified, even tentatively, without a standardized means for measuring technological complexity.

The entries in this table indicate that the most important distinction between instruments for obtaining wild plants and those for domestic plants is in terms of use rather than structural complexity. To foster the development of plants a single form was used in foraging activities; the Owens Valley Paiute cleaning pole was used in irrigation ditches to channel water to wild seed-bearing plants. All the other instruments used in association with wild plants were for harvesting. Farming instruments, by contrast, usually were employed in clearing and tending a plot rather than in the actual harvest of a crop. Instrument usages among farmers required a long-range planning that rarely was indicated in the use of instruments for foraging. Likewise plant collectors seldom used two forms in coordinated combination, but just the opposite was true for farmers.

The least specialized one-part instrument is the digging stick. It occurs widely among foragers, and farmers often used it to plant seeds or cuttings and to harvest root crops as well as to obtain wild species of edibles. Digging sticks (Fig. 4-1*a–d*) seldom included more than a single technounit. Among the more elaborate forms the Surprise Valley Paiute placed a skin grip around the handle of their digging stick (*a*), and the Chenchu made two iron-pointed varieties that had three technounits each. One Chenchu form was end hafted (*b*), and the other was hafted in a slot along the lower end of the shaft (*c*). The most developed form, that of the Klamath, included a crosspiece attached to the shaft with a line and pitch binder (*d*). It is noteworthy that each of the forms used by farmers in association with cultivated plants consisted of a single technounit. In spite of the occurrence of compound forms, the one-piece digging stick is certainly one of the most versatile, if not one of the most elegant, artifacts ever made by people.

Instrument technology seldom was applied to the harvest of plant products from water, which suggests the relatively minor importance of aquatic plant species as food; this is in striking contrast with the technology for harvesting aquatic animals. Among foragers the most important species-specific instruments for taking plants were associated with cactus fruits, which is predictable since cactuses were the plants most capable of harming people during their harvesting. Other species-specific forms include the knife used to remove edible pine bark, the wild rice-harvesting sticks, and breadfruit-picking pole. The comparative scarcity of specialized forms indicates just how versatile most instruments were. The racketlike seed beaters for harvesting wild seeds on land

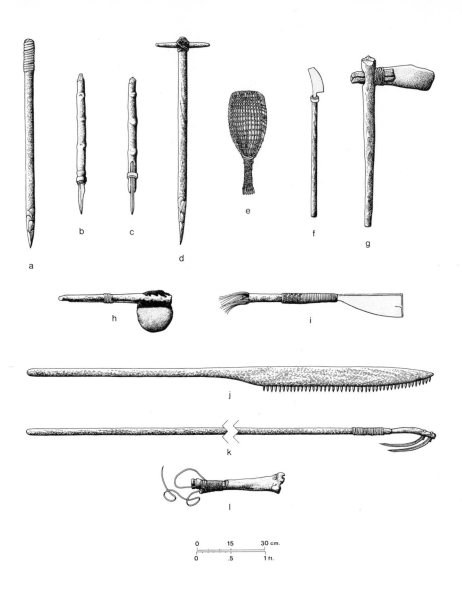

Figure 4-1 Instruments used to obtain plant and animal products as food: (*a*) Surprise Valley Paiute digging stick; (*b*, *c*) Chenchu digging sticks (Courtesy of Macmillan London and Basingstoke; from Fürer-Haimendorf, 1943); (*d*) Klamath digging stick; (*e*) Owens Valley Paiute seed beater; (*f*) Tanala plot-clearing ax; (*g*) Kapauku plot-clearing ax (Courtesy of *Yale University Publications in Anthropology* and Leopold Pospisil; from Pospisil, 1963); (*h*) Aranda ax for procuring animals or their products (Courtesy of Macmillan London and Basingstoke; from Spencer and Gillen, 1927); (*i*) Naga clearing knife and cultivator (Courtesy of the Government of Nagaland; from Hutton, 1967); (*j*) Twana herring rake; (*k*) Copper Eskimo fish snag; (*l*) Ingalik bear-killing club (Courtesy of *Yale University Publications in Anthropology* and Cornelius Osgood; from Osgood, 1940).

are among the most complex forms technologically, and the one used by the Owens Valley Paiute is illustrated (*e*). It is somewhat surprising that seed beaters, given their apparent usefulness, did not prevail more widely.

We find that among cultivators the specialization of instruments is best reflected in their diversity rather than in a high technounit average. For example, the Akamba used an ax and chopper to clear cultivated plots, while the Naga, Ojibwa, and Lepcha used two styles of hoes. Among the cultivators sampled the most complex instruments were cutting tools used for clearing during planting or harvesting. The metal-bladed clearing ax of the Tanala was the most developed form (*f*) followed by that of the Kapauku, which had a stone blade (*g*). The three-part metal-bladed knives used by the Akamba, Tonga, and Lepcha served primarily for harvesting, while the Naga form (*i*) was used to clear and cultivate the soil. Among the other instruments with relatively high technounit numbers were the Aymara plow, spade, and sickle. It is not inappropriate to note that the Aymara were one of the most acculturated peoples in the sample. The most impressive factor about all the instruments used to obtain plant foods, irrespective of whether the species involved were wild or domestic, is the technological simplicity of the examples.

Naturefacts Used to Obtain Animals or Animal Products (Table 4-3)   The danger posed to people by the claws and teeth of most animals and the ability of many species to escape from human predators make the use of natural instruments unlikely under most circumstances. This was predicted in an earlier chapter and certainly is supported by the data represented in the sample. The Surprise Valley Paiute alone used diverse instruments in this manner. Quite possibly some of these Paiute instruments should be grouped together, but there are equally good reasons for the separate listing of entries. The stick used to kill a deer trapped in a pitfall was presumably stout since an animal was jabbed to death. The straight stick for taking a squirrel was twisted in its skin and probably was relatively small. The form for taking rats appears to have been small and thin because as a rat bit it the stick was thrust down the throat to kill the rat.

Occasionally it was difficult to establish whether a particular naturefact was used as an instrument or a weapon, in which case the classification is at least partially arbitrary. For example, the Hopi used a stick to kill prairie dogs driven from their burrows with water. It is presumed that an animal emerging from a hole was capable of some effective movement, and therefore this stick was classed as a weapon. Somewhat similarly the Iglulik Eskimos drove geese that

Table 4-3   Naturefacts used as instruments primarily to obtain animals or their products as food

Form (1 tu each) and function	People
A. *Wild animals on land*	
Stick, kill deer in pitfall	S. V. Paiute
Stick, remove squirrel from hiding place	S. V. Paiute
Stick, impale rat in burrow	S. V. Paiute
Barbed stick, pull lizard from crevice	Walapai
Honey-removal stick	Ingura
Stick as club, used with weapon or facility	Klamath, Huron, Tanaina
B. *Domestic animals on land*	
Killing club	Kapauku
Killing stick	Naga
Braining stone	Lepcha
C. *Wild animals in water*	
Crayfish tongs	Tanala
Stick (club), kill fish, may be used with weapons or facilities	Pukapuka, Ingalik
Stone, kill fish, may be used with weapons or facilities	Pukapuka, Klamath, Copper Eskimos
D. *Domestic animals in water*	
None	

could not fly into an enclosure of stones and then killed them with sticks. The presumption is that the geese were capable of considerable movement, and the sticks served as weapons. What is most impressive about the list in general, if we ignore the Surprise Valley Paiute uses, is that there were very few different forms represented. Furthermore, and of far greater importance, most non-Paiute forms were employed with artifacts that first injured or maimed a species, the naturefacts serving to administer the coup de grace.

Artifacts Used to Obtain Animals or Their Products (Table 4-4)   Instruments never were used alone for taking animals in the wild that were dangerous to people, and this characteristic is shared by similarly employed naturefacts. An ax acted on the habitat of a wild species to obtain a species or its products rather than on the species or product itself. The Aranda ax (Fig. 4-1*h*) had a ground stone blade with a section of wood bent around the top and tied at its extensions to form the handle; the blade was held in place with plant resin. It was used to chop

Table 4-4   Artifacts used as instruments primarily to obtain animals or their products as food. All forms are simple except for the Akamba cattle-bleeding arrow, which is complex

Form (1–7 tu) and function	People
A. Wild animals on land	
Ax, cut wood to obtain animals (eggs, honey, etc.)	(4) Aranda, (4) Tiwi
Grub hook	(1) Aranda
Game-removal hook	(4) Naron, (5,3) Tanaina
Rat(rabbit)-removal stick	(2) Walapai
Honey-removal stick	(1) Tiwi
Knife (dagger), remove honeycomb (kill animals used with weapons)	(1) Ingura, (3) Twana, (4) Caribou Eskimos
Toggle and line, remove honeycomb used with spatula	(2) Chenchu
String shot into honeycomb with arrow, honey runs down string	(1) Chenchu
Spatula to cut honeycomb used with toggle and line	(1) Chenchu
Bird-striking pole	(1) Pukapuka
Hunting club used with weapon or facility	(1) Tonga, (1) Twana, (4) Ingalik
Paddle, scrape soil for moth chrysalids	(1) Klamath
Porcupine spear; barbed, pointed stick	(1) Tanaina
B. Domestic animals on land	
Knife, slaughter (brand, geld) animals	(3) Hopi, (1) Kapauku, (1) Naga, (3) Aymara
Cattle-bleeding arrow used with bow and lines to hold cattle; complex subsistant	(4) Akamba
Awl, castrate bulls	(1) Akamba
Needle, kill llamas as food	(1) Aymara
Pointed stick, kill livestock	(1) Lepcha
C. Wild animals in water	
Ice pick for fishing (sealing, etc.)	(3) S. V. Paiute, (3) Klamath, (3) Tlingit, (3) Huron, (3) Ojibwa, (4) Caribou Eskimos, (3) Ingalik, (5) Copper Eskimos, (3) Iglulik, (3) Tareumiut
Adz, free mollusks	(3) Andamanese
Hook-ended crabbing stick	(1) Andamanese
Probing (groping) stick	(1,1) Trukese, (1) Pukapuka
Crayfish leister	(3) Kapauku
Forked pole, lift weeds for crayfish (insects)	(1) Kapauku
Shellfish-dislodging knife	(1) Pukapuka
Fish-killing club	(1) Pukapuka
Shellfish-dislodging stick	(1) Tasmanians

Table 4-4   (Continued)

Form (1–7 tu) and function	People
Herring rake	(2) Tlingit, (2) Twana
Sharpened pole, kill deer driven into water	(1) Huron
Sea mammal club	(1) Tlingit, (1) Tanaina, (1) Iglulik
Fish-killing bodkin	(4) Caribou Eskimos
Sharpened stick, bullheads	(1) Tanaina
Crab-impaling pole	(1) Tanaina
Impaler, kill (remove) fish in traps	(3,2) Ingalik
Snag, fish (sea mammals)	(6) Copper Eskimos, (4) Iglulik
Seal-killing ice scoop	(4) Copper Eskimos
Capelin (mussel) scoop	(7,6) Angmagsalik
Stiletto, kill wounded sea mammals	(3,2) Angmagsalik

D. *Domestic animals in water*
    None

into the branches of trees to retrieve animals, eggs, and honeycombs. The Tiwi ax was generally similar in form and served largely to remove bandicoots and opossums from hollow logs or tree branches.

The counterpart of fruit-picking poles was the game-removal hook. As a group the examples in the sample are comparatively elaborate. The Naron form consisted of a number of reed poles bound together with sinew; at one end was tied a horn hook. The instrument was used to remove anteaters, snakes, and spring hares from their holes. The Tanaina used a gaff hook attached to a long pole to dislodge a porcupine from a tree or an ordinary gaff to take beavers from a lodge. The removal stick used by the Walapai is unusual because of one of its technounits. A pliable stick was moistened at one end with saliva and inserted into a hole in which a rabbit or rat was concealed. The animal could be obtained by twisting the stick into its fur.

Honey removal was most developed among the Chenchu, who found nests on cliffs as well as in inaccessible reaches of trees. To retrieve honeycombs from cliffs a man equipped with a wooden spatulalike instrument was lowered by rope over the cliff edge by one or two men. A separate fiber line with a bamboo toggle attached at the bottom was lowered beside the man, who skewered the honeycomb with the toggle. After the nest was cut free with the spatula, it was hauled up by the man or men above. The toggle line and spatula are considered as linked artifacts since the combination was essential for obtaining honey by this method. The rope on which the collector was lowered is an artifactual aid since it indirectly enabled him to harvest the honey. Another way honey in an inaccessible nest might be obtained was by shooting an arrow with a string attached into the honeycomb. The honey flowed down the string into a basket held by the collector. The bow and arrow combination served the same general purpose as the rope for lowering a man over a cliff and thus is judged as an aid. The basket likewise is an aid because it received the honey from the string but did not actually procure the honey in a direct manner.

Artifactual instruments such as clubs and knives may superficially seem to have served as weapons, but they were in fact used to kill wild or domestic animals that previously had been either injured or brought to hand by other means. It might be felt that still other instruments, which were used independently, might more properly be considered as weapons because the species involved usually were capable of effective movement. Yet escape does not appear to have been reasonable when the instruments cited were used. For example, the herring rake of the Twana (Fig. 4-1*j*) was used from a canoe in the midst of a herring school so thick that individual fish were unable to escape from the tines of the rake as it was moved about. The same was true for a fish snag used by the Copper Eskimos (*k*) at the base of a falls where char occurred in such large numbers that they could not escape. The hooks of this form were made of native copper. The hook-ended snag used by the Iglulik is another case in point. It was used to retrieve young seals from resting ledges sniffed out by dogs. The seals apparently were so frightened that they did not attempt to escape into the water below.

One form used against wild species on land, worthy of special comment because it included a liquid as a technounit, is the four-part Ingalik club. The Ingalik cut off the lower end of a moose tibia and inserted in the opening a wooden plug long enough to serve as a handle. The plug was bound to the bone with babiche lashings that ended in a hand loop (Fig. 4-1*l*). When the club was to be used, the plug was removed, warm oil poured into the marrow cavity, and the plug driven back in place. The oil soaked into the bone, which made it heavier. This club was employed mainly against enemies but also against bears, presumably bears that were relatively immobile. Although this club served as a weapon against a fleeing enemy, it is unlikely that clubs were used in the pursuit of bears, and thus they are not judged as weapons in this context.

The most important observation about artifactual instruments for obtaining animals or their products is that they most often were employed with other subsistants. The thirteen styles for taking wild species on land is significantly lower than the twenty styles employed for wild species in water. The techno-unit average for artifactual instruments used to take wild animal species on land is 2.3 compared with 2.6 for those taken in water. These averages support the notion that forms associated with water were more complex than those used on land; the data about weapons in Chapter 5 provide a further test.

Summary   The 210 instruments for the peoples sampled included 407 techno-units for an overall average of 1.9 technounits per form. A synopsis of the naturefact and artifact information in the tables follows:

	Plants			Animals		
	Forms	tu	Average	Forms	tu	Average
Wild on land	45	75	1.7	28	53	1.9
Domestic on land	79	151	1.9	11	18	1.6
Wild in water	2	5	2.5	44	104	2.4
Domestic in water	1	1	1.0			
	127	232	1.8	83	175	2.1

The contrast between clusters is obvious: Many forms were used in association with domestic plants on land, while few were used for domestic animals on land. Few forms were employed against wild plants in water, but many forms were used to obtain wild animals in water. The most numerous instruments for food getting were those used to obtain domestic land plants. Finally the complexity of the forms used for wild plants on land approximates that of the forms for taking wild animals on land.

Conclusions   Instruments were both extensions of human hands and competitors with hands. Because of the manipulative abilities of hands, arms, and legs, these anatomical features were highly adaptive for obtaining nondangerous, relatively immobile species. It will be recalled that a distinction was drawn in Chapter 3 between simple and complex subsistants. Those that are simple do not change their form during use, but complex forms include at least two technounits that change their relationship with one another during use. It is worthy of special note that only one complex instrument was identified in the sample. It is the arrow used by the Akamba to bleed cattle; the employment of an arrow in this context seems more "ceremonial" than practical. The reason simple instruments dominate appears to be the versatility of human hands. Instruments that operated in a mechanical manner could not compete with hands.

In plotting the evolution of food-getting technology, the use of naturefacts as instruments by the sampled populations is not very informative. These people were far removed from the point of human origins and had learned to make a host of artifacts. Natural instruments used without the aid of other subsistants were few and served humble purposes. Natural instruments most often were used to kill species that already had been wounded with artifacts. Furthermore it is difficult to conceive of many additional ways in which naturefacts could have been used as instruments. That natural instruments supplemented weapons suggests that natural forms were not effective as weapons, a consideration to be explored further in Chapter 5.

In terms of technounit numbers the one-part average for naturefacts as instruments is the absolute minimum in both logical and actual terms. These or similar forms used in the remote past are as basic as one might reasonably expect in a technological sense. The adaptive advantage that their use may have offered in the actual procurement of food may not have been great. Yet advantage there no doubt was, if only in terms of the experience gained in handling things. Presumably this was essential before more complicated subsistants could be made.

As technologically elementary as artifactual instruments were for taking wild plant species on land, they nonetheless averaged 1.8 technounits each. As a group they had nearly twice the average number of technounits as naturefacts used for the same purpose, a clear indication of their comparative complexity. Yet it is quite clear that even the developed food-getting technologies of the peoples sampled did not include complicated forms for harvesting wild plants. Perhaps they were either maladaptive or could not be developed with nonindustrial technologies. For domestic plants on land the technounit average for artifactual instruments was 1.9. New forms undoubtedly would have been conceived if the lifeways of the users had not been interrupted. Yet the evidence suggests that innovations more often would be in terms of different forms for cultivating rather than the addition of more technounits on existing subsistants. This is not to deny that more technounits could be added to forms, reflecting an ever-increasing specialization as was true for digging sticks.

The instruments for harvesting wild plants clearly are humble and unexciting. They usually were versatile in their uses and uncomplicated in form.

They stand in striking contrast with weapons and facilities used against wild animals, which were both complicated and specialized by comparison. Yet in the evolution of material culture it was the application of instrument technology used for wild plant foods to the cultivation of plants as food that led to surpluses and remarkable elaborations in other aspects of human life. In terms of long-term trends in cultural evolution it is the digging stick, not the spear, that has served mankind best.

▲▲▲▲▲▲▲▲▲

CHAPTER 5

WEAPONS

Of all the manufactures by aboriginal peoples weapons best represent their achievements, both in popular and technical terms. Weapons are favored by artifact collectors, they frequently serve as the focal point for museum exhibits, and they often are objects of dramatic interest in action photographs. Anthropologists pay greater attention to weapons than to most other items of material culture because of their importance in survival. A prime example is the evolutionary taxonomy centered on the development of weapons for the hunt and war by Lane Fox. The use of weaponry technology integrated skill and daring. Thus it is for good reasons that the spear and bow and arrow are the hallmarks of primitive hunters.

A weapon is a form that is handled when in use and is designed to kill or maim species capable of significant motion. In terms of this definition the user must hold or manipulate a weapon as he seeks to obtain a food animal that is capable of effective movement at the time the form is brought into play. Spears, bows and arrows, harpoons, and leisters are typical aboriginal weapons.

In introducing weapons we may review those major characteristics of animals and their habitats that have a direct bearing on the procurement technology.

The basic dichotomy between mobile and immobile animals already has been drawn, and a distinction has been made between harmless and physically dangerous species. The terrestrial-aquatic division likewise is significant, and it is apparent that terrestrial animals are far less mobile than are species capable of flying or swimming. This in turn affects accessibility, the time and energy required to locate species, and the nonsubsistant technology reflected in the use of conveyances during food getting. Another aspect of accessibility concerns the luring of species and whether or not disguises or blinds can be employed effectively. The amount of time normally available to employ a weapon requires consideration. In the predator-prey relationship there is also the matter of a species' relative abundance and whether it is concentrated or dispersed. The size of the units harvested and the seasonal variability of habitual numbers are major concerns. The degree to which the appearance and behavior of a species is predictable cannot be ignored, and the same is true for a prey's morphology with reference to the kill. Within a particular habitat these rather obvious variables for all pertinent species affect the resource base on which the weapons of people impinge. The qualities of their weapons emerge from technological traditions and from their fund of knowledge about the species sought. These factors are discussed more fully when the inventories for the sampled peoples are considered with reference to their habitats and foods.

We now turn to the text and tables in which the structural characteristics of weapons are set forth. As was true for instruments, weapons are separated on the basis of whether they were used primarily on land or in water and whether in foraging or farming contexts. Among instruments used by the peoples sampled, a single form was identified as complex, but complex weapons were important for taking wild animals. Once again, a complex subsistant is one with two or more technounits that change their physical relationship with one another, in a mechanical sense, when the form is used.

Naturefacts Used as Weapons (Table 5-1) It has been asserted that in logical terms natural weapons were probably of limited utility within the scope of technohistory. This appears to be true for the aboriginal peoples sampled, yet it is likely that sticks and stones were used as weapons more often and more widely than has been reported by ethnographers. Clubs and sticks, whether hand held or thrown, have been listed together in the table because a form may reasonably have functioned either way depending on the immediate context of usage. According to the ethnographic accounts consulted, these naturefacts were not very important; they appear to have been used only occasionally, compared

Table 5-1 Naturefacts used as weapons

Form (1 tu each) and function	People
A. *Wild animals on land*	
Stick (short stick, missile stick, club), kill small game (birds)	S. V. Paiute, S. V. Paiute, Walapai, Hopi, Hopi, Tiwi, Chenchu, Tonga, Aymara, Iglulik
Missile stone, small game (birds, snakes)	Walapai, Hopi, Tiwi, Ingura, Chenchu, Kapauku, Tasmanians, Caribou Eskimos, Tanaina, Copper Eskimos, Iglulik, Angmagsalik
Pole, kill ducks	Aymara
B. *Protect domestic species from wild species on land* None	
C. *Wild species in water*	
Stone, stun (drive) fish from beneath rocks, taken by hand (net)	Lepcha
D. *Protect domestic species from wild species in water* None	

to other weapons, to take birds and small game. These sticks and stones were used to batter and smash rather than cut and pierce, the more usual pattern with weapons.

Artifacts Used as Weapons on Land (Table 5-2) A remarkably small number of simple weapons are identified as used mainly to obtain wild species on land. The thirty-one forms average 2.5 technounits each, which is a slight increase in complexity over the 2.3 average for simple artifactual instruments used against animals on land. What is most apparent from the inventory of weapons is that aboriginal peoples generally had complex forms that appear to have served their purposes better than simple ones.

Missile sticks (Fig. 5-1a–e) are not distinguished from boomerangs in the reported gradations. The Aranda made straight missile sticks with round cross sections (a), others that were slightly curved and ovoid in cross section, and still others that would be termed boomerangs (b) because they are distinctly curved with flat cross sections. The Hopi forms, thrown to rotate through the air as boomerangs, served primarily to kill rabbits. One type was slightly curved (c), and others are distinctly curved (d); gradations are reported between these extremes. The Tiwi appear to have produced two distinct styles of missile sticks. One was long and straight for killing geese, and the second graded from

An Anthropological Analysis of Food-Getting Technology

Table 5-2   Artifacts used as weapons on land

Form (1–13 tu) and function	People
A. *Simple forms for wild species*	
Missile stick (boomerang, throwing-stick, digger, club)	(1) Aranda, (1) Naron, (1) Hopi, (1,1) Tiwi, (1) Tasmanians
Spear (lance, club)	(3) Naron, (1) Tiwi, (5) Naga, (2) Tanala, (5) Tonga, (1) Tasmanians, (3) Tlingit, (3) Huron, (5) Lepcha, (2) Nabesna, (3) Ingalik, (3) Tanaina, (4) Copper Eskimos, (5) Iglulik, (4,3) Tareumiut
Bear spear made from knife	(4) Nabesna
Club	(1) O. V. Paiute, (1) Pima, (1) Aymara
Hunting knife	(2) Yuma, (1) Ojibwa, (3) Ingalik, (4) Iglulik, (3) Tareumiut
B *Complex forms for wild species*	
Spear used with throwing-board	(9) Aranda, (1) Ingura
Throwing-board used with spear	(6) Aranda
Bows	
sinew-backed (may also be composite)	(5) S. V. Paiute, (4) O. V. Paiute, (4) Twana, (6,5) Caribou Eskimos, (7) Tanaina, (9) Copper Eskimos, (8) Iglulik, (6) Tareumiut
self	(5) Naron, (2) O. V. Paiute, (3) Pima (2) Walapai, (3) Hopi, (2) Yuma, (6) Andamanese, (2) Kapauku, (4) Akamba, (2) Tanala, (3) Klamath, (2) Tlingit, (2) Huron, (3,3,3) Ojibwa, (3) Lepcha, (6) Nabesna, (3) Ingalik
composite	(4) Chenchu
crossbow	(10) Naga
Arrows	
birds (small game)	(3) S. V. Paiute, (8,6) O. V. Paiute, (4) Pima, (5,5) Walapai, (4,4) Kapauku, (7,7,6) Akamba, (4) Klamath, (3) Twana, (5) Ojibwa, (2) Lepcha, (7,6) Ingalik, (4) Tanaina, (5,5) Tareumiut
big game	(6) S. V. Paiute, (5) Pima, (12,10) Walapai, (13) Andamanese, (6,6) Kapauku, (6) Klamath, (7) Twana, (5,5) Ojibwa, (8) Ingalik, (6) Tanaina, (7,7,5,3) Iglulik, (8,5,5) Tareumiut
game	(5,5) Naron, (10) O. V. Paiute, (5) Hopi, (6,5) Yuma, (6,6,4,4) Chenchu, (5,4) Naga, (13) Akamba, (2) Tanala, (4) Tlingit, (5) Huron, (9,7,7) Lepcha, (5) Caribou Eskimos, (6,5,5,5) Nabesna, (7,4) Copper Eskimos

Table 5-2 (Continued)

Form (1–13 tu) and function	People
Blowgun	(5) Jivaro, (3,2) Tanala
Blowgun dart	(9) Jivaro, (3) Tanala
Bolas, birds (game)	(3) Pukapuka, (4,3) Aymara, (4) Tareumiut
Sling, deer (birds)	(2) Tlingit, (3) Caribou Eskimos, (1) Tanaina, (2) Iglulik, (2) Angmagsalik
Missile for sling (slingshot)	(3) Tlingit, (1) Lepcha, (1) Caribou Eskimos, (1) Tanaina, (1) Iglulik, (1) Angmagsalik
Slingshot	(2) Lepcha
Lance, bear on ice	(9) Angmagsalik
C. Simple forms to protect domestic species from wild species	
None	
D. Complex forms to protect domestic plant species from wild species	
Sling	(3) Akamba, (4) Tanala, (1) Aymara
Missile for sling (pellet bow)	(1) Akamba, (1) Tanala, (1) Aymara, (3) Lepcha
Pellet bow, used with missile	(8) Lepcha

slightly curved to straight with a sharp point at one end (*e*). A Naron missile stick is termed a knobkerrie and is characterized by a rounded head at one end and a point at the opposite end. A knobkerrie was used by a man to hurl at game, to club an animal, or to dig plant products. As has been observed often, multipurpose natural sticks used as weapons probably developed into missile sticks, and some of these emerged as boomerangs in Australia and the southwestern United States. The hurtling motion of a missile stick through the air is equivalent in function with the graceful movement of a boomerang, and one technounit is represented. The temporal priority of one form over the other cannot be considered pertinent since both served the same purpose and were made from a single part.

Spears (Fig. 5-1*f–j*) were the most widely distributed simple weapons, as would be expected. However less than half of the people sampled used spears as their primary weapon against wild game on land. This is a smaller number of users than might have been anticipated. The Tasmanians and Tiwi made the simplest spears; these consisted of shafts sharpened at one end. This very elementary style must have been highly effective judging from ethnographic accounts about the Tasmanians. Their spears were from five to eighteen feet in length and were cut from the long straight shoots of certain trees. A shaft

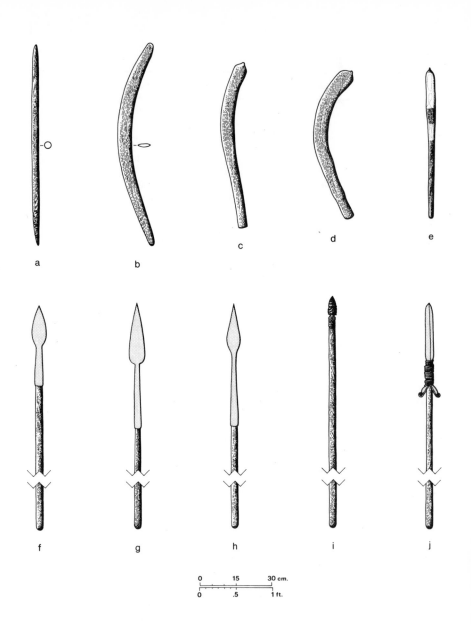

Figure 5-1 Simple weapons used on land: (*a*, *b*) Aranda missile sticks; (*c*, *d*) Hopi missile sticks; (*e*) Tiwi missile stick; (*f–h*) Tanala varieties of spears; (*i*) Tareumiut caribou spear; (*j*) Nabesna hunting knife hafted as a spear (Courtesy of *Yale University Publications in Anthropology* and Robert A. McKennan; from McKennan, 1959).

that was somewhat crooked was heated over a fire and straightened by holding a section between the teeth and bending it by hand. One end of a spear was pointed with the aid of a stone knife and later was hardened in a fire. The bark apparently was peeled off with a notched stone flake, and the shaft planed with a stone scraper. Typically a Tasmanian spear could be thrown from forty to sixty yards with great accuracy.

The two-part Nabesna spear is unusual because it was short, about three feet in length, and because oil was an essential technounit in the finished form. The spear was a long caribou antler tine impregnated with oil for added weight. It was used by brave men against bears and also served as a club. The only other two-part spear is the Tanala form; it had a shaft and an iron point with a sleeved tang that fit over the shaft. These people identified three varieties of spears (*f–h*) on the basis of point shape, but in terms of technounits they represent one style. An example of a three-part spear is one used by the Tareumiut for caribou. They distinguished their whaling lance from a caribou spear, but since both have the same structural configuration and technounit number, they represent a single form in this presentation. It is nonetheless an arbitrary decision to label the form as a caribou spear. It had a chipped stone point attached to a shaft with a strip of baleen (*i*). The Tareumiut bear spear was more developed since it included wedges of skin fitted in the haft between the point and shaft. A bear spear made by the Nabesna is designated as a different style of spear because a separate artifact, a knife, was lashed to a shaft to make a spear as the need arose. The knife blade and handle were fashioned from a single piece of native copper, and to the handle was added a strip of leather as padding (*j*); the handgrip was nonfunctional in terms of the spear's overall design. From the data at hand the technounit maximum for land-use hunting spears was five.

Artifactual clubs and hunting knives possibly were made more often than the accounts mention, but on the basis of the sample we would conclude that they had limited popularity. It is possible that general-purpose knives often were used by hunters to make kills.

Bows and arrows (Fig. 5-2, 3) dominate as complex weapons, and the diversity among arrows is striking. The self bow, meaning that the shaft is made from a single piece of raw material, was the most popular form, and the bowstring frequently was made from sinew or vegetable fiber. The Kapauku bow, as an example of the two-technounit style (Fig. 5-2*a*), consisted of a palm-wood shaft with the bowstring, a section of split rattan vine, tied directly to the shaft. A ring of rattan often was placed near the shaft ends of the Kapauku bow as decoration, but because of its artistic purpose it is not included as a technounit.

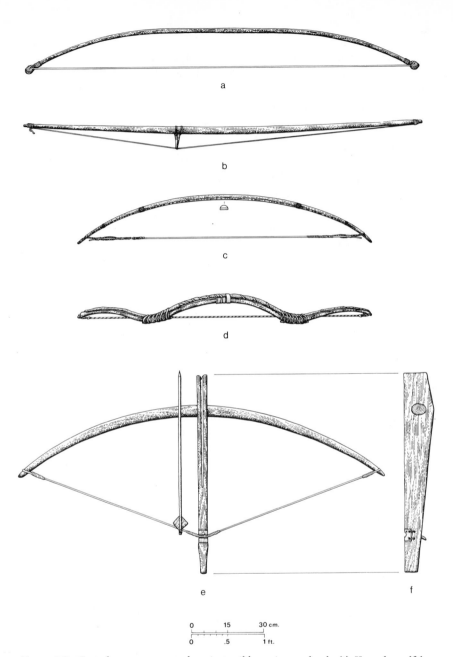

a

b

c

d

e   f

```
0        15        30 cm.
|----|----|----|
0        .5        1 ft.
```

Figure 5-2 Complex weapons used against wild species on land: (*a*) Kapauku self bow (Courtesy of *Yale University Publications in Anthropology* and Leopold Pospisil; from Pospisil, 1963); (*b*) Nabesna self bow with bow guard (Courtesy of *Yale University Publications in Anthropology* and Robert A. McKennan; from McKennan, 1959); (*c*) Chenchu composite bow (Courtesy of Macmillan London and Basingstoke; from Fürer-Haimendorf, 1943); (*d*) Copper Eskimo composite bow with sinew backing; (*e*) Naga crossbow and arrow; (*f*) Naga crossbow mounting [(*e, f*) Courtesy of the Government of Nagaland; from Hutton, 1968].

The technounits most often added to the self bow were shaft-string binders and midshaft handgrips. The Andamanese and Nabesna self bows with six technounits each are the most elaborate examples. The Andamanese form not only had nock strings but a fingerhold on the bowstring, a loop binder on the bowstring for stringing the bow, and a protective coat of wax on the string. The Nabesna bow was coated with blood and grease to toughen the wood, and it included a wood bow guard tied to the shaft (*b*). Among the Ojibwa we find that three different styles of self bows were produced; one was used against big game, the second for taking squirrels, and the third for an unstated purpose. The question of whether to include certain bows as subsistants is posed by the Tanala data. Their adolescent boys used a self bow for hunting; it is judged a subsistant since they presumably were able to kill game on a reasonably frequent basis.

The shaft of a composite bow includes at least two separate pieces which may or may not be made from the same material. The form made by the Chenchu had outer and inner strips of bamboo (*c*); the rings of skin placed around the two parts are described as decorative only. The bowstring consisted of a long sliver of bamboo attached to the composite shaft with sinew. The two styles of Caribou Eskimo bows were composite and sinew backed. One was light and used against birds, and the other was of heavier construction and designed to kill large game. In both instances pieces of wood were spliced and joined to form the shaft. In their habitat long sections of wood were rare, and this apparently led to the development of composite shafts that may include pieces of antler or musk-ox horn as wood substitutes. These bows were backed with strips of sinew for added strength. Wood was equally scarce among the Copper Eskimos, and their composite, sinew-backed bow consisted of nine technounits (*d*). The sections of wood were bound with sinew, and wood reinforcement pieces were placed at the joints plus separate binders for the reinforcements. Loops of sinew prevented the backing from slipping, and sealskin strips beneath the loops reduced friction. Wood wedges were fitted in place to tighten the sinew backing, and the bowstring was made from sinew. A crossbow with ten parts was made by the Naga (*e, f*), and its accuracy range was about sixty yards. The technounits of this crossbow are listed in the Appendix.

Because of the limited size and diversity of the bow sample, it probably is presumptive to rank the entries in terms of complexity, yet at least interim conclusions may be offered. The most elementary form is the self bow with only a bowstring, and elaborations on this two-part style appear to be limited to four additional parts. Composite, sinew-backed bows may have as many as nine parts, and the most developed form is the crossbow with ten technounits. In all likelihood crossbows with fewer technounits were used as weapons among some aboriginal peoples, and there well may be examples of self bows with more than six technounits. However this patterning among bows suggests the predominating numbers of technounits utilized.

Arrows are arranged in Table 5-2 by their use against birds and small game, big game, or, if ethnographic accounts were not specific for all the arrows made by a people, against game in general. This overlapping does not really matter since my primary purpose is to illustrate complexity among arrows relative to their technounit numbers. In terms of structure a basic arrow has five parts: a shaft, separate point, shaft-point binder, feather vanes (fletching), and vane binder. An elementary form with fewer technounits was made by the Lepcha to stun birds. It consisted of a wood shaft with a conical metal tube fitted over one end. The Akamba examples (Fig. 5-3a–d) illustrate elaborations on the five-part model. One bird arrow had a barbed wood head, reed shaft, head-shaft binder, a band of sinew around the nock, feather vanes, and a shaft-vane binder (a). Many different arrangements of barbs occurred on similar Akamba arrows, but since each configuration was carved from a single piece of wood, the differences are ignored. Another bird arrow was barbless and had four pegs held in place with cords (b), and yet another arrow used for the same purpose had crossed sticks bound in place with vegetable fiber (c). In all other respects these arrows are like the style described first. Bird arrows such as these with six and seven parts have significant structural differences that are reflected in technounit totals. The thirteen-part big-game arrow (d) consisted of an iron point attached to a wood foreshaft with sinew. The foreshaft fit into a sinew binder at one end of the wood shaft, which also was bound with hair. The three feather vanes were attached near the base of the shaft with gum and thread, and a leather ring was positioned just above the nock as well as another binder of hair. The point was tipped with a poison consisting of three technounits.

The most developed form of arrow, made by the Andamanese for hunting wild pigs (e), had a shell point and bone barbs bound separately to a wood fore-shaft. The wood shaft into which the foreshaft was fitted had a binder at the joint and at the nock end. A cord from the foreshaft to the shaft was covered with wax, and three-technounit waterproofing was added to the lower part of the point and barb lashings. The head of this arrow detached from the shaft when a pig was struck, but the shaft dragged along by the cord as the pig attempted to escape. The shaft caught on undergrowth to hold the pig fast until the hunter arrived to kill it.

The sixty-six arrows in the sample average 5.8 parts each, which approximates

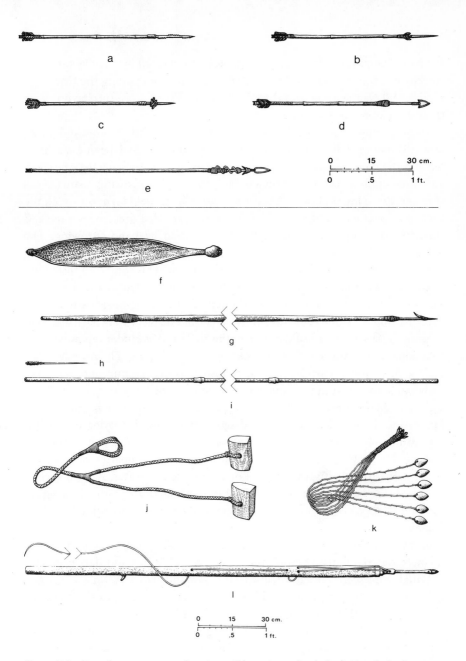

Figure 5-3 Complex weapons used against wild species on land: (*a–c*) Akamba bird arrows; (*d*) Akamba big game arrow; (*e*) Andamanese pig arrow (Courtesy of Cambridge University Press; from Radcliffe-Brown, 1948); (*f*) Aranda throwing-board (Courtesy of Macmillan London and Basingstoke; from Spencer and Gillen, 1927); (*g*) Aranda spear; (*h*) Tanala blowgun dart; (*i*) Tanala blowgun; (*j*) Aymara bola; (*k*) Tareumiut bola; (*l*) Angmagsalik bear lance.

the basic five-part model. Specialization is best indicated by the differences in structure of the forms used. The existence of four styles among the Chenchu, Iglulik, and Nabesna suggests that their arrows served more specific purposes than those of peoples with fewer styles.

Among complex weapons used for wild species on land the bow and arrow clearly dominated. In regions where relatively large terrestrial game was hunted and the bow and arrow were unknown, as in most of Australia, the spear and throwing-board combination was likely to occur. A throwing-board (spearthrower, throwing stick, atlatl) is a rectangular, hand-held form on which the base of a spear was cradled. Use of the board provided greater leverage and thrust for hurling a spear than could be realized by hand throwing. The Aranda throwing-board (Fig. 5-3f) was used to cast a spear (g) that had a long foreshaft, wood point, and barb bound to the point. This spear and throwing-board combination included fifteen parts that are detailed in the Appendix. The most unusual characteristic of the Aranda throwing-board is that it included a chipped stone blade near the hand grip. The blade may have served to balance the spear, but if it did not, then the blade and its binder represent nonfunctional technounits in terms of the subsistant's purpose. The Aranda spearhead with a separate barb lashed to it consisted of three technounits, but if the barb had been cut from the same piece of wood as the head, only one technounit would be represented. Thus a barbed spearhead with one technounit, as opposed to three, reflects a different design concept. By identifying and analyzing distinctions such as these the process of change in material culture may be evaluated by technounit numbers. The Ingura throwing-board was used with either a one-part shaft spear on land or with leisters in water. A form such as this throwing-board, with land- and water-connected uses, must be assigned to one category or the other; in this case it was included with land-use subsistants.

It appears that for most peoples a single complex weapon dominated for taking terrestrial fauna. Among the Tanala the blowgun and dart prevailed, although adolescent boys hunted with the bow and arrow. A Tanala blowgun dart was made from a sliver of bamboo to one end of which foss was tied (h). One style of Tanala blowgun consisted of a bamboo tube with rawhide reinforcement bands at the joints (i). The blowgun was the only complex weapon for terrestrial game among the Jivaro. The style that they produced included a separate mouthpiece and a wax sight; the darts were tipped with poison.

Given the absence of land game on Pukapuka and its scarcity among the Aymara, it is not surprising that their complex weapons are atypical for the sample. The Pukapukans did use a bolalike weapon to take birds flying over land. It consisted of a pole as much as nine feet long with a length of fiber rope tied to the far end. To the free end of the rope was tied a piece of stone. The weighted pole-line combination was cast at birds to entangle their wings. The Aymara made a small bola for entangling birds (*j*) and appear to have had a bigger and more complex form for large game. The Tareumiut bola (*k*) was used against waterfowl, but their bow and arrow formed a far more important land-use weapon.

The sling and missile combination was most developed among the Tlingit, who had a special missile for taking deer, but it is not reported in detail. The Lepcha slingshot consisted of a Y-shaped piece of wood with a band of rubber tied at the ends of the projections to propel a missile. The final weapon used against wild species is the Angmagsalik lance, employed against bears on ice. It consisted of a stone point pegged to a bone foreshaft that fit into a bone socketpiece at the end of a wood shaft (*l*). A line leading from the foreshaft base through two holes in the shaft was tied to a long harpoon line with a bone grip at the end. A bear was struck with the point-foreshaft combination, and then the weapon was pulled free from the wound with the handline. It was cast again and again until the animal was killed. Dogs prevented a bear from escaping between casts of the weapon.

A few complex weapons were used by farmers, or their children, to protect crops from wild species. Slings and missiles dominated, although the Lepcha had a special bow that shot clay pellets at predators. The absence of additional forms suggests that there were more effective means to protect domestic plants than by using weapons. This makes good sense since crops require protection from predators particularly at night, a time when weapons usually could not be used efficiently.

Artifacts Used as Weapons in Water (Table 5-3)   Of all the simple weapons the leister was by far the most widely distributed and important style. The word *leister* is used to identify any fish spear (Fig. 5-4*a–e*) that has a single point, prongs, a point and prongs, or prongs alone as in a trident. The most elementary form is a shaft pointed at one end such as that used by the Trukese to kill and drive fish. The one-part Jivaro leister was a pointed, barbed shaft. A Pukapukan form (*a*) had a barbed wood point attached by fiber to a shaft, but most leisters had multiple prongs or points. A rudimentary pronged leister, made by the Tanala (*b*), consisted of a wood shaft split at one end to form the prongs and wedges to hold the prongs apart, plus a binder to keep the wedges in place. The three-part Ingalik leister had two similar bone points lashed to a wood shaft with a

Table 5-3   Artifacts used as weapons in water

Form (1–26 tu) and function	People
A. Simple forms for wild species	
Leister	(3) S. V. Paiute, (5) Aranda, (3) O. V. Paiute, (4) Andamanese, (1) Jivaro, (4,1) Trukese, (4,3) Pukapuka, (3) Tanala, (5,3) Klamath, (5,3,3) Twana, (3) Huron, (3) Aymara, (3) Ojibwa, (6) Caribou Eskimos, (3) Nabesna, (3) Ingalik, (9,4) Copper Eskimos, (10) Iglulik, (7) Tareumiut, (5,3) Angmagsalik
Fish-killing club	(1) S. V. Paiute, (1) Tiwi, (1) Ojibwa
Fish gaff (snag)	(3) Tlingit, (3) Iglulik
Sea mammal (caribou) spear (lance)	(3) Twana, (7) Caribou Eskimos, (3) Tanaina
Waterfowl spear	(8) Twana
Wood hammer, stun (drive) fish from beneath rocks	(1) Lepcha
B. Complex forms for wild species	
Arrows	
fish (sea mammal, waterfowl)	(1) S. V. Paiute, (7,3) O. V. Paiute, (3) Yuma, (8) Andamanese, (1) Trukese, (9) Klamath, (7) Twana, (3) Ojibwa, (6) Ingalik, (5) Tanaina
arrow dart	(6) Ingalik, (7) Tanaina
Self bow	(2) Trukese
Toggle-headed harpoon, fish (sea mammal)	(6) S. V. Paiute, (5) Klamath, (14,9) Twana, (7) Ingalik, (11,11) Tanaina, (15) Copper Eskimos, (26,17,13,12) Iglulik, (21,17,16,12) Tareumiut, (14,10,8,7,5) Angmagsalik
Leisters used with throwing-board	(3,3) Ingura
Harpoon dart, dugong (fish, etc.)	(6) Ingura, (4) Jivaro, (3) Tonga, (5,3) Tlingit, (5) Ingalik, (10,6) Tanaina
Throwing-board, used with leisters (or other weapons in water or on land)	(5) Ingura, (2) Caribou Eskimos, (3) Ingalik, (2) Tanaina, (2) Iglulik, (2) Tareumiut, (8,3) Angmagsalik
Detachable-headed hook (gaff)	(4) Tanala, (4) Twana
Bird (sealing) dart used with throwing-board	(3) Caribou Eskimos, (4) Ingalik, (7) Iglulik, (5,5) Tareumiut, (11,7) Angmagsalik
Arrowlike lance used with throwing-board	(5) Tanaina
Lance	(8) Iglulik
Toggle-headed harpoon used with throwing-board	(25,25) Angmagsalik
Lance used with throwing-board	(7) Angmagsalik
C. Simple forms to protect domestic species from wild species	
None	
D. Complex forms to protect domestic species from wild species	
None	

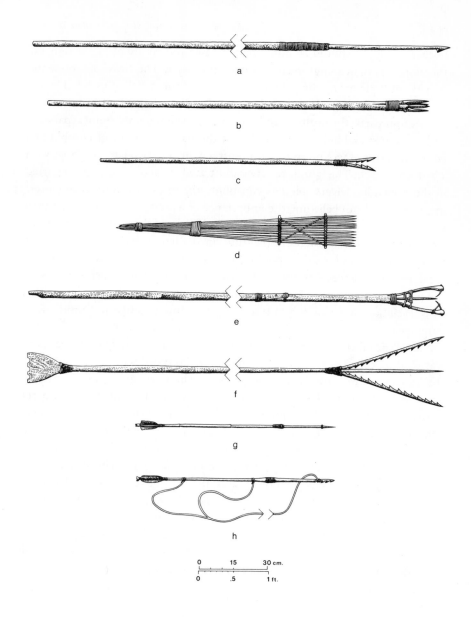

a

b

c

d

e

f

g

h

0 15 30 cm.

0 .5 1 ft.

Figure 5-4   Simple (*a–f*) and complex (*g, h*) weapons used against wild species in water: (*a*) Pukapuka leister; (*b*) Tanala leister; (*c*) Ingalik leister (Courtesy of *Yale University Publications in Anthropology* and Cornelius Osgood; from Osgood, 1940); (*e*) Andamanese leister (Courtesy of Cambridge University Press; from Radcliffe-Brown, 1948); (*e*) Iglulik leister; (*f*) Twana duck spear; (*g*) Klamath waterfowl arrow; (*h*) Tanaina arrow dart (Courtesy of *Yale University Publications in Anthropology* and Cornelius Osgood; from Osgood, 1937).

leather line (c). It should be noted that the two prongs are of like design and therefore represent a single technounit in the analysis. The "loss" of representation by multiple prongs or points is even more dramatically illustrated by the Andamanese leister (d). It included about twelve impaling points but consisted of only four parts: the multiple and similar wood splint points, splint separation sticks, splint-stick binders, and binders at the handle. The most complicated leisters in terms of technounits had a central point and two lateral prongs with a barb set in each. The Iglulik variety is illustrated (e), and its parts are reported in the Appendix. Diverse binders contribute the most technounits to leisters in general. Without belittling the importance of leisters, we can note that they probably were not an important means for obtaining fish except under certain circumstances. When fish were plentiful, in shallow water, and restricted in their movement as by a tidal pool or weir, the harvest with leisters could be great. However, since a leister usually was designed to impale one fish at a time, the form was a rather inefficient means for taking most fish on a large-scale basis. Facilities such as nets and traps were far more effective and more often employed.

A small number of spears were designed for use in water. The Twana spear was used to kill a sea mammal that had been wounded with a harpoon, and the Tanaina form served the same purpose. The Caribou Eskimo spear was used from a kayak for killing caribou as they swam. Three of the seven parts were the foreshaft and shaft binders. The fish gaffs and snags used by the Tlingit and Iglulik are considered weapons and stand in contrast with forms of broadly similar design that were classed as instruments (Twana and Tlingit herring rake, Copper Eskimo fish snag, Iglulik young seal snag). The instrument–weapon distinction is made on the basis of the mobility of the prey. The char taken with an Iglulik snag seemingly were capable of considerable movement, and this was even more clearly the case with the Tlingit gaff for salmon. The gaff, with its bone point, pole handle, and presumed point-handle binder, was used in cloudy water. As coho salmon swam upstream, a fisherman drifted downstream in a canoe and no doubt snagged for fish whenever he saw ripples in the water; thus the use clearly is as a weapon. The only other simple weapon of note is the Twana duck spear (f). The wood side prongs and bone center prong were lashed to a shaft and had a pitch and ash binder as well. A separate butt plate with indentations as finger rests was lashed to the base of the shaft.

These simple artifacts used as weapons in water against wild species averaged 3.7 technounits each, which may be compared with the 2.6 average for instruments for taking wild aquatic species. This marked increase in complexity is impressive but not nearly as striking as the 7.7 average for complex weapons used to harvest wild species in water. Complex water-use forms unquestionably were the most technologically sophisticated of all aboriginal weapons.

The arrows used for taking species in aquatic settings (Fig. 5-4*g*–*h*) occasionally were uncomplicated. Only the Trukese bow is considered in an aquatic context since their only arrow was used against fish. The Trukese fish arrow, like that of the Surprise Valley Paiute, was a shaft of wood pointed at one end. Arrows used for waterfowl were likely to be far more complicated, as was the case for the seven-part forms used by the Owens Valley Paiute and Twana, or the nine-part waterfowl arrow of the Klamath. The latter had a wood head with a ring of pitch and sinew near the point. The head was attached to the shaft with sinew as well as pitch, and the feather vanes were fastened on the shaft with sinew and pitch (*g*).

The Tanaina and Ingalik arrow darts were the most developed forms of arrows because they represent complexity compounded. The bow and arrow combination is complex, and the arrows with detachable points are likewise complex. The seven-part Tanaina form, probably used for fish, consisted of a bone point fitted into a bone socketpiece that was bound to the shaft with sinew (*h*). Feather vanes were bound with sinew to the base of the shaft, and a sinew line led from a hole near the base of the point to the shaft, where it bifurcated and was tied at separate places on the shaft. When a fish was struck, the point detached from the shaft, which was dragged through the water to tire the fish and facilitate retrieval.

Of all the subsistants used by the sampled peoples, the toggle-headed harpoon is technologically the most complex form, and it was most highly developed among Eskimos. Iglulik and Angmagsalik forms had twenty-six and twenty-five technounits respectively. These weapons typically were designed to injure and then to impede the movement of sea mammals. A species may have died after being harpooned repeatedly, or it may have been dispatched with a lance or knife. Thus a toggle-headed harpoon usually did not kill in as direct a manner as a typical spear or arrow.

Because of the technological complexity of the toggle-headed harpoon, it is desirable to introduce the different styles with an abridged description of the more common forms (Fig. 5-5). A stone point (*a*) was fitted into a slot in an ivory harpoon head (*b*), and the point was pegged in place (*c*). In a hole beneath the harpoon barbs was fitted an ivory foreshaft (*d*), its opposite end fitting into a hole at the top of an ivory socketpiece (*e*). Through a hole in the foreshaft was passed a loop of rawhide line (*f*) that was bound tightly to the wood shaft (*g*). A second line, the headline (*h*), was passed through a hole in the harpoon head. This is the basic unit at the forepart of a harpoon. As the weapon was

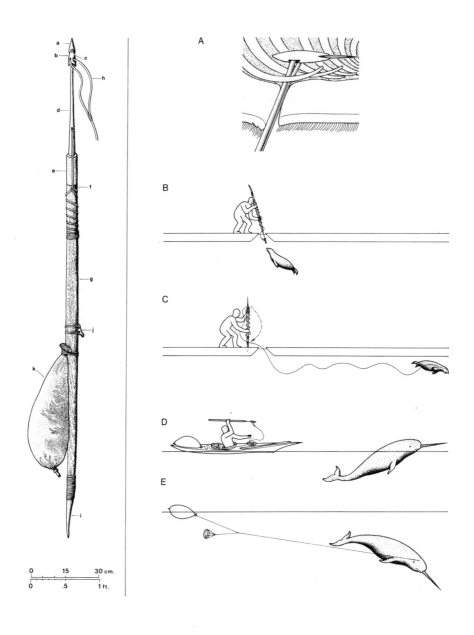

Figure 5-5 Toggle-headed harpoon composite (*a–k*); (*A*) the manner in which a harpoon head toggles beneath an animal's flesh; (*B, C*) hunting a seal at a hole in sea ice; (*D, E*) hunting a narwhal from a kayak, using a harpoon with a drag anchor and sealskin float attached.

thrust or thrown, the blade cut through a seal's skin, and the harpoon head entered the wound from the force of the blow. As the injured animal pulled away in an effort to escape, tension was placed on the line, and the head toggled beneath the seal's flesh (A) in the manner of a button in a buttonhole.

The arrangement for securing the headline (h) varied with the harpoon's design and use. For hunting seals at holes in sea ice an ivory ice pick (i) was lashed at the base of the shaft, and the headline may have been tied to the shaft. In this case, as soon as the harpoon was thrust (B) the shaft was reversed, and the ice pick was driven into the ice. The seal then was played to exhaustion with the shaft-tied line (C) and killed with a knife. Alternatively the headline may have been long and coiled in one hand as the harpoon was thrust; the wounded animal was played with this line. When a seal was hunted from a kayak, there was no ice pick at the base of the harpoon shaft, but a finger rest (j) may have been lashed to the shaft. This permitted the hunter to gain a firm grip on the harpoon as it was thrown. In this case the headline was tied directly to the shaft, and there may have been a small inflated bladder (k) tied to the shaft. When the headline was not tied to the shaft, it was attached to a long line at the end of which was an inflated sealskin float. A drag anchor may have been attached to the same line. The Iglulik harpoon for hunting beluga and narwhal included both a drag anchor and sealskin float (D, E). The twenty-six parts of this Iglulik weapon and a list of the specific technounits for all their other subsistants are recorded in the Appendix.

Most toggle-headed harpoons had far fewer technounits (Fig. 5-6a, b) than the typical Eskimo forms used against sea mammals. The five-part Klamath fish harpoon had double bone points and two foreshafts attached to a single shaft (a). The points were designed to toggle after they had passed through a fish. Double-headed toggle harpoons with eight and five technounits each also were used against fish by the Angmagsalik. The Tanaina harpoon for beluga and sea lions (b) had a stone blade and bone socketpiece fitted directly onto a wood shaft in addition to an inflated float attached to the shaft.

A second style of harpoon is the harpoon dart (Fig. 5-6c, d), which averaged far fewer technounits and had a much wider distribution than the toggle-headed form. A dart head was designed with one or more barbs to hold firm in a wound after it detached from the shaft. As the headline tied to the shaft was dragged behind, the wounded animal soon tired and could be harpooned again or killed with another weapon. The Tonga hippopotamus harpoon had an iron head with a tang fitted into a wood shaft and a stout head-shaft line (c). The Ingura harpoon dart for dugong and sea turtles had a long barbed point attached to a light wood float by a heavy fiber line (d). Half of the technounits

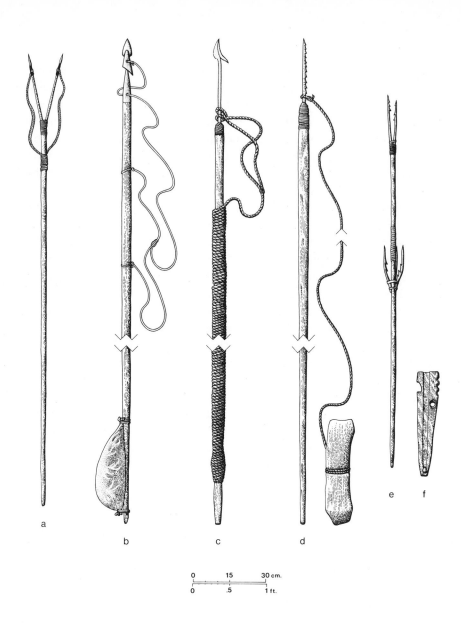

Figure 5-6 Complex weapons used against wild species in water: (a) Klamath toggle-headed fish harpoon; (b) Tanaina toggle-headed beluga harpoon (Courtesy of *Yale University Publications in Anthropology* and Cornelius Osgood; from Osgood, 1937); (c) Tonga hippopotamus harpoon dart (Courtesy of The National Museums of Zambia; from Reynolds, 1968); (d) Ingura dugong harpoon dart; (e) Iglulik bird dart; (f) Iglulik throwing-board used with bird dart.

for the ten-part form used by the Tanaina were parts of a bladder attached to the shaft for flotation. Some darts were hurled with the aid of throwing-boards. A dart having multiple barbed points resembled a multipronged leister. The Iglulik bird dart, like others reported among Eskimos, had two sets of barbed points. If the end points did not strike a duck, there was the chance that one of the three side prongs would pierce it (*e*). This dart was hurled with a two-part throwing-board (*f*) that had an iron peg at the end to receive the ivory ferrule at the base of the dart shaft. The lances used by the Iglulik and Angmagsalik functioned in much the same manner as harpoon darts.

The *ultimate* weapon in terms of its technological complexity was surely the toggle-headed harpoon made by the Angmagsalik to be used with a throwing-board and sealskin floats for hunting large seals from a kayak. The combination consisted of thirty-three parts, most of which are illustrated in Figure 5-7. The stone blade (*a*) was attached to the toggle harpoon head of bone (*b*) with a peg (*c*), and the fore end of the ivory foreshaft (*d*) was fitted into a hole at the base of the harpoon head. The base of the foreshaft was fitted into a hole in the top of the short bone socketpiece (*e*) and held in place by thongs (*f*). The thongs were passed through a hole in the foreshaft and on through two holes in the wooden shaft (*g*). Two bone pegs on the shaft (*h*) held the throwing-board (*i*) in place. At the base of the shaft was a bone receiving block (*j*), pre-sumably pegged to the shaft, to receive the hooked end of the throwing-board. The counterweights or "feathers" (*k*) were pegged to the receiving block. The harpoon headline (*l*) was attached to the harpoon head through two holes, and the line extended through two holes in a bone clasp (*m*). A third hole in the clasp was fitted over a bone peg (*n*) which fit into the shaft. The line ex-tended to another bone clasp (*o*), to which the end was tied through one of two holes. The floats (*p*) were held together by a single line (*q*) that was strung through the bone clasp on the harpoon lead line and held with a toggle bar (*r*). The double floats consisted of two inflated sealskins that were bound together at the middle with a thong, and thongs closed the openings at the head of each (*s*). A section of wood (*t*) which served to join the floats at the front was forked on the ventral surface in order to fit over a strap across the rear decking of the kayak. A hole was made near the right forepaw section of each sealskin, and into each hole was bound a bone plug with an opening drilled through it lengthwise. A sealskin was inflated by blowing through a tube—which is not counted—and then the opening was plugged with a wooden stopper. In Figure 5-7 the nozzle assemblies are illustrated but not lettered. The throwing-board (*i*) consisted of a section of wood with a bone inset at the rear (*u*) and bone side plates (*v*) held in place with a series of bone pegs (*w*). A bone hook (*x*) at

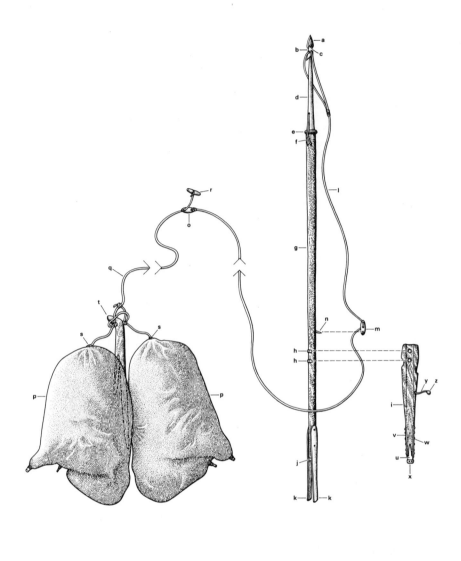

Figure 5-7 Angmagsalik toggle-headed "feather" harpoon and throwing-board for hunting large seals from a kayak.

the base of the throwing-board was pegged in place to engage the receiving block (j). The throwing-board also included a short strap (y) with a bone button at the end (z) to attach the weapon to the kayak decking. A harpoon of this form was placed on one side of the kayak decking in front of a hunter. The harpoon line was coiled in a special wood frame in front of the manhole. When a seal came within range, the harpoon was launched, the line uncoiled, and the floats released.

Summary. The 288 weapons included 1375 technounits for an overall average of 4.8 technounits per form. A synopsis of the naturefact and artifact information in the tables follows:

	Simple			Complex		
	Forms	tu	Average	Forms	tu	Average
Take wild species on land	54	101	1.9	121	592	4.9
Protect domestic species on land				8	22	2.8
Take wild species in water	38	141	3.7	67	519	7.7
	92	242	2.6	196	1133	5.8

What is most striking is the comparative complexity of forms used on water as opposed to those used on land and the difference between simple and complex forms. We also are struck by how few weapons were employed primarily to protect domestic species from wild ones.

Conclusions Weapons were capable of doing what human hands and teeth could not. They bashed and battered or cut deep into flesh to wound and kill. Instruments were most effective as extenders of human arms to gain access to harmless food products. Weapons, by contrast, had the capacity to reach dangerous edibles, and they partially protected the user irrespective of whether the form was thrust or thrown. Weapons most often were cutters by extension and projection.

With an average of 4.8 technounits each, weapons were far more developed than instruments, which had a comparable average of 1.9. The greater the possible movement of a species on land, in water, and in the air, the more complex the weapon used against it was likely to be. The most species-specific weapons, especially those used in water, tended to have greater numbers of parts. For aquatic species, such as sea mammals in the arctic, that live in water but may bask on ice, maintain breathing holes in ice, or seek air at the surface of water between ice cracks, the situational variability for the prey appears to have been far greater than could be exploited effectively with a single form of weapon. The styles of Eskimo harpoons illustrate the diversity of weapons developed for such specialized hunting.

The naturefacts used as weapons appear to have been forms picked up when no useful artifact was at hand. The increase in technounit averages for simple artifactual weapons used on land clearly illustrates the greater technological knowledge involved in their production. Before more complicated weapons could be made, it was essential for the idea of composite forms to emerge. However the maximum number of parts for any simple land-use weapon was five, which is fewer than probably would be predicted. Apparently very little improvement was possible on a point + shaft + point-shaft binder in the creation of a spear without making forms with moving parts, such as a lance with a detachable point. More typical of complex weapons are the spear and throwing-board or the bow and arrow. In their production the upper limit for part numbers by the time of historic contact was about fifteen for each subsistant in a linked usage. The greater technounit average for simple subsistants used against animals in water is again a significant increase over comparable forms used on land. Yet for simple water-use forms the highest number of technounits represented was ten. The far higher technounit average for complex subsistants used in water indicates that they were the most complicated weapons in terms of part numbers.

The data on the complexity of weapons yield the following conclusions based on the number of parts and the naturefact–artifact distinction. The supposition is that the greater the number of parts for a cluster of forms the more developed the cluster and the more recent its origin. It would appear that naturefacts were used first (1 tu average) and that they were followed by land-use forms that were simple artifacts (2.5). Simple artifactual forms used in water (3.7) were followed by complex land-use weapons (4.9). The most recently developed cluster would be water-use weapons (7.7).

A part-by-part analysis of weapons verifies some widely held impressions about aboriginal technologies and contradicts others. The ethnological truism that weapons are most complex among Eskimos is verified fully. The only qualification necessary is that the complexity of their weapons varied widely from one population to the next. Assertions that Australian technology is uniformly elementary has no support, at least insofar as weapons are concerned. The Aranda spear and throwing-board combination with a total of fifteen technounits is one of the most highly developed weapons used against terrestrial animals. The Andamanese also have the reputation of possessing a simple material culture, yet their thirteen-part pig arrow is the most complicated arrow in the sample.

The adaptive advantages that weapons offered for obtaining animals were without doubt great achievements in the cause of culture. We must at the same time realize that weapons had severe limitations. The presence of a person was essential for a weapon to function, and when its use was against fierce animals, considerable physical danger was involved. Furthermore most weapons were capable of harvesting only one animal at a time. For the more efficient use of human energy in food getting another class of forms was in many respects far superior to weapons. These are defined as facilities and are considered in the chapters that follow.

▲▲▲▲▲▲▲▲

FACILITIES:
TENDED

Many of the qualities of facilities have a negative connotation in modern American English. We speak of life's "pitfalls," being "trapped," "surrounded" by enemies, and "snaring" a spouse. It is unkind to "bait" or to "lure" others, and a "disguise" suggests some devious purpose. In one way or another these purposes served by facilities are considered unfair because they take advantage of individuals. This interpretation has justification with reference to other persons, but for obtaining food, facilities are elegant manufactures. To take wild and vicious animals with facilities rather than with weapons minimizes or may even eliminate the physical danger involved. Another advantage of facilities is that they often are capable of harvesting several animals at once, while weapons usually kill one animal at a time. Even more impressive is the fact that many facilities quite literally work to obtain food for people while the people themselves are occupied with other activities.

A facility is a form that controls the movement of a species or protects it to man's advantage. The concept of *movement control* is fundamental to understanding the qualities of facilities, which are highly varied in both structure and function. The reasons for such variety are based on the morphological and physiological differences among species and the contrasts in their habitats. For controlling the movement of such different species as cattle, crayfish, fish, gulls, and kangaroos, the technological forms must be varied more than instruments or weapons designed to be employed in a direct manner. Facilities nearly always were associated with animals, but even when plants were involved, movement control of harmful external elements was critical.

Movement control takes many forms, and although wild species may be killed when facilities are used, their capture rather than their death is the primary result of the way in which the facility functions. The movement of a wild animal may be controlled in terms of loose physical guidance as is provided by game fences, fish sweeps, or weirs. The control may be more restrictive, as that afforded by a fishnet, fish trap, or rabbit net. Effective movement may even become impossible, as when a deadfall or snare is used. Whether a captive species is dead or alive when the facility is checked is not nearly as important as the animal's inability to escape. Control may shift from loose to restrictive. An example is the formation of a large circle by many persons playing musical instruments and the gradual closing of the circle to surround and then kill game.

The effective control over movement of species is involved when a sticky gum (bird lime) is placed on tree limbs to hold the body, feet, or wings of birds. The same is true when poison is thrown into a pond to stupefy fish, or a torch is used to hold a deer spellbound. A beehive constructed to attract a swarm of wild bees is an effort to control the bees' movements. Hunting blinds are designed to deceive animals so that they will venture into the range of weapons. Hunting disguises serve the same general purpose, and all lures are designed to affect the movement of prey. The management of domestic animals depended to a large extent on movement control. Corrals, crooks, hobbles, and tethers are facilities that direct the activities of livestock. The protection of domestic plants from wild and domestic animals was exceedingly important. To this end fences were built, traps were set to prevent predators from eating crops, and thorny cactuses were placed around individual plants.

Weapons were designed to kill or maim species rather than to direct their movement. Although movement control was involved when certain weapons were used, it served a secondary purpose in their operation. The flotation devices attached to harpoons are an example. A toggle-headed harpoon was thrown by an Eskimo to wound a seal, and the sealskin float to which the lead line was attached partially controlled the seal's subsequent movement. The cutting quality of the harpoon dominates, however; the sealskin float supplemented and expanded the harpoon's capacity. By contrast we expect facilities to control movement first and foremost.

Protection was afforded domestic animals by administering or applying medicines to cure diseases; animals likewise were protected by nests, pens, and other forms of housing. Check dams, terraces, and windbreaks protected domestic species from the elements, and torches, used to burn the weeds on a plot, protected seeds to be planted.

The Lepcha use of stones for fishing illustrates how a single stone could serve as an instrument, weapon, or tended facility. Fish often hid beneath rocks, and a person might pound on the stone above a fish with another stone. If an immobile fish were stunned by the blow, the pounding stone served as an instrument. The stone functioned as a weapon when it was thrown at and killed a swimming fish. The same stone thrown at a fish to guide its movement toward a net was used as a tended facility. The deciding factor in classifying this stone was the mobility potential of the fish involved. The Eskimo harpoon and the Lepcha fish-taking stone were classified according to their primary purpose as reported in the ethnographic accounts consulted. And so it was for all the other subsistants analyzed.

A useful distinction may be drawn between facilities that require the presence of a person or people and those that function in the absence of anyone. When the physical presence of one or more persons is essential, the form is a *tended facility*. Examples include a game blind, hunting disguise, stones thrown to drive fish, flutes played and drums beaten to drive game, a lasso to capture an animal, and a whistle to scare predators from crops. *Untended facilities*, by contrast, function in the absence of people. Examples include spring-pole snares, a stone terrace or wood fence around a cultivated plot, a livestock corral, and housing for domestic animals. Some facilities may be either tended or untended; included are fish weirs and traps, deadfalls, pitfalls, and certain forms of snares. This chapter deals with tended facilities, and the one to follow focuses on untended forms.

Distinguishing certain facilities from instruments may seem difficult, but the difference is quite clear when it is remembered that an instrument never acts on things that move. A digging stick functioning as an instrument is used to dig immovable grubs and roots from the ground or dislodge stable earth to plant seeds. A groundhog is forced from its burrow with a hooked stick, but it is killed with another form. The hooked stick is a facility because it guides the mobile groundhog. If an escaping groundhog were killed with a hooked stick, the stick would be a weapon. A pointed stick used to impale and kill a rat in its nest is an instrument if the rat cannot avoid the fatal thrust of the stick.

A stick beaten against ice to drive beavers into a lodge and a stick beaten on water to drive fish into a trap are facilities because the beavers and fish are directed by them but actually are harvested with other forms.

Under many conditions the advantages provided by facilities over instruments and weapons are unprecedented. Fishing serves as a typical example. A fish may be trapped in a tidal pool and clubbed with an instrument, or a leister may be used to impale a swimming fish. In each instance the catch consists of a single fish. However facilities such as nets and seines may catch hundreds of fish in a short time. The same applies to setting a net into which rabbits are driven as opposed to the use of a missile stick. Driving caribou into a surround where snares are set and arrows shot to kill individual animals at close range is more efficient than killing them with a bow and arrow.

Untended facilities had even greater potential against wild animals than did tended facilities, instruments, or weapons. One or many deadfalls or snares could be set for game at one time, left unattended, and then checked. The same was true for set nets or weir and trap combinations for fish. Traps also could be set to protect crops against predators, especially nocturnal ones. The species taken usually were eaten, and if so an untended set of this nature served a twofold food-getting purpose.

Naturefacts Used as Facilities (Table 6-1)   Few naturefacts were employed in this

Table 6-1   Naturefacts used as facilities

Form (1 tu each) and function	People
A. *Simple tended forms for wild species on land*	
Stick, drive (hook, prod) animal from burrow	S. V. Paiute, S. V. Paiute, Pima, Walapai
Stones, drive game killed with bow and arrow	Chenchu
Sticks, drive game killed with weapons (facilities)	Chenchu, Huron, Lepcha
Sticks slapped together as a lure, simulate the call of rutting moose	Ingalik
B. *Simple tended forms for wild species in water*	
Stones (pebbles) drive fish into net	Trukese, Aymara
Fish-driving stick (pole) used in water (above ice to drive into net)	Trukese, Klamath, Aymara
C. *Simple tended forms to protect domestic plants from wild species on land*	
Missile stone	Akamba, Huron

manner. They always were simple, were never left untended, and functioned only against wild species. Once again the examples are sticks and stones used alone except in the case of an Ingalik lure. The Ingalik slapped sticks together to simulate the call of a rutting moose so that an animal would move within range of their weapons.

Anthropologists long have hypothesized that sticks and stones were the forms likely to have been used most intensively by emerging human populations. That aboriginal peoples at the time of historic contact did pick them up and use them as instruments, weapons, and tended facilities in highly diverse ways suggests that sticks and stones were versatile subsistants.

Artifacts Used as Tended Facilities on Land (Table 6-2) In terms of the land–water, simple–complex, and wild–domestic distinctions, tended facilities are far more diverse than any other comparable category. The 175 forms with 404 techno-units averaged 2.3 technounits per form. The essential human involvement in the use of tended facilities helps to explain their low technounit average, but even so a higher average probably would have been anticipated.

A lure, the first entry in Table 6-2, as a tended facility is designed primarily to attract an animal that is then captured or killed by other means. The Aranda made a form designed to look like the head and neck of an emu. Although the description is incomplete, the form presumably was used to lure emus so that they could be killed with weapons. During the caribou mating season a Caribou Eskimo hunter held antlers over his head as a lure. A Copper Eskimo hunter held a walking stick and a bow above his head to simulate caribou antlers. In this instance the walking stick functioned as a lure, and the bow served the same purpose secondarily to its use as a weapon. A three-part lure was used by the Ingalik when they located a hibernating bear. A bundle of willow sticks was tied to a rawhide line, the willows were thrown into the bear's den, and the other end of the line was tied to a tree. The bear grabbed at the willows but was unable to move them, and as it crawled from its hole the willows partially blocked the way. Hunters waiting at the entrance killed the bear with spears as it emerged.

Baited blinds designed to take birds were used by three of the peoples sampled. In the southwestern sector of Tasmania a blind large enough to conceal a person was built. It was covered with grass and probably framed with poles. Bait was placed at the top if crows were sought or at one side to attract ducks. Presumably worms were placed on a stone for ducks, and for crows a fish was concealed partially by a stone. When a bird landed to take the bait, the hunter

Table 6-2   Artifacts used as tended facilities on land

Form (1–10 tu) and function	People
A. *Simple forms for wild animal species*	
Bird (game) lure	(3) Aranda, (1,1) Caribou Eskimos, (3) Ingalik, (1) Copper Eskimos
Baited bird blind	(4) Tasmanians, (3) Iglulik, (3) Angmagsalik
Game (bird) guide (with surround)	(1,1) S. V. Paiute, (2,1) Aranda, (2) Hopi, (2) Pukapuka, (3) Huron, (3,2) Caribou Eskimos, (1) Nabesna, (3) Ingalik, (2) Copper Eskimos, (1) Iglulik, (1,1) Tareumiut
Poison	(1) Aranda
Blind, above ground	(1) Aranda, (5) O. V. Paiute, (1) Walapai, (3) Chenchu, (6,5) Kapauku, (3) Akamba, (2) Tasmanians, (1) Klamath, (1) Twana
Blind, pit	(2,1,1) S. V. Paiute, (3) Naron, (1) Klamath, (1) Copper Eskimos, (1) Tareumiut
Torch, drive (attract, blind) game	(1) S. V. Paiute, (1) Aranda, (1) Naron, (1) O. V. Paiute, (1) Walapai, (1) Hopi, (1) Tiwi, (1) Ingura, (3) Chenchu, (1) Tasmanians, (1) Klamath, (1) Twana, (5) Ojibwa
Spread net	(6,3) S. V. Paiute, (4) O. V. Paiute, (3) Walapai, (6) Klamath
Pole-handled net	(6) Pukapuka, (5) Nabesna, (6) Iglulik
Disguise	(5) S. V. Paiute, (3) O. V. Paiute, (1,1,6) Walapai, (1) Hopi, (2) Klamath, (1) Caribou Eskimos
Pitfall (hole trap)	(4) S. V. Paiute, (1) Naron, (4,3) Caribou Eskimos, (4) Tareumiut
Surround (enclosure, with guide)	(3,1) S. V. Paiute, (1) O. V. Paiute, (3) Hopi, (3) Huron, (3) Aymara, (4) Ingalik, (1) Iglulik
Plug, restrict movement of animal	(1) S. V. Paiute, (1) Walapai, (1) Huron
Water poured (diverted) down hole of burrowing animal to drive it	(1) Pima, (1) Hopi, (1) Aymara
Probe, crook (pole) remove species from hiding place	(1,1) Walapai, (1) Tiwi
Natural surround and man-made gate	(0+1) Hopi
Snare, land crab (bird, caribou, hare, mountain sheep)	(4) Trukese, (4,1) Pukapuka, (2,2,2) Nabesna, (5) Ingalik, (1) Copper Eskimos
Land crab trap	(3) Trukese
Bird, pole snare	(2) Pukapuka, (2) Ojibwa, (2) Angmagsalik
Kangaroo tripping device	(1) Tasmanians
Game (bird) call	(1) Klamath, (1) Twana, (3) Ojibwa, (1) Angmagsalik
Crossed poles, subdue bear emerging from hibernation	(1) Klamath, (2) Nabesna
Sticks hit together to drive game	(1) Huron

Table 6-2 *(Continued)*

Form (1–10 tu) and function	People
Musical instruments to drive game	(6+4,3,2,1) Aymara
Basket trap for burrowing animals	(5) Aymara
Wild pig-impaling stakes	(1) Lepcha
Caribou frightening board and beater sticks	(3+1) Copper Eskimos
Adz, open muskrat house	(3) Nabesna
Beaver dam–breaking log	(1) Ingalik
Forked stick, hold trapped lynx	(1) Ingalik

B. *Complex forms for wild animal species*

Deadfall, birds (monkeys)	(5) Pima, (4) Akamba
Arrow used with bow to decoy game	(6) Chenchu
Game-bird enclosure trap	(7) Twana
Deer net	(4) Twana
Bird net and stone to drop net	(6) Lepcha

C. *Simple forms for wild plant species*
None

D. *Complex forms for wild plant species*
None

E. *Simple forms for domestic animal species*

Crook, herd sheep (catch calves)	(1) Hopi, (1) Akamba
Lasso, capture domestic animal (obtain mountain sheep)	(1) Hopi, (1) Aymara
Piglet-carrying bag	(3) Kapauku
Rope (strap, line), lead (hold) animal	(1) Naga, (2,1) Akamba
Cattle-slaughtering post assembly	(7) Naga
Cow-milking stand for unruly animals	(4) Akamba
Medicines	(2,2,2,2,2,2,2,2,1,1) Akamba
Stuffed calf skin, milking aid	(3) Akamba

F. *Complex forms for domestic animal species*
None

G. *Simple forms for domestic plant protection*
(clear plot)

Torch, clear plot	(1) Yuma, (1) Jivaro, (3) Trukese, (1) Kapauku. (1) Naga, (1) Akamba, (2) Tanala, (1) Tonga, (1) Huron, (1) Aymara, (1) Lepcha
Musical scares	(1,1) Naga, (3) Tanala, (6+1,4,3,2) Tonga
Mole-taking pole, protect crop	(1) Akamba
Watchtower with scares attached, protect crop	(6) Akamba
Leaf scare, protect crop	(3) Tonga

H. *Complex forms for domestic plant species*

Pit-fall trap, protect crop from birds	(5) Aymara

grabbed and killed it. The Iglulik and Angmagsalik baited bird blinds were made from snow with bait placed on top, and they functioned in much the same manner as the Tasmanian form. This is but one among numerous instances of subsistants that served the same purpose, with like or similar technounit totals, being reported for unrelated peoples separated by great distances.

Artifactual guides are arrangements on the landscape designed to direct species toward other forms that trap or kill. Guides often were nothing more than piles of brush, as among the Surprise Valley Paiute and Hopi, that led to a surround, natural enclosure, or hunters concealed in blinds. The Aranda configuration was somewhat different. Their brush guide for emus led to a dammed section of a water hole into which poisonous leaves had been crushed. Birds that drank the water became stupefied enough for the hunters to kill them with relative ease. Guides might be felled trees, as among the Nabesna, to direct caribou and moose, or rock pile cairns for guiding caribou, as among the Iglulik. Rock piles might be topped with turf as were the Caribou and Copper Eskimo caribou guides. For taking deer the Huron guides were more elaborate. Vertical posts were erected, and horizontal poles apparently were bound between the posts to form a v-shaped guide. The guide led to an enclosure in which the animals could be killed with weapons. The most developed guide and surround combination was made by the Ingalik for taking caribou (Fig. 6-1). The crossed-pole guide fence with snares at openings led to the surround where additional snares were set. Hunters drove caribou into the area between the arms of the guides and snared animals that attempted to escape through apparent openings in the fence. Those caribou that moved into the surround were snared there or shot with arrows.

Blinds are designed to allow the normal movement of animals while concealing the nearness of hunters. Both aboveground and excavated blinds occurred. Aboveground blinds most often were made of brush or stone, and the individuals hiding there used weapons. One of the most developed forms, made by the Owens Valley Paiute, consisted of a bent pole frame tied in place and covered with willows, boughs, and grass siding. The Kapauku ground-level and platform blinds for hunting birds had five and six parts respectively; these are listed in the Appendix.

The term *torch* is used to designate any form that carried fire. The most common practice, especially in dry areas, was to set grassland on fire to drive animals toward hunters, who killed them with weapons. Fire drives were carried out by the Aranda, Klamath, Naron, and Tasmanians among others. The Surprise Valley Paiute used torches not only as they encircled deer and killed

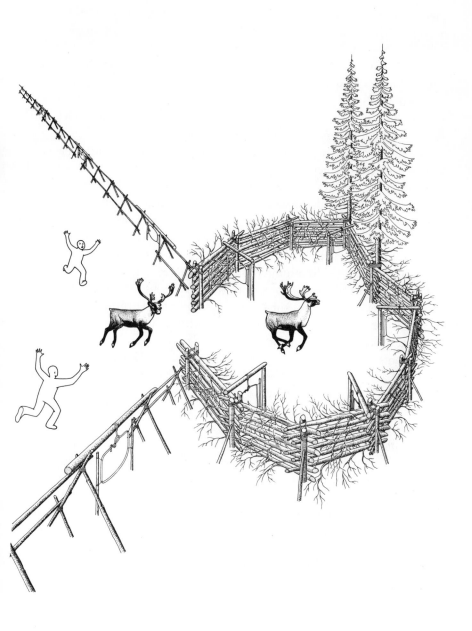

Figure 6-1 Ingalik caribou guide fence and surround with snare sets (Courtesy of *Yale University Publications in Anthropology* and Cornelius Osgood; from Osgood, 1940).

them with arrows but also to attract porcupines and to suffocate skunks in their burrows. A torch served as an aid for hunting wombats at night in Tasmania, and the Chenchu smoked bees from their nests to facilitate the retrieval of honey. The Owens Valley Paiute used smoke to bring caterpillars down from a tree in order to trap them in a pit dug around the base of the trunk. The most elaborate torch was used by the Ojibwa for hunting deer at night and appears to have been of Euro-American inspiration. It consisted of a hazel stick with cloth and pitch wrapping and a bark light reflector.

Two styles of nets are identified for taking species in terrestrial habitats: spread nets with the general appearance of tennis nets and bag nets attached to poles in the manner of a butterfly net. The Surprise Valley Paiute, Owens Valley Paiute, and Walapai set spread nets into which rabbits were driven. Only the Klamath took large game with spread nets. They drove antelope with torches, shot them with arrows whenever possible, and caught the survivors in nets. Bag nets were used against birds except by the Nabesna, who fashioned a form used by a hunter to take muskrats on land.

A hunter wore a disguise to control the movement of a species as he approached close enough to kill it with a weapon. A Surprise Valley Paiute hunter wore an antelope's skin and head with the horns attached, and also smeared white paint on himself. He carried a stick as an aid in imitating the movements of antelope as he approached his quarry. The same disguise was used with a stick to approach and kill sage hens. The Walapai had doeskin and deerskin disguises and also used an antelope disguise similar to that of the Surprise Valley Paiute. The Caribou Eskimos wore wolf skins as they directed the movement of caribou.

A pitfall is an opening into which a species falls and is trapped. Pitfalls usually are untended, but tended ones occasionally occur. The most elementary form was used by the Naron. After a heavy rain they dug a hole next to a termite nest, made an opening in the nest above the hole, and waited for the exiting termites to fall into the hole. The insects then were scooped up, roasted, and eaten. One Caribou Eskimo pitfall was dug in deep snow and covered with brush and moss, with human urine on the covering as bait. The second form included a snow cairn to lure caribou, a shallow pit in the snow with built-up sides of snow blocks, and a thin snow cover on top. The set was most effective when caribou were numerous and the pits were watched closely. If a caribou was not killed soon after being trapped, it was likely to escape.

Most of the remaining simple tended facilities listed in Table 6-2 were restricted to one or comparatively few peoples. The uses of many forms are clear from their labels, but some merit comment or even discussion. Water was used as a simple tended facility when it was poured or diverted into the hole of a burrowing animal, such as a guinea pig or prairie dog, to force the animal to the ground surface where it was killed with another form. The water is evaluated as representing one technounit since it functioned as an integrated fluid mass to dislodge an animal. Since the water moved only unto itself, it is judged a simple form. If water were poured down a hole to drown an animal, it would be evaluated as a one-technounit simple weapon. The Trukese land crab trap consisted of a long pole to which a bundle of leaves was tied as a lure. The leaves were dangled before a crab, and after it had grasped them, it could be captured by hand. The tripping device of the Tasmanians was used on grasslands frequented by kangaroos. Over an open area tussocks of grass were tied together at the top. Kangaroos being pursued by hunters might trip over these ties and could be speared more readily or struck with a missile stick. Thus the grass ties partially controlled the movement of fleeing animals.

Perhaps the most unusual tended facilities were musical instruments. They were used by the Aymara, among whom hunting was relatively unimportant, to drive foxes, vicunas, and viscachas. A locality likely to contain game was surrounded by dogs, men, and women. Two different flutes and panpipes apparently were blown and drums beaten to drive game; the kill was made by dogs or with clubs. The four instruments included sixteen technounits, with the drum and its stick made from ten parts. Considering the number of subsistants and technounits represented by these instruments and the minor importance of hunting among the Aymara, we might think that this example does violence to the system of analysis. I would suggest, however, that the high number of technounits is especially meaningful because it indicates that something very different is represented by this Aymara tended facility.

Snares usually are thought of as being set and left unattended, but they sometimes were tended. The simplest style was a noose made of a single line. The Copper Eskimos held a one-part noose at the entrance of a ground squirrel's burrow to strangle an uncautious animal leaving the hole. Among the Nabesna three different styles of tended snares with two parts each were identified. One was large, made from rawhide, and set in series for caribou or moose at guide fences toward which animals were driven. The second was small, fashioned from sinew, and set in series to take hares during drives. The third snare, probably of intermediate size, was set for mountain sheep during drives. The most complicated tended snare had five parts and was made by the Ingalik for use with a caribou surround and guides. In the surround rawhide nooses were hung from horizontal poles held in place between the surround fencing and vertical posts. Sets also were made between openings in the guide fence itself (Fig. 6-1). Each noose was held open with willow bark lines tied to noose-spreading stakes.

Six complex tended facilities were used against wild animals sought primarily as food. The nets and deadfalls involved most often required the presence of a person to pull a drop cord, except in the case of the Twana deer net. It consisted of a large-meshed net stretched between poles across a deer's path. A pursued animal thrust its head into a mesh and knocked over the poles, thereby becoming entangled. The Chenchu shot a particular style of arrow at a tree trunk to drive animals from dense foliage. Once the game was in view it was killed with another form of arrow used as a weapon.

The tended facilities for domestic animals were few in number but very important in terms of the purposes served. A Kapauku woman raising a small pig carried it in a special bag so that it could be with her during the day as she worked, and she fed it prechewed food. Pigs were very important in the Kapauku economy, and the carrying bag was the most important artifact involved for raising pigs. It was the Akamba, however, who used the most diverse forms of tended facilities for domestic animals. They not only had a special stand for milking unruly cattle, but when a calf died they stuffed its skin with hay and placed it near the mother, who then could be milked. Furthermore ten different medicines with a total of eighteen technounits were employed to cure the diseases of domestic animals. To include these medicines as subsistants seems reasonable since each represented an effort to protect afflicted animals.

Land clearance for cultivating crops usually was necessary, and for a number of peoples this was the most important use of torches. Domestic seeds and plants were protected by people playing musical instruments, and other forms were used to scare predators from crops. The form with the largest number of technounits was made by the Akamba especially for protection from baboons and birds. It consisted of a platform, presumably of two technounits, raised on four posts, with platform-pole binders assumed. Here a lookout was stationed to throw stones at predators and to shake long cords to which scare objects, such as banana leaves, were attached. The Akamba also drove a pointed stick through the underground passage of a mole to block its escape so that it could be dug up and killed before it damaged crops.

The only complex tended facility for plant protection was a fall trap employed by the Aymara to catch troublesome birds. A pit was excavated and baited with grain. A flat stone was propped up at an angle above the pit by means of a stick to which a long string was attached. A concealed person pulled the string to release the stone as soon as a bird entered the pit. The same form of trap also was used to catch wild doves for food.

Artifacts Used as Tended Facilities in Water (Table 6-3) The 187 forms were used only against wild species. Their technounit total was 773 for an average of 4.1 parts

Table 6-3   Artifacts used as tended facilities in water

Form (1–15 tu) and function	People
A. *Simple forms for wild animal species*	
Fish sweep	(1) Aranda, (3) Trukese, (1) Pukapuka, (2) Tonga, (2) Tanaina
Basket (splint, wickerwork, etc.) fish trap	(4) S. V. Paiute, (3) Jivaro, (3) Trukese, (4,3) Pukapuka, (3,3) Tanala, (9,5) Tonga, (5,4,3) Klamath, (10+2) Tlingit, (3) Twana, (4) Lepcha, (6) Caribou Eskimos
Blind	(1,1) S. V. Paiute, (2) Klamath, (4) Ojibwa
Lure, waterfowl (fish, crayfish, lobster, shark, seal)	(3) S. V. Paiute, (1) Trukese, (2,1) Pukapuka, (3) Kapauku, (3) Tanala, (5) Ojibwa, (5,3) Caribou Eskimos, (4) Copper Eskimos, (6) Iglulik, (4,4) Tareumiut, (4,3,1) Angmagsalik
Fish poison	(1) O. V. Paiute, (2) Chenchu, (1) Andamanese, (1) Jivaro, (1) Trukese, (1) Naga, (1) Tanala, (2) Tonga, (3,1) Lepcha
Fish poison container	(5) O. V. Paiute, (1) Trukese
Weir (dam, guide), may include platform or be a trap	(2) O. V. Paiute, (3) Ingura, (2) Jivaro, (4,4,3) Trukese, (4,2,1) Pukapuka, (1) Kapauku, (2,2) Naga, (1) Tonga, (1) Klamath, (1,1) Tlingit, (12,7,5) Twana (3) Aymara, (4,1) Ojibwa, (3) Lepcha, (1+1) Caribou Eskimos, (2+2) Copper Eskimos, (1) Iglulik, (1) Angmagsalik
Seine	(4) O. V. Paiute, (5) Yuma, (4) Pukapuka, (6) Tanala, (5) Huron
Fishhook assembly	(4) O. V. Paiute, (4) Yuma, (4) Ingura, (4) Jivaro, (5,5,5,4,4) Trukese, (15,14,5) Pukapuka, (4) Naga, (4) Tanala, (7,4) Klamath, (11) Tlingit, (5) Twana, (5) Huron, (3) Ojibwa, (4) Lepcha, (6) Caribou Eskimos, (10) Tanaina, (12,7) Copper Eskimos, (7) Iglulik, (8,6,6) Tareumiut
Drag net	(5,5) Naga, (4) Klamath, (8,7,7) Aymara, (12) Ingalik
Stationary bag net	(8) Aymara
Dip (scoop, bag) net for fish (muskrat)	(4) Yuma, (4) Andamanese, (6,5) Trukese, (6,5) Pukapuka, (5,4) Kapauku, (3) Naga, (7) Tanala, (9,6) Klamath, (5) Tlingit, (12,6) Twana, (7,7,5,5) Aymara, (6) Nabesna, (9,7) Ingalik, (5) Tanaina
Set net, fish (beaver, seal, sea turtle, waterfowl)	(7) Andamanese, (5) Trukese, (4) Twana, (4) Huron, (4) Ingalik, (6) Tareumiut

Table 6-3   (Continued)

Form (1–15 tu) and function	People
Thrown net, fish	(5) Jivaro, (5) Lepcha
Kite-fishing rig	(7) Trukese
Fish-driving sticks	(1) Pukapuka, (1) Klamath
Fish (gull) gorge	(3,3) Pukapuka, (5) Klamath, (4) Lepcha, (4) Angmagsalik
Jig-fishing rig	(3) Pukapuka, (4) Ojibwa
Fish snare	(2) Pukapuka, (2) Naga, (2) Iglulik
Torch, fish	(1) Pukapuka, (2) Ojibwa
Fuel, fire built in canoe to attract birds at night	(1) Klamath, (1) Twana
Weir and gate	(1+2) Tlingit
Waterfowl hunting headdress	(7) Twana
Seal-impaling sticks	(1) Twana
Pole net, geese	(6) Twana
Pole for setting net beneath ice	(1) Huron, (2) Ingalik
Fishhook-lure	(5) Ingalik
Lamprey snag	(3) Ingalik
Fish trap-checking pole	(1) Ingalik
Oil poured on water to prevent swans from flying	(1) Angmagsalik
B. *Complex forms for wild animal species*	
Waterfowl-hatchling net	(4) Klamath
Seal net	(7,6) Twana

each; the comparative average for tended facilities used on land for wild species is 2.4. Presumably the qualities of water led to the much higher average for aquatic forms. Most were used in fishing, and the functions of many are explained by their identifying labels. The first entry, a fish sweep, was designed to envelop or to drive fish before the manipulators. For two months following heavy rains in the arid Aranda country, fish sometimes were abundant at water holes. When they were plentiful, people pushed tree branches or brush through the water and literally swept the fish before them. The Tonga pushed large rolls of grass through ponds as sweeps and then were able to catch the fish by hand. For use within the fringing reef, the Trukese attached coconut palm leaflets to a long length of vine and drove fish into weirs, where they were taken with leisters or netted. The additional sweeps follow the same patterning.

Since tended fish traps (Fig. 6-2a–b) were handled or watched when in operation, their holding capacity usually was small. A fish need only be confined in such a trap long enough for someone to grasp, club, or impale it. Diverse materials were combined in many different ways to construct these

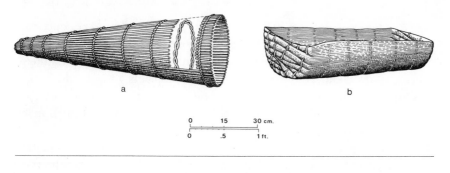

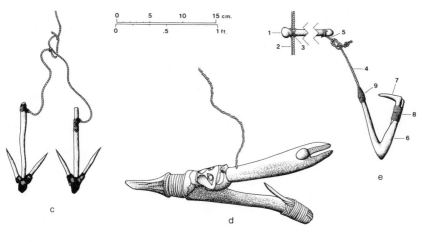

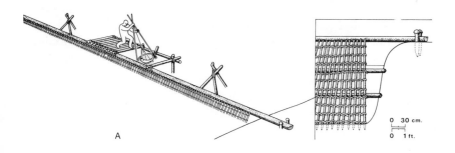

Figure 6-2 Tended facilities used in water: (*a*) Tanala cone-shaped fish scoop; (*b*) Tanala half-cylinder fish scoop; (*c*) Klamath composite fishhook; (*d*) Tlingit halibut hook; (*e*) Pukapukan deep-sea fishhook; (*A*) Twana salmon weir and dip net platform with dip net.

119

traps. The Jivaro made a trap of bamboo poles, set it at a weir, and poisoned the water. Among the Trukese a satchellike basket was used with a rock pile lure. Within the fringing reef Trukese women erected piles of rocks and left them unattended for about a month. During this time plants grew on the rocks, fish were attracted to the spot, and then women caught them in basket traps. On Pukapuka fishing baskets were used with rock pile traps, and small mats served as weirs. For taking small fish and larvae Tanala women used either a cone-shaped fish scoop trap (*a*) or one woven into a half-cylinder shape (*b*). The only other forms worthy of brief comment are the woven Lepcha trap with a short handle and the Caribou Eskimo trap of skin set at a weir. The most complicated example was made by the Tlingit for taking salmon, and it was used at a weir with a separate closing gate. The description is not entirely clear, but it appears that the trap was about twenty-five feet wide and perhaps seventy-five feet in length. It was made from cedar splints lashed together with spruce roots, and within this frame was a separate inner portion. Salmon were caught as they were driven downstream by people, some of whom fitted the gate in place to close the trap.

The only blinds similar in form to those designed for land species were used by the Surprise Valley Paiute. A brush blind concealed a hunter as he attempted to harpoon fish, and a blind of tules was associated with hunting ducks with duck skin lures and bows and arrows. The Klamath and Ojibwa partially shielded ice fishing holes with covers that functioned as blinds since they prevented light from entering the hole and frightening the fish away.

Fish poisons apparently were used only when people were present to retrieve the catch. Poison was dispersed in still water by the Chenchu and Tonga or in rivers, as among the Tanala and Lepcha. The Trukese placed poison in containers, from which it seeped into the water, as did the Owens Valley Paiute, who poisoned fish at weirs. The Andamanese poisoned streams and used hand nets to retrieve fish and prawns. The general impression is that the use of poison seldom was an important fishing technique.

The term *weir* is used as the generic designation for obstructions in water that serve to guide or hold fish. Fish dams and fences or mats and screens as guides are included in this definition of a weir. Weirs alone may take fish, as in tidal areas, but most often they were used in conjunction with leisters, nets, poison, or traps. Weirs usually were made from one material. The Kapauku stuck reeds in streambeds for use with dip nets, and the Tlingit constructed weirs of stones or poles at fish traps. The Trukese stone weirs built within lagoons were more complicated, and three different forms are identified according to the way in which the stones were arranged. One form consisted of a half circle of stones, another was a three-quarter circle with stone wings from the openings, and the third had a three-quarter circle of stones with a line of stones leading to the middle of the opening. At each form leaves and branches were used to close the openings as the tide ebbed. Fish were stranded in shallow water and taken by hand or captured with hand nets, leisters, or traps.

The most complex weir identified had twelve technounits and was made by the Twana for taking salmon. A dip net platform constructed in conjunction with their weir contributed to its complexity. Tripods of poles held the weir in place, and against the two upstream sides of each tripod were lashed three sets of stringers, horizontal poles that spanned the river (Fig. 6-2A). Latticework made from sections of poles with cedar limb binders faced the stringers and prevented any salmon from swimming above the weir when dip nets were being used. At other times the latticework sections were removed to allow salmon access to their spawning grounds. On the downstream side of the weir the dip net platform was constructed, with a stake to support the net handles.

Seines are small meshed, usually rectangular, nets with the ends drawn together to envelop fish or to strand them as the seine is pulled ashore. They usually are poorly described, and it has been assumed, perhaps incorrectly, that they included sticks at each end to spread the mesh. In all instances they were manipulated by a number of persons. Seines were used in ponds by the Owens Valley Paiute, in river waters by the Yuma, and along the beach or a reef on Pukapuka. The Huron made holes in ice and set a seine with a pole. None of these forms included more than six technounits, and it is possible that fewer parts normally were involved.

Among tended facilities used in water there was more diversity of form and technological complexity in fishhook assemblies than in any other cluster of forms. Fishhook assemblies averaged 6.3 parts, but because they tend to be described poorly in ethnographies, numerous assumptions have been made about the parts involved. Furthermore metal fishhooks received in trade often had replaced aboriginal forms entirely. This was true for the Ingura and Tanala among others. The most elementary assemblies in terms of technounit number were lines and hooks, such as the Ojibwa probably used, fashioned from one material and baited. The Trukese fishhook assemblies are of particular interest because of the part combinations for specific conditions. Unfortunately informants could not recall the particulars of aboriginal hooks since they had been replaced by metal hooks. Each of the five styles of assemblies included baited hooks and lines. For deep-water fishing a stone weight was added to the line, and for fishing along the shore a pole was used. In surface fishing free bait was used as well as a weighted line, and a float assembly included a pole and float. For trolling a lure was added to the baited line. Thus there were situation-specific fishhook assemblies with relatively few parts combined in a variety of ways.

Composite hooks were most likely used when large fish were sought. The seven-part Klamath hooks for large fish were used in pairs (Fig. 6-2c). A bone shank was attached to a pair of bone barbs with sinew and pitch as the binder. A fiber lead line was tied to the main fiber line, and bait was stuck on the barbs. Another composite hook assembly, this one with eleven parts, was made by the Tlingit for halibut. A bone barb was wedged in a wood side prong and bound in place with root; the bait was tied on the barb. The prong was bound to a shank with a root line, and there was a lead line of root (Fig. 6-2d). Multiple hooks were tied to a secondary lead line, and the main line was weighted with a stone near the bottom. The surface end of the main line was attached to either an inflated seal stomach or wood float.

The most complicated fishhook assembly had fifteen parts and was made by the Pukapukans for deep-sea fishing. The handline, up to 300 fathoms in length, had a secondary lead line tied with a separate binder to spreading sticks with a composite hook attached to each line (Fig. 6-2e). The spreading stick (1) was tied to the secondary lead line (2) with fiber cord (3). The primary lead line (4) was tied to the end of the spreader stick with another fiber line (5). The wood hook shank (6) included a wood barb (7) lashed in place (8), and there was a separate shank–lead line binder (9). Attached to the line was a block of coral serving as a sinker and held by a separate line. Each hook was baited, and the bait was tied on with a string.

A drag net is moved through the water from a boat or hand carried by two or more persons. Seines and drag nets are not clearly separable, but seines usually are rectangular and designed to encase fish. Drag nets, which are either roughly cone-shaped or rectangular, hold fish by their gills or by the net's motion through water. The Naga forms illustrate the gradations. They made long rectangular nets with large mesh and similar short nets with small mesh. When used in combination, the large-meshed nets were dragged through the water, entangling large fish and often frightening small fish into the smaller nets. The small nets seem to have functioned as seines and possibly should be so designated. The Klamath drag net was pouch-shaped with two poles attached to it, and it was dragged through river water by two men holding the poles vertically. It was the Aymara who fished most intensively with drag nets (Fig. 6-3a–c). They made three styles, and the technounits of each are detailed in the Appendix. The two-man drag net was pulled by men in different balsas (a),

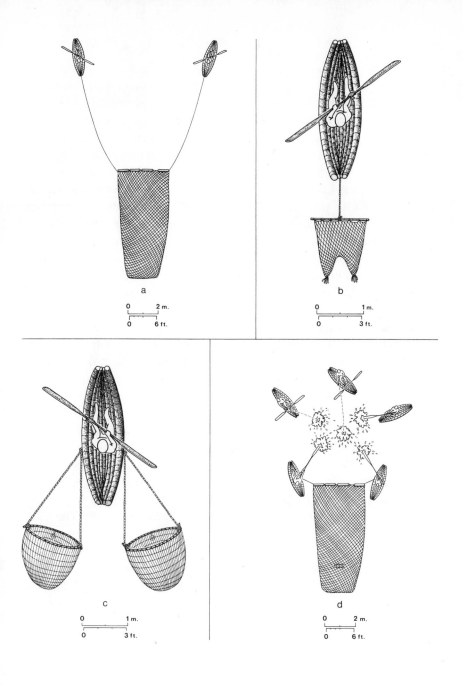

Figure 6-3 Aymara drag and bag nets: (*a*) two-man drag net; (*b*) one-man drag net; (*c*) basketry drag nets; (*d*) stationary bag net.

and the lobed form was pulled by one man in a balsa (*b*). They also made basketry drag nets that were pulled in pairs behind a balsa (*c*). A stationary bag net (*d*) was used by the Aymara, who drove fish into it by tossing pebbles and beating the water with poles. The Ingalik drift net, whose parts are detailed in the Appendix, was a drag net. One end was tied to a canoe, and the net was drifted down a river at right angles to the current. When a salmon struck, the net was hauled in, the salmon killed, and the net paid out in another drift.

Dip or scoop nets have handles (Fig. 6-4) and most often were used against fish at weirs or with poison. A four-part Kapauku form with the scoop and handle made from a single piece of wood (*a*) was used with a baited stick as a lure for crayfish. The seven-part Tanala dip net (*b*) included a wood frame, separate handle, handle extension, and extension-handle binder. More diverse dip nets were used by the Aymara than by anyone else. One form had wood crosspieces to hold the netting (*c*), and another had the netting held inside a wood frame (*d*); it was used at a weir from a balsa. The most complicated dip net (*e*) by far was made by the Twana for use at a weir platform. The hoop frame (*1*) was lashed together (*2*), and the netting (*3*) was attached directly to the frame. The crossed pole handles (*4*) were bound with cord near the upper ends (*5*) and at the sides of the hoop (*6*). U-shaped wood prongs (*7*) were lashed (*8*) near the lower ends of the sharpened pole bases. The pole points and prongs were forced into the river bottom to hold the net in place. Across the frame was a horizontal trigger string (*9*) tied to a vertical trigger string (*10*), and between the two were diagonal trigger strings (*11*). Finally a finger loop (*12*) was attached near the top of the vertical trigger string. The purpose of the trigger strings was to indicate to a fisherman when a salmon was in the net.

Set nets used as tended facilities were rectangular, and their primary purpose was to take species such as beavers, ducks, and sea turtles, not fish. The basic net consisted of netting, mesh-separation poles at the net ends, netting-pole binders, and backing lines, which often were assumed to have been present. The Tareumiut form with six parts was set at leads in ice to take seals. It included sinkers as well as a backing line extension anchored to a wood stake on the ice. The Andamanese set net (Fig. 6-5*a*) for sea turtles and large fish had the most parts, seven, because it included three-part floats and stone sinkers lashed to the net. It is probable that the nets were tended because the species taken were capable of damaging or destroying the net. However similar nets set for fish usually were untended.

Gorges are designed to be swallowed by a species and to hold fast either by barbs or more often by toggling in an animal's stomach. A Pukapukan gorge for small fish consisted of a spined section of pandanus leaf tied to a hand line

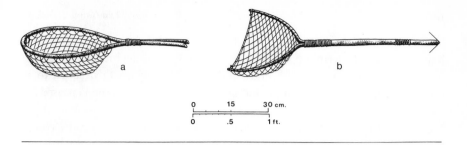

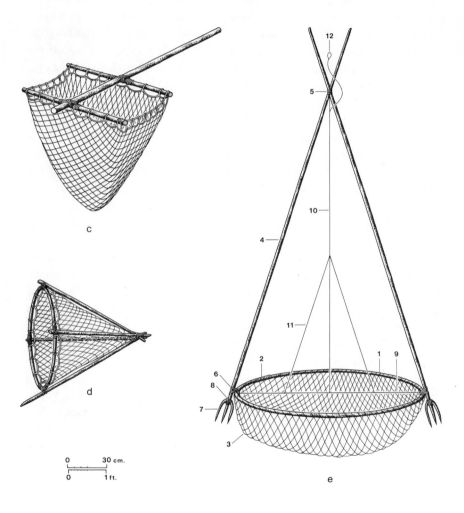

Figure 6-4   Dip (scoop) nets: (a) Kapauku (Courtesy of *Yale University Publications in Anthropology* and Leopold Pospisil; from Pospisil, 1963); (b) Tanala; (c, d) Aymara; (e) Twana.

by half hitches. The bait was tied to the gorge with a lower section of the line (Fig. 6-5*b*). The Klamath fish gorge included the most technounits. A piece of bone was sharpened at both ends, and the middle of it was attached to a fiber line with sinew cord and pitch (Fig. 6-5*d*). The gorge was then encased in bait.

Lures to attract aquatic species were far more varied and usually more complicated than those used on land. An elementary form, a tree branch with leaves attached, was used by the Trukese when they took lobsters with leisters. When the moon was full and the tide low, a lobster was lured within range by holding the branch so that it cast a shadow. The lobster moved within the shadow and was impaled. The Pukapukans used loose bait to lure fish, or may have tied bait to a line to attract a fish so that it could be snared. When fishing with leisters, the Copper Eskimos used a bear tooth to which small pieces of bone were attached; these fluttered like fins as the lure was moved through the water (Fig. 6-5*c*). The Surprise Valley Paiute used stuffed duck skins at their duck blinds, and two different forms of seal lures were made by the Tareumiut. One consisted of a wood handle to which a seal's claws were attached, and the second was a wood rattle with ivory clappers. Seal nets were set at leads in ice, and the surface of the ice nearby was scratched with the claw lure to attract seals, which then were taken in nets. The rattle also appears to have been shaken to attract the attention of seals. The most complicated lure was fish-shaped and was used with leisters by the Iglulik to take char; its parts are reported in the Appendix. For taking sharks at leads in ice where they could be harpooned, the Angmagsalik placed bloody seal meat at the edge of the ice. The blood dyed the water and attracted sharks. These Eskimos tied blubber to weighted stones and dropped them down in the water for the same purpose.

On Pukapuka torches were used to fish at night. In fishing for some species the use of torches appears to have been to provide light; less often fish were lured to the light. In either case they were taken with leisters or in nets. The Ojibwa used a torch that consisted of a pole with strips of birch bark at the end. They set these strips on fire when they fished at night with leisters. Another use of fire was by the Klamath for taking birds at night. They built a fire in a canoe to attract birds, which then became entangled in a large triangular fishnet arranged in the bow of the canoe. The Twana too used fire to take waterfowl at night. A fire was built in the stern of a canoe, and a paddler sitting in front of it wore a headdress which cast a shadow over the rest of the canoe. Waterfowl swimming into the lighted area were both frightened and temporarily blinded. As they swam back into the shadow, they were killed with a bird spear or captured with a pole net.

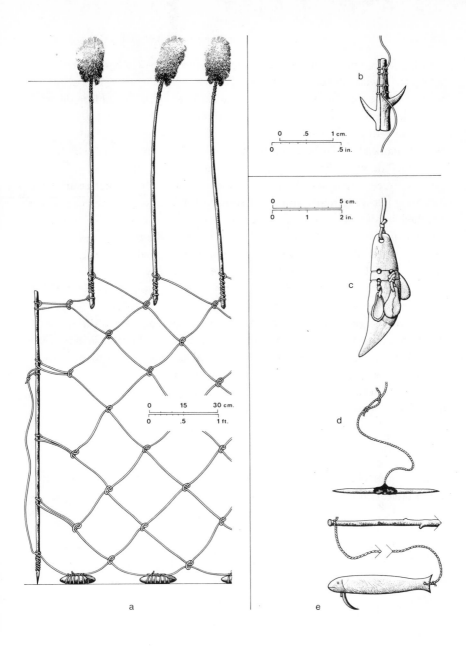

Figure 6-5   Tended facilities for aquatic species: (a) Andamanese sea turtle net (Courtesy of Cambridge University Press; from Radcliffe-Brown, 1948); (b) Copper Eskimo fish lure; (c) Pukapukan fish gorge; (d) Klamath fish gorge; (e) Ingalik lure-hook (Courtesy of *Yale University Publications in Anthropology* and Cornelius Osgood; from Osgood, 1940).

At localities where seals gathered on shore and dove off a bank to reach the water, the Twana drove stakes beneath the bank at low tide. The stakes were pointed at the top, and when seals on the bank were frightened into diving at high tide, some became impaled on the stakes.

The only lure and hook combination prevailed among the Ingalik. A fish-shaped shank of antler had a bird claw hook wedged into a hole with a piece of wood. The sinew line was tied to a wood pole (Fig. 6-5e).

Only three complex tended facilities were identified. The Klamath waterfowl-hatchling net was circular and about three feet in diameter. At the edges were attached small rods with pointed bottoms. The upper ends of the rods fitted into a shaft, and when the shaft was cast to launch the net, the net spread to envelop small ducks or geese, the pointed ends of the rods sticking in the ground. The Twana nets for seals were set out at low tide near the shore. A net was stretched and tied between two logs. Crossed stakes were placed over the logs and driven into the bottom. A trip line tied near the tops of the crossed stakes led to the shore and to the hands of a concealed hunter. With the incoming tide a seal swam over the net, and the hunter dislodged the crossed stakes with the trip line. The logs and the net floated to the surface beneath the seal and held it long enough for men in canoes to reach the net and kill the seal. A variant of this set had a single log float, and one side of the net was pegged to the shore bottom.

Summary   The 378 tended facilities included 1193 parts for an overall average of 3.2 technounits per form. A synopsis of the naturefact and artifact information in the tables follows:

	Simple			Complex		
	Forms	tu	Average	Forms	tu	Average
Wild species on land	134	288	2.1	6	32	5.3
Domestic animals on land	21	43	2.0			
Domestic plants on land	24	47	2.0	1	5	5.0
Wild species in water	189	761	4.0	3	17	5.7
	368	1139	3.1	10	54	5.4

The most obvious observations are that complex forms rarely were employed and that tended facilities were numerically unimportant for use with domestic species. The greater importance and elaboration of tended facilities for aquatic use as opposed to those employed on land also are striking.

Conclusion Tended facilities remind me of huge, versatile human hands and arms used to direct wild species to their doom or conversely to protect domestic species by warding off danger. Their technounit average of 3.2 may be compared with 1.9 for instruments and 4.8 for weapons. We would predict that tended facilities would be more complicated on the average than instruments if only because these facilities were used against creatures in motion. We might also predict that tended facilities would have a lower technounit average than weapons, the reason being that the vital quality of most tended facilities, to hold, required fewer parts than a lethal weapon need have. It would seem that it is technologically less difficult to gain a loose or firm hold on wild species than to kill it by other means.

Simple tended facilities used for wild species on land had an average of 2.1 technounits, while comparable forms in water averaged 4.0. The implication is that more technounits are required for aquatic tended facilities than for their counterparts on land because of the greater prey escape potential in water and the greater limitations of human pursuit. According to current paleoethnographic evidence, the systematic exploitation of aquatic resources is a comparatively recent development among technoeconomic patterns. If so we would expect that experience in using tended facilities emerged in a terrestrial context and then was extended to uses in water. Thus the higher technounit averages for tended facilities in water are compatible with the more recent emergence of these forms as structural-functional clusters as well as with the need for escape deterrents in aquatic forms.

That only 10 of the 378 tended facilities were complex is somewhat surprising but seems to be explainable. When people were present to handle facilities, their manipulations were a substitute for the use of forms that operated in a mechanical manner. Thus human manipulations are antithetical to technological mechanization, and when viewed in this manner the existence of any complex tended facilities must be considered an extreme in facility elaboration.

As a subsistant cluster, one of the important functions of tended facilities is to increase the effectiveness of weapons by first guiding and partially controlling the movements of wild animals. Another characteristic is the comparative importance of coordinated human effort in the effective use of diverse tended facilities. The use of weapons may sometimes have involved cooperation among people, but tended facilities often required such cooperation. Conversely, the most important inherent limitation of instruments, weapons, and tended facilities alike is that they require the presence of human operators.

CHAPTER 7

▲ ▲ ▲ ▲ ▲ ▲ ▲ ▲

FACILITIES:
UNTENDED

U ntended facilities are constructed in such a manner that they can function without the presence of humans, although people must check their performance. Tended and untended facilities alike control the movement of species or protect them. An untended facility was designed to restrict the movement of a species, material, or force to the point that it usually was prevented from changing position, which is the ultimate in motion control. A stone terrace stopped the earth in a garden from moving, soil placed on weeds prevented their growth, and a deadfall, net, or trap stopped or nearly stopped the movement of wild animals. A few forms, such as hobbles for domestic animals or windbreaks around cultivated land, are untended facilities that permit limited movement.

The most widely prevailing untended facilities already have been introduced in their use as tended facilities. These include deadfalls, fish traps, guides, nets, pitfalls, and snares. These and all the other identified forms in this category are artifacts. In the discussion that follows those forms that closely resemble tended facilities reported in Chapter 6 will not be detailed except when their form or use may not be apparent.

Untended Facilities Used on Land (Table 7-1)   The 223 forms with a total of 1023 parts averaged 4.6 technounits each. The comparable average for tended facilities is 2.3. It is averages such as these that indicate the "cost" of substituting techno-units for people.

Pitfalls, the first entry in the table, usually were holes in the ground, and except for the simplest forms, most were covered with more than one material. The most elementary form listed is a trench dug around a tree to trap cater-pillars as they crawled away from the trunk. Caterpillar trenches were made by the Owens Valley Paiute, who used a torch to produce smoke and thereby induce the caterpillars to abandon the tree. The Tonga dug a pit next to a termite mound, made a hole in the mound, and placed a torch just beyond the pit. The swarming termites struggled from the hole toward the torch light and fell into the pit. The Twana pitfall for deer had a cover of branches and an impaling stake at the bottom of the pit. Impaling knives, spears, and stakes often were placed in pitfalls, where they operated as untended weapons in killing an animal. However they are more correctly listed as integral parts of facilities since they functioned only after the trap had worked. The most complicated pitfalls were made by the Iglulik, and the parts of each are described in the Appendix. An Iglulik set for wolves was made by building an enclosure of snow at the top of a snowbank and then digging a hole in its interior. The hole was covered with a thin slab of snow, and bait was placed on top. A wolf jumped over the enclosure to reach the bait, fell through the cover, and was trapped in the pit until retrieved by a hunter. For taking foxes a cone-shaped stone tower was built with a stone slab opening at one side. A stone slab roof was placed on the cone, with one stone slanted diagonally down into the cone. The chamber was baited, and the diagonal stone was covered with water, which froze. As a fox attempted to reach the bait, it slid down the ice-covered stone and was trapped in the chamber. Since the fox could be retrieved by removing the slab of stone on one side, the pitfall was ready to function again as soon as it was rebaited.

The development of increasingly complicated pitfalls may have occurred in the following manner. The most elementary form was a pit, or simply a small hole in the ground such as those designed to take insects. When a deep pit for large game was developed, one or more materials were added to cover the opening. The form became more involved when impalers were added to ensure the animal's immobility. When artificial "pits" were constructed, as among some Eskimos, the form sometimes included still more technounits.

Untended snares (Fig. 7-1a–e) have a minimum of two parts, the line and a line holder, as was the case when a noose line was tied to a separate guide

Table 7-1   Untended facilities used on land

Form (1–14 tu) and function	People
A. *Simple forms for wild animals as food*	
Pitfall	(4) Aranda, (1) O. V. Paiute, (6) Naga, (5,4) Tanala, (1) Tonga, (3) Klamath, (3) Twana, (4) Lepcha, (4,3) Caribou Eskimos, (6) Copper Eskimos, (7,6,4) Iglulik
Snares	(2) S. V. Paiute, (4) Naron, (2) Walapai, (4) Hopi, (6,6) Trukese, (3) Pukapuka, (5) Akamba, (6,2,2) Tanala, (4,4,2) Tonga, (1) Twana, (2) Huron, (3,3) Lepcha, (3,3) Caribou Eskimos, (2) Nabesna, (6,6,5) Ingalik, (4) Tanaina, (2) Copper Eskimos, (3,2) Iglulik, (2) Tareumiut
Guide to deadfall (snare)	(1) Walapai, (3) Naga, (1) Tanala, (1,1) Tonga, (1) Tlingit, (2) Twana, (1) Ojibwa, (1,1) Ingalik
Lure (bait, caged live birds)	(1) Pukapuka, (5) Tonga
Captive animal (bird) pen (cage)	(3,2) Pukapuka, (6) Twana, (1) Huron
Bird gorge	(4) Pukapuka
Impaling spikes (spears)	(1) Naga, (1) Tasmanians
Beehive	(6) Akamba, (4) Tanala
Bird lime trap	(2) Trukese, (4,3) Tanala, (2) Tonga, (5) Lepcha
Bird cage trap	(4) Tanala
Bag net, burrowing animal	(3) Tonga
Spread net, rabbit	(3) Ojibwa
Blood knife (glass)	(4) Caribou Eskimos, (6,3) Iglulik
B. *Complex forms for wild animals as food*	
Spring-pole snare	(3) S. V. Paiute, (7) Naron, (4) O. V. Paiute, (9) Trukese, (9,8,6) Naga, (7) Akamba, (8,4) Tanala, (8,6) Tonga, (4) Twana, (4) Huron, (6) Lepcha, (4) Nabesna
Deadfall	(6) S. V. Paiute, (7) O. V. Paiute, (8) Walapai, (8,5) Hopi, (6) Jivaro, (9) Akamba, (10,7) Tonga, (13,6) Tlingit, (7) Twana, (8,5) Ojibwa, (8,6,2) Lepcha, (14,7) Nabesna, (12,11,10) Ingalik, (10,9,8,7) Tanaina, (6) Copper Eskimos, (4) Iglulik, (7) Tareumiut
Trap, unknown style	(4) O. V. Paiute
Snare with moving parts, not tossing-pole or spring pole	(4) Jivaro, (7,5) Tlingit, (3) Nabesna, (11,10) Ingalik, (6) Tanaina
Pitfall & spring-pole snare	(4+2) Akamba
Spear trap	(11) Akamba, (9) Lepcha
Cage trap	(10) Akamba, (9,6) Tanala, (4) Ojibwa, (5,4) Caribou Eskimos, (5) Iglulik, (7) Angmagsalik

Table 7-1 (Continued)

Form (1–14 tu) and function	People
Tossing-pole snare	(9) Tlingit, (6) Nabesna, (9) Ingalik, (8,6) Tanaina
Torque trap, fox	(12) Tanaina
Spring bait	(3) Iglulik, (3) Tareumiut

C. *Simple forms for wild plant species*
None

D. *Complex forms for wild plant species*
None

E. *Simple forms to control or protect domestic animals from wild species or the elements*

Hobbles (tether) for horses	(1) Hopi, (1) Aymara, (2) Lepcha
Corral for livestock	(2) Hopi, (5,2) Akamba, (4) Tanala, (3,2) Tonga, (3,2) Aymara
Bell for grazing animal	(3) Hopi, (3) Akamba
Snare, protect poultry from hawks	(5) Tanala
Domestic animal housing	(3) Tanala, (11+2,11,10,4) Tonga, (7+2+1,4) Lepcha
Scare, protect poultry (livestock)	(2) Akamba, (3) Tonga

F. *Complex forms to protect domestic animals from wild species or the elements*
None

G. *Simple forms to protect domestic plants from wild species or the elements*

Protective barrier (cactus, stones, wrappings, etc.) around individual plants	(1) Pima, (1+1) Hopi, (2) Trukese, (1) Kapauku, (1) Tonga
Fence around cultivated plot	(2,2) Pima, (1) Walapai, (7) Kapauku, (3) Tanala, (3) Tonga, (4,1) Lepcha
Scarecrow (scare)	(13,7,1) Hopi, (5) Yuma, (4) Naga, (3) Akamba, (3) Tanala, (3) Tonga, (4) Aymara, (3) Ojibwa
Terrace (barrier to form cultivated plot)	(1,1) Hopi, (1) Aymara, (2,1) Lepcha
Windbreak	(1) Hopi
Soil from irrigation ditch to kill weeds	(1) Kapauku
Boar (deer) impaling trap	(11) Kapauku, (5) Naga
Substances to repel predators from seeds	(2) Naga, (3) Tonga
Pitfall	(4) Kapauku, (6) Tonga
Fuel for fire, protect garden from predators	(1) Tonga
Poisoned bait	(3) Lepcha

Table 7-1   (Continued)

Form (1–14 tu) and function	People
H. *Complex forms to protect domestic plants from wild species*	
Spring-pole snare, rat (mole)	(7+4 tu house) Kapauku; (11) Pukapuka, (7) Akamba
Deadfall, monkey (guinea pig, mice)	(6) Naga, (5) Aymara
Cage trap, monkey	(7) Lepcha
Crossbow	(6) Lepcha
Arrow for crossbow	(2) Lepcha

fence. Simple untended snares never included more than six parts, exclusive of guide fences, and yet there were diverse kinds of parts. An elementary form, used by the Tonga for small animals and birds, consisted simply of a fiber noose suspended from a branch across a trail (*a*). Bait was included with some forms, as exemplified by the Pukapukan bird snare with the noose anchor serving as the bait container. The Pukapukans cut off the upper portion of a coconut shell and removed the meat near the rim of the remaining portion. Holes were drilled near the opening, and a noose line, arranged over the opening, was tied through each hole (*b*). A bird that attempted to reach the coconut meat in the lower half of the shell was caught in one of the nooses. On Truk half a coconut shell was set upright, and a piece of fish was placed inside as bait. Stakes held the shell upright, and one stick anchored the noose line. The noose rested on two other sticks that extended over the top of the shell (*d*). The Trukese coconut shell set with six parts clearly is more complicated than the Pukapukan form with three parts. As usual, however, the addition of technounits is not lineal for snares or most other forms. A four-technounit Tongan snare was a multiple set for small birds seeking grain among the chaff left from threshing. The grain served as "natural" bait. On a circular wood frame with its binder were strung netlike strips of bark, and hair nooses were tied to these (*c*). The set was buried in the chaff, and birds were caught by their feet as they searched for grain. The design of simple snares may move in still other directions, as illustrated by an Ingalik example. Their ptarmigan snare was set in connection with a guide fence of brush. A pole was stuck in the ground diagonally, and the noose was suspended from a point along the diagonal (*e*). The pole was tied to a vertical stake, and gate sticks were placed on each side of an opening in the fence. The noose was held open with grass ties fastened to the gate sticks. When a bird stuck its head through the noose, it broke the grass ties, and the noose tightened as it struggled.

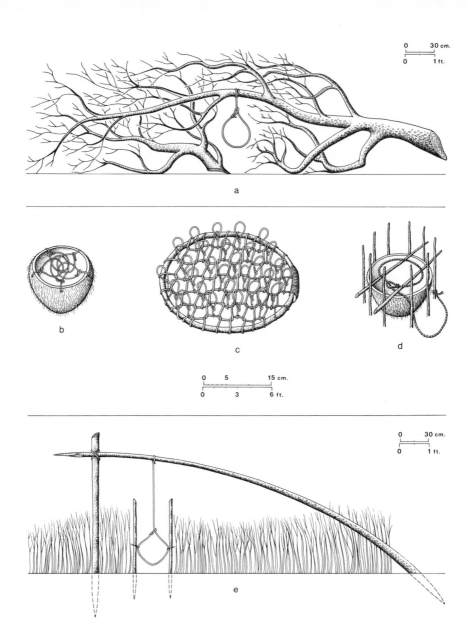

Figure 7-1 Simple snares as untended facilities: (a) Tongan small-animal snare (Courtesy of The National Museums of Zambia; from Reynolds, 1968); (b) Pukapukan baited coconut shell bird snare lines; (c) Tongan multiple small-bird snares (Courtesy of The National Museums of Zambia; from Reynolds, 1968); (d) Trukese baited coconut shell set (Courtesy of *Yale University Publications in Anthropology* and Frank M. LeBar; from LeBar, 1964); (e) Ingalik ptarmigan snare and guide fence (Courtesy of *Yale University Publications in Anthropology* and Cornelius Osgood; from Osgood, 1940).

136

Bait was used as a lure for taking land crabs on Pukapuka. Crabs were attracted by the odor of toasted coconut gratings which had been placed in the brush, and after a few hours the person returned to the spot and collected the assembled crabs. The Tonga made a cage in which wild birds were placed to lure others. The birdcage was hung in a tree, and bird lime was spread on nearby branches to hold fast any birds that perched there. Immature wild animals also were caged, to be fed until they were large enough to eat. On Pukapuka land crabs were raised in pens, and birds were raised in cages. The Twana and Huron caged bears for the same purpose.

A number of additional simple untended facilities require brief comment. The Akamba and Tanala made wooden beehives that they hung in trees to attract wild, or perhaps more properly semiwild, colonies of bees. Bamboo spikes as impalers were placed in the paths of deer by the Naga, and the Tasmanians implanted crossed spears in game trails to impale animals. One of the most famous untended facilities is the "blood knife" used by Eskimos for taking wolves. The Caribou Eskimos coated a metal-bladed knife with blood and placed the knife, with the sharp edge up, in snow. As a wolf licked the blood, its tongue was cut, and the taste of its own blood led it to lick more and more until it bled to death. The Iglulik also used the blood knife for wolves; alternatively they sometimes placed a piece of a broken bottle in the snow and poured blood over it to accomplish the same end.

A small number of facilities killed in the manner of weapons, but since their functioning did not require the presence of persons they are classed as untended facilities. Included are the set spears of the Naga and Tasmanians, set crossbows of the Lepcha, and blood knife sets of Eskimos. The cluster also includes automatic spear traps and spears set at garden fences for predators. All of these are "untended" weapons that might legitimately be distinguished as a separate class of subsistants. Since they are so few in number, however, they have been listed as untended facilities, with due recognition of their qualities as weapons. In many respects untended weapons are "ultimate" weapons because of their killing capacities in the absence of any direct human involvement at the time of a kill.

Snares (Fig. 7-2) and deadfalls predominated among complex untended forms, but the ethnographic descriptions are not always precise concerning the parts involved. The first group, spring-pole snares, were most effective against species capable of wiggling free from a simple noose or chewing through a snare line. A spring pole hurled a small captive completely into the air by its neck or feet or held one or more legs of a larger animal high enough to make escape very difficult. At least three parts were involved: a noose line, spring

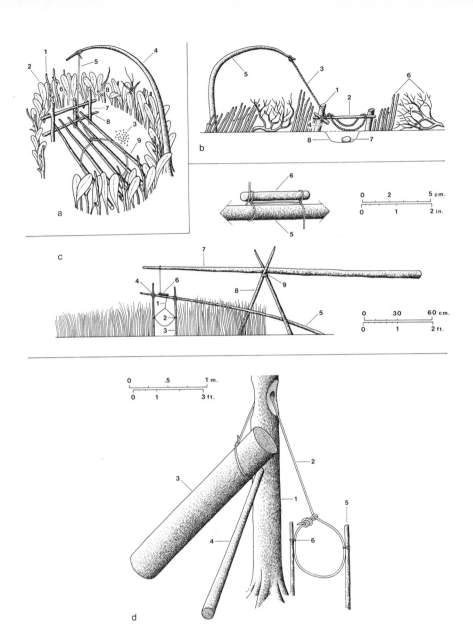

Figure 7-2 Complex snares: (*a*) Trukese wildfowl spring-pole snare (Courtesy of *Yale University Publications in Anthropology* and Frank M. LeBar; from LeBar, 1964); (*b*) Tongan baited spring-pole snare (Courtesy of The National Museums of Zambia; from Reynolds, 1968); (*c*) Ingalik tossing-pole snare (Courtesy of *Yale University Publications in Anthropology* and Cornelius Osgood; from Osgood, 1940); (*d*) Tanaina bear snare and fall log (Courtesy of *Yale University Publications in Anthropology* and Cornelius Osgood; from Osgood, 1937).

pole, and trigger to release the spring pole. Additional structural characteristics vary widely, but two illustrated examples should be sufficient to explain how they operate. The Trukese form (*a*) included an enclosure, presumably of sticks (*1*), which was covered with leaves (*2*) and baited (*3*) to attract wildfowl. In an effort to reach the bait a bird was forced to walk across the set, which consisted of a bent spring pole (*4*) with a noose line (*5*) tied to the spring pole and a trigger stick (*6*). The spring pole was held in place by a pair of vertical sticks (*7*) with upper and lower cross sticks (*8*). The noose was placed on four treadle sticks (*9*). As a bird stepped on the treadle sticks, the lower cross stick was forced down to release the trigger stick, which tightened the noose around the bird's leg or legs as the spring pole sprang upward to hold the bird captive.

Tongan spring-pole snares ranged in size from very small sets for rats to very large ones for buffalo. Since there appears to have been continuity from small to large varieties, they are considered as a single unbaited style despite the use of different materials. The baited form is entered as a separate style since it had two additional technounits, the bait and a small bait pit; it is the illustrated form (Fig. 7-2*b*). Two vertical sticks (*1*) held a horizontal trip stick (*2*), and the noose line (*3*) was attached to a trigger stick (*4*) and then to the spring pole (*5*). A guide fence of brush (*6*) and a small baited (*7*) pit (*8*) completed the actual set. In addition, however, leaves from a particular plant were rubbed on the noose line to deter white ants from destroying it. As the bait in the pit was disturbed, the trip stick was moved, releasing the trigger stick and tightening the noose line around the game as the spring pole righted itself.

Another form that hoists game into the air at the end of a noose is the tossing-pole snare. It appears to have been used most often when the spring-pole snares of a people would not function effectively because of their loss of elasticity in cold weather. The tossing-pole snare of the Ingalik was set across a hare's trail at an opening in a brush fence (Fig. 7-2*c*). A hare that stuck its head through the noose (*1*) broke the grass ties (*2*) to the gate sticks (*3*) tied (*4*) to a diagonal support pole (*5*), and dislodged the trigger (*6*), which unbalanced the tossing pole (*7*) from its fulcrum at a pair of crossed poles (*8*) that had been tied together (*9*). The heavy end of the pole dropped to the ground and thereby tossed the strangling hare into the air.

Other snares, such as the one used by the Jivaro for game birds, had trip sticks as triggers. The Nabesna might set a snare for caribou with a drag attached at the end of the noose line. When a caribou was snared, the drag, probably a pole, was pulled along until it caught on an obstruction to hold the animal firmly or choke it to death if the noose were around its neck. Another style used by the Tanaina for bears included a snare and fall log (Fig. 7-2*d*). The purpose of the fall log appears to have been to prevent a snared bear from chewing through the noose line. A hole was cut through a tree (*1*) and the noose line (*2*) passed through the hole. The free end was tied to a heavy log (*3*) propped against the tree with a pole (*4*). The noose was held open at gate sticks (*5*) with ties (*6*). A bear walking along the trail put its head through the noose and broke the ties to the gate sticks. As the bear struggled, the fall log dropped to the ground and hoisted it into the air.

Deadfalls (Fig. 7-3*b*, *c*) are constructed in such a manner that a weight, usually a log or stones, falls on an animal as soon as it moves the bait and trigger that releases the fall. Occasionally bait is not included, as in the Jivaro example; in this instance the trigger was dislodged by an animal's movements. Deadfalls were relatively complicated, and their technounit average among the peoples sampled was 7.8. The most elementary form reported had only two parts and was used by the Lepcha. Across a game trail they raised one end of a wooden beam and supported it with a stick. An animal that brushed against the stick while running along the trail released the fall log and was crushed. The Tanaina and Ingalik made more different deadfalls than any other peoples, and theirs were among the most complicated forms. A Tanaina deadfall for grouse (*b*) had a three-part pole frame on which debris was placed for added weight. The figure-four trigger mechanism, which reportedly was aboriginal, supported the deadfall, and beneath it were placed plants that were favored food of the grouse. A bird pecking at the bait brushed against the trigger stick, released the weight, and was crushed. Sometimes more than one grouse was taken at a time, but this set seems to represent an example of overkill in terms of its design and the game birds harvested.

The parts of the Ingalik deadfalls are detailed in the Appendix, but it is desirable to illustrate one form, the eleven-part samson-post deadfall used for bears (Fig. 7-3*c*). The fall log (*1*) was supported by a Y-shaped stick (*2*) at one end and a samson post (*3*) at the opposite end; the fall log also was held in place by two sets of vertical guide posts (*4*). Between the barrier logs (*5*) and samson post was wedged a trigger stick (*6*) to which rotten fish bait (*7*) was tied (*8*). Additional weight for the fall log was provided by logs (*9*) leaned against it. A bear could not reach the bait from the rear of the set because of a wooden barrier (*10*) covering the back and a barrier at the top (*11*). Neither could a bear step over the high barrier logs (*5*). Instead it was forced to extend its head over the barrier logs and beneath the fall log to reach the bait. As it ate the bait, the bait stick moved, the samson post was displaced, and the fall log crashed down on the bear's head or neck.

Spear traps set across game trails included spearlike devices that were re-

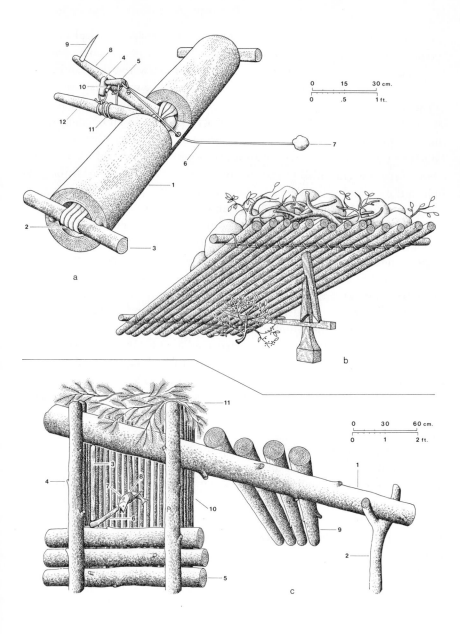

Figure 7-3   Complex traps: (*a*) Tanaina torque trap; (*b*) Tanaina grouse deadfall with figure-4 trigger mechanism (Courtesy of *Yale University Publications in Anthropology* and Cornelius Osgood; from Osgood, 1937); (*c*) Ingalik samson-post deadfall for bears (Courtesy of *Yale University Publications in Anthropology* and Cornelius Osgood; from Osgood, 1940).

leased automatically when an animal moved a trip cord. For elephants the Akamba set an eleven-part spear trap with a poisoned projectile point, and the Lepcha used a nine-part spear trap for deer. Cage traps were baited, and when the bait was disturbed, a cage or door dropped to hold a species captive.

The torque trap of the Tanaina (Fig. 7-3a), probably of Siberian origin, consisted of a split log (1) hollowed out along its length, with an opening at the middle. Stout thongs (2) were passed from one side to the other along the hollowed-out center and wrapped around crosspieces at each end (3). A hole in a block (4) was fitted with a pin (5) attached to a cord (6) that passed through a hole in the log and led to the bait (7) at the end of the bait cord. In the trigger arm (8) was fitted an impaling spike (9), and a peg (10) was inserted in the side of the trigger arm. Tension was obtained by twisting the end crosspieces (3) in opposite directions, presumably with the trigger-arm base attached to one set of thongs and the trip-arm (11) base to another set. When an animal pulled at the bait, the bait cord (6) and trip-arm cord (12) released the trigger and drove the impaler into an animal's brain.

The final complex untended facility used against wild species was the spring-bait set employed by the Iglulik and Tareumiut. The Iglulik rolled up a strip of baleen, tied the roll with sinew, and covered it with blubber. These lethal balls were distributed where they were likely to be found by wolves, who swallowed the set whole. As the sinew dissolved in a wolf's stomach, the baleen sprang out to its original shape, pierced the wolf's stomach, and killed it. The Tareumiut followed the same practice except that the baleen strips they used were pointed at each end.

The simple untended facilities used to protect domestic animals were few in number and are largely self-explanatory. Corrals often were poorly described, but they never appear to have been very complicated in technological terms. The Tonga made two different styles of chicken coops with a combined total of twenty-two technounits as well as a pigeon coop with eleven technounits and pigeon nesting cones with two parts. They also constructed a four-part goat house.

For the protection of domestic plants eleven styles of simple untended facilities were identified, few of which require comment from a technological point of view. Perhaps the protective barriers for individual plants merit the most attention. To guard them against nocturnal predators the Pima sometimes ringed plants with cholla cactuses, while the Hopi piled stones around peach saplings and also placed wrappings around each plant. To foster plant growth the Trukese wrapped transplanted shoots with leaves that were tied in place. The Kapauku rubbed dirt on plant cuttings to prevent rot, and the Tonga spread ashes on young plants for their protection. The only predator scare worthy of special comment was made by the Hopi. It was a scarecrow dressed in Western clothing, which helps explain the technounit count of thirteen.

A number of traps were used primarily to prevent predators from entering gardens. The Naga and Kapauku both placed impaling spikes at low sections in garden fences. A boar attempting to jump a Kapauku fence was impaled, and the same was true for deer attempting to enter Naga gardens. The Tonga built fires near their gardens in an effort to protect crops from nighttime marauders. The general configurations of complex traps used primarily to protect crops are similar to those already described to take wild species. However the forms listed in Table 7-1, *H*, served primarily to protect crops, not to obtain meat.

Untended Facilities Used in Water (Table 7-2) Many less complicated forms of similar design already have been encountered as tended facilities used in water. The first untended entry, a weir-trap combination, was reported only twice. In a stream the Surprise Valley Paiute built a wood-framed weir with crossed sticks projecting above the water. The projecting sticks on the upstream side were higher than those on the downstream side. A fish swimming upstream attempted to jump the barrier and cleared the downstream sticks but not those beyond; it was caught between the rows of sticks. The Twana built a tidal impounding weir-trap of poles and latticework. At high tide seals pursued herring along the shore; some swam into the converging arms of the weir and were led on to the circular trap, where they were trapped as the tide ebbed.

Untended and tended fish traps sometimes partially merge, as illustrated by a Pukapukan example. In the shallow waters of a lagoon the Pukapukans placed four stones on the bottom to support a rock slab and then covered the slab and supporting stones with other stones. About two weeks later two fishermen returned with a cone-shaped basket trap that was placed near the rock pile. After a mat had been arranged around the rock pile and the basketry trap, the stones were disarranged so that the fish would swim from the piled rocks into the basket trap. The rock pile attracted the fish and controlled their movement, but the basket trap and mat combination, which functioned as tended facilities, were essential to actually retrieve fish. The Trukese also piled stones to attract and hold fish, but their trap consisted of a single technounit since there was no apparent difference in the purposes served by particular stones. A Naga trap of stones was tunnel-shaped and led away from a pool of cold river water; the far end was blocked with stones. The morning after the

Table 7-2   Untended facilities used in water

Form (1–15 tu) and function	People
A. *Simple forms used for wild species*	
Weir-trap	(3) S. V. Paiute, (7) Twana
Fish (eel) trap (basket, poles, splints, roots, etc.)	(8) O. V. Paiute, (3) Yuma, (8,4,1) Trukese, (3) Pukapuka, (3,3) Naga, (11,10,5) Tanala, (7,3) Tonga, (6) Klamath, (9) Tlingit, (9,7) Twana, (7,4,4,4,3) Lepcha, (5) Nabesna, (12,12,12,8) Ingalik, (15,5) Tanaina, (4) Tareumiut
Fishhook assembly	(4) Tonga, (7) Klamath, (5) Lepcha, (12) Tanaina
Roe-collection bundle	(5) Twana
Fish-catching platform	(2) Ingura
Hatchling sea turtle pen	(3) Pukapuka
Entangling (holding) nets, crayfish (fish, waterfowl, otter)	(10) Kapauku, (8,7) Tonga, (8,4) Klamath, (8,3) Huron, (8,7,4) Ojibwa, (8) Ingalik, (8) Tareumiut
Weir used with trap (net, dip net)	(3) Naga, (5,2) Tonga, (8) Twana, (2) Huron, (1) Lepcha, (4) Nabesna, (8,4) Ingalik, (8) Tanaina
Gorge (gorgelike, hook) set, waterfowl (gull, fish)	(5) Tlingit, (3) Twana, (4) Caribou Eskimos, (3) Copper Eskimos, (5) Iglulik, (4) Tareumiut
Snare, waterfowl	(1) Kapauku, (2) Twana, (3) Aymara, (7) Ingalik, (6) Angmagsalik
Snare guide fence	(1) Kapauku, (1) Ingalik
Screen used with fish trap	(3) Ingalik
Octopus trench	(1) Tanaina
B. *Complex forms used for wild species* None	
C. *Simple forms used to cultivate or protect domestic species* None	
D. *Complex forms used to cultivate or protect domestic species* None	

trap had been built, fish that had entered the tunnel were numb with cold and could be taken by hand.

Traps, which usually were cylindrical or cone-shaped, were placed in water with or without an accompanying weir. One Tanala trap for eels was made from a roll of bark that had a funnel-shaped opening of bamboo splints (Fig.

7-4*a*). It appears to have consisted of ten parts and was baited and set in conjunction with a weir. The Lepcha made five different styles of fish traps from bamboo, of which three were set in conjunction with weirs. The trap with the greatest number of parts, fifteen, was made by the Tanaina for salmon and was set at a weir. The trap body (Fig. 7-4*b*) was constructed of alder poles, with encircling hoops bound to the poles. The funnel-shaped entrance of poles was bound in place, as were poles at the rear of the trap. A door was placed at the top to remove fish, and the front of the trap was bound to poles that formed the weir. On one side at the rear of the trap a post was driven into the streambed. A line was tied around it as well as to a rock on the opposite side of the trap.

In terms of technounit totals the four Ingalik fish traps included forty-four parts, which are listed in the Appendix. Their chum salmon trap (Fig. 7-4*c*) was set at a weir with a separate screen above the trap. The trap body consisted of spruce splints, with other splints coiled around the body splints and lashed in place with spruce root line. The trap sometimes included three or four separate sections fitted and bound together, and fish were removed through a door at the top. The trap was set with the mouth against the current, and there was no funnel-shaped entrance. Fish entering the trap were unable to escape because of the force of the flowing water, and because they were so numerous, there was not sufficient space for individuals to swim free.

The purposes served by most of the remaining forms usually are apparent, and only a few need be discussed. One of these is the twelve-part Tanaina fish-hook assembly set for halibut. Much of its complexity is contributed by the anchor assembly. The roe-collection device used by the Twana for herring consisted of branches, presumably bound together and weighted with an anchor. The bundle was placed in tidal water to attract herring to lay their eggs on the set. Among the Ingura an unusual fish trap prevailed. At the base of a small waterfall, the people placed a piece of paperbark supported by sticks. Any small fish that fell back in its attempt to leap the falls was trapped on the paperbark.

Nets designed to hold or entangle diverse aquatic species have been lumped together because there were comparatively few different varieties. The most developed form, used by the Kapauku for taking crayfish (Fig. 7-4*d*), consisted of a wood frame with fiber netting bound to the frame with grass ties. Bait was skewered to the net with slivers of cane, and a horizontal pole was bound across the frame. A forked stick held the net down and was lashed to an anchor pole on shore. When the set was checked, any crayfish eating the bait were trapped as the net lifted them from the water.

A reasonably typical set net for fish is the one used by the Ingalik for white-

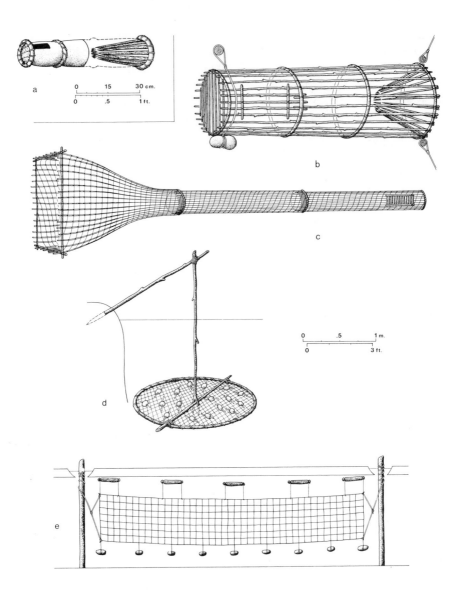

Figure 7-4 Untended facilities in water: (*a*) Tanala baited eel trap; (*b*) Tanaina salmon trap set at a weir (Courtesy of *Yale University Publications in Anthropology* and Cornelius Osgood; from Osgood, 1937); (*c*) Ingalik chum salmon trap set at a weir (Courtesy of *Yale University Publications in Anthropology* and Cornelius Osgood; from Osgood, 1940); (*d*) Kapauku baited crayfish net (Courtesy of *Yale University Publications in Anthropology* and Leopold Pospisil; from Pospisil, 1963); (*e*) Ingalik whitefish net set beneath river ice.

fish at holes in river ice. The holes were made with an ice pick, and the net was passed under the ice with a net-setting pole. The fiber net had upper and lower backing lines with bark floats and stone sinkers bound to them (Fig. 7-4e). The net was anchored with lines extending from the net to posts, and the fisherman exercised particular care to arrange the net so that the floats did not freeze into the ice.

Summary The 299 untended facilities included 1443 technounits for an overall technounit average of 4.8. A synopsis of the information about these forms in the tables follows:

	Simple			Complex		
	Forms	tu	Aver-age	Forms	tu	Aver-age
For wild species on land	76	246	3.2	73	505	6.9
To protect domestic animals on land	26	98	3.8			
To protect domestic plants on land	39	119	3.1	9	55	6.1
For wild species in water	76	420	5.5			
	217	883	4.1	82	560	6.8

Among the simple forms to take wild species, those used on land were far less developed than the ones used in water. The absence of complex forms for taking wild animals in water is especially noteworthy, as is the fact that few complex untended facilities were associated with domestic species. Thus the potential utility of untended facilities appears to have been much greater among intensive foragers than among farmers.

Conclusions To employ instruments, weapons, and tended facilities people must be at the right place at the proper time; otherwise these classes of subsistants will not function. Not only is a human presence required, but people are linked to wild prey or domestic species in a direct manner. Untended facilities, however, call for human involvement of a different order because they serve as substitutes for people, and prey must go to them. As human surrogates it would appear that untended facilities resulted from thinking of a different order than that required to produce and use other classes of subsistants.

Untended facilities must do more than control prey and function well in a technological context; they, not people, must be in the proper place at the right time.

For harvesting wild species with untended forms we find that deadfalls and snares predominated for land use, and fish traps were most important among the forms used in water. Likewise all three were represented among tended facilities. We would expect that when comparisons are reasonable, untended facilities would have higher average numbers of technounits than their tended counterparts to compensate for the absence of a human operator. For example, the five tended pitfalls averaged 3.2 technounits, whereas the average for the seventeen untended forms was 4.2, perhaps a smaller difference than one might predict. For tended snares on land the average for the eleven forms was 2.5, but for the sixty-nine untended snares, whether simple or complex, the average was 4.9. Thus untended snares averaged about twice the number of parts as tended forms, and the difference is the human replacement cost.

The 225 untended facilities used to take or hold wild species compares with 74 used in association with domestic species. The number of forms involved with domestic animals or plants seems high, especially when the nature of the sample is considered. Twenty of the peoples selected were exclusive foragers, and most of the farmers chosen did not rely on domestic animals. We would expect that, as the importance of wild species for food declined with more intensive farming, there would be an increase in untended facilities used with domestic species, but we did not anticipate as large an increase. What this seems to reflect above all else is a continuity of subsistants in the shift from foraging to intensive farming.

The analysis of untended facilities points up the technological limitations of the forms. Simple artifacts alone served to protect domestic animals; coops, corrals, and pens appear to have functioned well in the absence of mechanical components. For protecting domestic plants the only complex subsistants were wild animal traps, which most often appear to have been perfected for harvesting wild species and then applied to plant protection. Complex untended facilities were numerous and seemingly important for taking wild species on land, but no such forms were used in water. Even among tended facilities, only five complex ones were associated with water usage (Klamath waterfowl-hatchling net; deer net, game bird enclosure trap, and two seal nets of the Twana). It appears that none of the peoples sampled conceived of ways to set complex untended facilities in water.

Now that the detailed description of instruments, weapons, and facilities has been completed, important characteristics of the technounit approach bear reconsideration. The amount of detailed information required for the analysis of a particular form is quite limited. Specific measurements in terms of size and shape are not required; it need only be known that one form was small and another of the same style was large, with or without continuity between the sizes. One need not have precise measurements for the parts of subsistants in order to analyze a form. Materials too play a very subordinate role in the analysis. The details of parts are not considered, and the same is true of the manufacturing process itself. Since these characteristics of artifacts often are unreported in ethnographic accounts, it is fortunate that their absence is of no great consequence for the analysis of technounits. In sum an ethnographic account may be deficient in terms of details, yet adequate for our analytical approach. What is essential is that all the forms be described with their uses and the actual parts identified with clarity.

The 1175 subsistants analyzed included 4418 technounits with an overall technounit average of 3.8 parts per form. The breakdown by major taxonomic groups is as follows:

	Subsistants	Technounits
Instruments	210	407
Weapons	288	1375
Tended facilities	378	1193
Untended facilities	299	1443

Instruments were the simplest forms, with an overall average of 1.9 technounits each. The most complicated instrument was the Angmagsalik capelin scoop with seven parts. Tended facilities averaged 3.2 technounits each, and the most developed form was a Pukapukan fishhook assembly with fifteen technounits. For weapons, with an average of 4.8, the most complicated form was the twenty-six-part Iglulik toggle-headed whaling harpoon. For untended facilities the average was 4.8, and the most complicated form was the Tanaina salmon trap with fifteen parts.

There is clear verification that the food-getting technologies of all the sampled peoples were comparatively simple. However, as amply demonstrated in Part 3, the range of differences between groups who foraged or farmed and lived in very different habitats was great. Therefore, with rare exceptions, it is unwise to label any food-getting technology as uniformly simple.

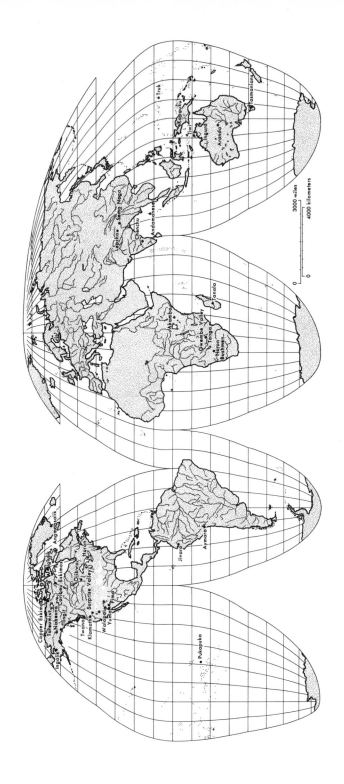

Societies selected for analysis of aboriginal food-getting technology

PART 3

EXPLOITATIVE
NETWORKS

CHAPTER 8

▲▲▲▲▲▲▲▲

DESERT AND
TROPICAL HABITATS

Whether the setting of a people was tropical, arctic, or temperate, the forms used to obtain food were attuned to the realities of environmental conditions. The earlier descriptions of subsistants suggest that these forms and their parts were of highly utilitarian design. Artistic embellishments were rare, and superfluous parts seldom were noted. Subsistants appear to have been made in an economical manner if only because they had to work effectively for people. Breakage and breakdown were minimized by a form's design, the materials used in its construction, the craftsmanship involved, and patterns of care and use. No matter how crude or complicated, a subsistant's only reason for existence was to make a positive contribution to a group's survival. Practicality of form and purpose best characterize these artifacts.

The materials used for making subsistants usually came directly from the habitats exploited, and each form served to extract food from the local setting. Subsistants for the sampled peoples are detailed in Part 2 in terms of their structural and functional characteristics. This section familiarizes the reader with the range of variability among subsistants for the peoples sampled. Part 3 presents the inventories of the thirty-six populations sampled as integrated technological configurations, and references to specific forms are avoided. The peoples are grouped by the similarities of their biomes, and whenever appropriate they are distinguished on the basis of whether they were foragers or farmers. A detailed analysis of their habitats is beyond the scope of inquiry. I seek instead to relate subsistant technologies to their environmental backdrops. Peoples in desert and tropical regions form one unit, and those in temperate to arctic settings comprise another. The habitats of each people are considered with special reference to the foods harvested. Dietary percentages of foods are presented for specific peoples when the figures are reasonably reliable, and these are summarized later in a table covering all the peoples. Ethnographers seldom provided detailed information along these lines. In most instances the percentages are based on my uncertain judgments from reading the pertinent ethnographies and from consulting similar estimates prepared for many peoples by George P. Murdock (1967). The ethnographic sources consulted for each people are recorded in the Appendix, along with the page references for each subsistant by taxonomic unit.

The subsistant technology of any people presumably represents an orderly sociocultural response to food resources available in their setting. It is proposed that a high positive correlation exists between the complexity of food-getting forms, as measured by technounits, and the biomes occupied by foragers or farmers. Above all this means that peoples who occupied broadly similar habitats exploited edibles in similar ways. The supposition is that this was true whether there was a presence or absence of cultural bonds for geographically proximal or widely dispersed populations.

Desert Foragers   In extremely arid deserts the distribution of people was dictated largely by the availability of dependable sources of water. Water holes, springs, and seepages not only provided water for people but attracted prey, especially birds and mammals. In the Macdonnell Ranges of central Australia, where the Aranda lived, and in the Kalahari Desert of southern Africa, the home of the Naron Bushmen, the annual rainfall was less than ten inches, and water sources were critical to survival. These deserts are among the driest in the world that supported aboriginal populations. Plant growth was thin and scattered, an important factor affecting hunting with weapons. Furthermore few species of large mammals were represented, and they appear to have been rather widely dispersed. Burrowing animals, such as lizards, rodents, and snakes, were reasonably common however. For the Aranda the most important sources of meat were emus, lizards, and kangaroos, and these animals were taken whenever possible. The pattern of exploitation was for small family groups to locate near one source of water, exhaust the nearby food resources, and then move on to another water hole. The same pattern prevailed among the Naron; they too killed animals whenever the opportunity arose. The most important animals taken by the Naron were anteaters, hares, ostriches, paauws, porcupines, and tortoises. The impression is that for the Aranda and Naron alike small animals contributed much more to the diet than did larger ones. Because rainfall was largely unpredictable and animal resources were limited, their economies were based primarily on wild plant products. It seems too that since relatively small numbers of persons lived together, cooperative hunting would not be well developed, and few tended facilities would be expected. Given the habitats of the Aranda and Naron, we would anticipate that their subsistant technologies would share many common features in spite of the distance that separated them and their very different cultural backgrounds.

In the United States, along the western fringe of the Great Basin in eastern California and adjacent states, lived the Surprise Valley Paiute and the Owens Valley Paiute. Their habitats were marginally desert, and the amount of precipitation there was much greater than for the Aranda and Naron areas. In addition these Paiute could rely on streams and rivers flowing from the Sierra Nevada Mountains for dependable supplies of water. Yet the Owens and Surprise Valleys were arid and supported drought-resistant plants. During the summer the Owens Valley Paiute lived in the valley, where they fished and collected seeds. Gathering seeds was especially important in the fall, and people wintered in the mountains when the pine nut harvest there was good or lived in the valley and ate seeds collected earlier in the year. They sought game throughout the year, and cooperative hunts, especially for rabbits, were conducted in the fall, when small groups of people assembled. These people lived primarily on wild plant products, and some wild grasses were cultivated in irrigated plots at select localities. For the Surprise Valley Paiute the food quest appears to have been more intensive throughout the year. In the early spring they fished, and the summer was devoted largely to the collection of roots, which were dried and stored for winter. In the late summer berries and seeds were collected, while the fall was devoted to hunting, especially cooperative rabbit drives. Antelope, deer, and smaller species were taken throughout the year. Winter was a time of scarcity, and food stress was common with the approach of spring. Given the common cultural background of these Paiute groups and the similarity of their habitats, we would expect their subsistant technologies to exhibit much the same patterning.

As indicated in Table 8-1, the number of subsistants represented among these four groups of desert foragers ranged from 12 to 39 with from 40 to 107 techno-units. The technounit average, based on dividing the number of technounits by the number of subsistants, ranged from 2.5 to 3.8. In these terms the Surprise Valley Paiute had the least developed subsistant technology (2.5), the Owens Valley Paiute exhibited the greatest degree of complexity (3.8), and the Aranda (2.6) and Naron (3.3) were intermediary. The most striking difference is the large number of tended facilities used by the Surprise Valley and Owens Valley Paiute; they had 29 such facilities with 71 technounits compared to 10 tended facilities with 15 technounits for the Aranda and Naron. The explanation appears to be that the settings of the Aranda and Naron differed significantly from those of the Paiute. The Paiute populations exploited diverse life zones ranging from high mountains to low deserts with varied and localized animal populations. Then too the number of Paiute concentrated in one locality for particular times of the year appears to have been greater than for the Aranda and Naron, which increased the likelihood that tended facilities could be used effectively.

In spite of the distance between the Aranda and the Naron and the difference in the species exploited, their subsistants shared a similar patterning by sub-sistant totals, taxonomic unit, and technounit totals. Furthermore the Paiutes parallel each other along similar dimensions. However, in terms of overall subsistant complexity measured by the average number of technounits per form, the Surprise Valley Paiute and Owens Valley Paiute are at opposite extremes for these desert groups. Further comparisons are most appropriately offered after additional peoples have been analyzed.

Desert Farmers   All the sampled peoples lived in the southwestern United States, along either the Colorado River or one of its drainages. In this extremely arid region about three inches of rain fell in Yuma country along the lower Colo-rado River and up to about ten inches in the areas where the others lived. All were farmers, but for the Walapai of northwestern Arizona the cultivation of plants was marginally significant at best. Only a small percentage of Walapai food came from domestic crops. These were raised by some families who main-tained irrigated plots near springs. The Pima of south-central Arizona chan-neled river water into canals to irrigate plots. When the Gila River dried up, reportedly once every five years, or when floods destroyed the canals or crops, they turned to wild plant products, especially cactuses and mesquite beans, as food. The most important animals among these peoples were antelope, deer,

Table 8-1 Summary of subsistants used by the sampled foragers in desert and tropical settings. The first number in each set refers to the subsistant total, and the number in parentheses is the corresponding technounit total

	Simple instruments	Weapons		Facilities				Total	Average
				Tended		Untended			
		Simple	Complex	Simple	Complex	Simple	Complex		
Deserts									
S. V. Paiute	7 (15)	4 (6)	5 (21)	19 (41)		2 (5)	2 (9)	39 (97)	2.5
Aranda	4 (7)	2 (6)	2 (15)	7 (10)		1 (4)	1 (7)	16 (42)	2.6
Naron	2 (5)	2 (4)	3 (15)	3 (5)		1 (4)	1 (7)	12 (40)	3.3
O. V. Paiute	4 (9)	2 (4)	7 (40)	10 (30)		2 (9)	3 (15)	28 (107)	3.8
								95 (286)	3.0
Tropics									
Tiwi	3 (6)	6 (6)		2 (2)				11 (14)	1.3
Ingura	3 (3)	1 (1)	5 (18)	3 (8)		1 (2)		13 (32)	2.5
Chenchu	7 (13)	2 (2)	5 (24)	5 (10)	1 (6)			20 (55)	2.8
Andamanese	4 (8)	1 (4)	3 (27)	3 (12)				11 (51)	4.6
								55 (152)	2.8

quail, and rabbits. The Hopi along the southern fringe of Black Mesa in northern Arizona practiced floodwater farming and took advantage of moisture from seepages, as well as water from springs, in their farming activities. Since burros, cattle, goats, horses, and sheep of European origin were integrated into their economic life by ca. 1900, about the time they were described in reasonable detail, the subsistants associated with these animals are included; for the other peoples the livestock that they possessed has not been considered since it was not well integrated into their economic lives for the time periods detailed by ethnographers. Yuma settlements lay near the banks of the lower Colorado River, but they moved to higher ground temporarily during the yearly floods. The land that they cultivated flooded annually, and the layer of silt deposited frequently remained moist throughout the summer. Their farming techniques were very elementary, as was vividly conveyed by an early observer: "The river rises and carries off the rubbish, and as soon as the water goes down and recedes, with a stick they make holes in the earth, plant their seeds, and do nothing else to it" (Forde, 1931a, 97). When the river did not flood sufficiently to provide moisture for their cultivated lands, the Yuma were forced to depend largely on wild plants for food, especially mesquite and screw beans. Game was less plentiful among them than among the others, but the Yuma did take fish from the Colorado River. None of the other peoples possessed subsistants identified with fishing. Among these Indians the Hopi were the most sedentary; they, the Pima, and the Yuma occupied the same settlements for generations. The Walapai, because of their primary dependence on wild animals and plants, were the most mobile, but they maintained winter villages at relatively well-watered sites.

These peoples were concentrated largely in Arizona, and in a broad sense they shared a similar cultural background. The Yuma exhibited close linguistic ties with the Walapai, and although the Hopi and Pima languages belonged to another phylum, they were related to each other. With respect to subsistence patterns the Hopi, Pima, and Yuma each derived at least fifty percent of their food from cultivated plants, especially beans, maize, and squash. It is doubtful that the Walapai as a whole obtained as much as ten percent of their food from cultivated plants, and in some respects it may seem inappropriate to include them with the other farmers. However the Walapai, unlike any of the desert foragers considered, did farm and were selected precisely because farming was unimportant among them. Their inclusion makes it possible to gain some idea of the subsistant technologies of both marginal and intensive farmers in deserts.

The most striking summary statistic in Table 8-2 is that all the subsistants for

Table 8-2 Summary of subsistants used by sampled farmers in desert and tropical settings. The first number in each set refers to the subsistant total, and the number in parentheses is the corresponding technounit total

| | Simple instruments | Weapons | | Facilities | | | | Total | Average |
| | | | | Tended | | Untended | | | |
		Simple	Complex	Simple	Complex	Simple	Complex		
Deserts									
Pima									
Foraging	3 (5)	1 (1)	3 (12)	2 (2)	1 (5)			10 (25)	2.5
Farming	4 (6)					3 (5)		7 (11)	1.6
								17 (36)	2.1
Walapai									
Foraging	12 (16)	2 (2)	5 (34)	10 (17)		1 (2)	2 (9)	32 (80)	2.5
Farming	2 (2)					1 (1)		3 (3)	1.0
								35 (83)	2.4
Hopi									
Foraging	1 (1)	4 (4)	2 (8)	6 (9)		1 (4)	2 (13)	16 (39)	2.4
Farming	5 (8)					8 (26)		13 (34)	2.6
Animal husbandry	1 (3)			2 (2)		3 (6)		6 (11)	1.8
								35 (84)	2.4
Yuma									
Foraging		1 (2)	4 (16)	3 (13)		1 (3)		9 (34)	3.8
Farming	3 (3)			1 (1)		1 (5)		5 (9)	1.8
								14 (43)	3.1

Table 8-2 (*Continued*)

	Simple instruments	Weapons		Facilities				Total	Average
				Tended		Untended			
		Simple	Complex	Simple	Complex	Simple	Complex		
Tropics									
Jivaro									
Foraging		1 (1)	3 (18)	5 (15)			2 (10)	11 (44)	4.0
Farming	4 (6)			1 (1)				5 (7)	1.4
								16 (51)	3.2
Trukese									
Foraging	2 (2)	2 (5)	2 (3)	21 (75)		6 (27)	1 (9)	34 (121)	3.6
Farming	6 (10)			1 (3)		1 (2)		8 (15)	1.9
								42 (136)	3.2
Pukapuka									
Foraging	6 (6)	2 (7)	1 (3)	25 (95)		7 (19)		41 (130)	3.2
Farming	3 (3)						1 (11)	4 (14)	3.5
								45 (144)	3.2
Kapauku									
Foraging	2 (4)	1 (1)	5 (22)	6 (24)		3 (12)		17 (63)	3.7
Farming	7 (10)			1 (1)		5 (24)	2 (11)	15 (46)	3.1
Animal husbandry	2 (2)			1 (3)				3 (5)	1.7
								35 (114)	3.3

	1	2	3	4	5	6	7	Total	Mean
Naga									
Foraging	6 (12)	1 (5)	3 (19)	8 (24)		5 (16)	4 (26)	21 (90)	4.3
Farming	2 (2)			3 (3)		3 (11)	1 (6)	13 (32)	2.5
Animal husbandry				2 (8)				4 (10)	2.5
								38 (132)	3.5
Akamba									
Foraging	6 (10)		5 (37)	1 (3)	1 (4)	2 (11)	6 (43)	15 (98)	6.5
Farming			2 (4)	4 (9)		1 (3)	1 (7)	14 (33)	2.4
Animal husbandry	1 (1)	1* (4)		15 (29)		4 (12)		21 (46)	2.2
								50 (177)	3.5
Tanala									
Foraging	1 (1)	2 (5)	6 (16)	7 (27)		12 (60)	5 (28)	33 (137)	4.2
Farming	5 (10)		2 (5)	2 (5)		2 (6)		11 (26)	2.4
Animal husbandry						3 (12)		3 (12)	4.0
								47 (175)	3.7
Tonga									
Foraging	1 (1)	2 (6)	1 (3)	5 (19)		14 (57)	6 (33)	29 (119)	4.1
Farming	4 (8)			7 (20)		6 (17)		17 (45)	2.6
Animal husbandry						8 (46)		8 (46)	5.8
								54 (210)	3.9

* Complex instrument.

161

farming in deserts averaged only 2.0 technounits and that the average is 2.4 for all the subsistants of desert farmers combined. The Walapai, as marginal farmers, used the same number of total subsistants, with nearly the same technounit total and the same average (2.4), as the Hopi, who probably derived about seventy-five percent of their food from domestic crops. When only farming subsistants are considered, their totals are very different, but their technologies are equally complex in overall terms. The distinctiveness of each is reflected in the uses of their subsistants: the Walapai used far more instruments and more complex weapons than did the Hopi in foraging activities, and the Hopi employed many more facilities for farming. It is worthy of special note that the overall technounit average for desert foragers was 3.0 compared with 2.4 for desert farmers; the Pima average of 2.1 is lower than for any of the desert foragers. In the same context the Hopi and Walapai averages (2.4) approximate that of the Aranda (2.6) but are considerably lower than that of the Naron (3.3). The 3.1 average of the Yuma, the highest among farmers, is below the high of 3.8 for the Owens Valley Paiute.

How can we explain the similar degree of subsistant complexity for desert foragers and farmers? First, we would expect that these peoples, and all other aboriginal populations, depended most heavily on food resources that were the most predictable. Because of the apparent low density of large terrestrial game, even among the Paiutes, and the scarcity of fish, all eight peoples concentrated on species incapable of effective motion. Thus domestic or wild plants and small animals with little potential for mobility under harvest conditions dominated their economic lives. Among both foragers and farmers the instruments for harvesting wild or domestic plants and small game were uncomplicated, yet they contributed the bulk of the food. In sum the digging stick, among the simplest of all subsistants, was the most critical subsistant for aboriginal peoples living in deserts.

Ethnologists have set aside the food-getting technologies of aboriginal peoples by reason of the often bland and pervasive similarities of forms fashioned in uncomplicated ways. The usual judgment is that these manufactures are simple, with rare exceptions, quite uniform, and thus do not merit detailed study. In general terms this position seems reasonable, at least with reference to the data at hand for desert peoples. If nothing else the technounit approach for measuring comparative developments in subsistant technologies validates these feelings based on impressions. The admittedly laborious analysis of technounits for desert peoples nonetheless yields some unanticipated conclusions. The subsistant technologies of the Aranda and Naron are indeed simple but not quite as simple as those of the Hopi and Pima. Thus the technology for farming in deserts may be less developed than that employed by people who lived exclusively by foraging. Technounit averages for the subsistant inventories of these peoples, based on a parallel analysis of all the forms involved, yield a quantitative measure of technological complexity on a cross-cultural basis. The interim conclusions contribute greater systematic understanding to the technological achievements of aboriginal peoples in deserts.

Tropical Foragers Tropical regions and arid deserts share a number of rather obvious and important characteristics. Each has comparatively little seasonal variability, high mean annual temperatures, and considerable species diversity with relatively few individuals represented.

The Tiwi occupied a tropical forest habitat on Bathurst and Melville islands, located off northern Australia some thirty miles from the mainland town of Darwin. The lifeways on both islands were so similar that they have been described as having a single population by ethnographers. Ethnographic studies of aboriginal Tiwi life began in 1911 and continued intermittently until 1954; thus the information about them spans more than forty years. They resisted intrusions by outsiders until comparatively recent times, and therefore many aboriginal customs continued into the 1950s. The indigenous fauna includes bandicoots, opossums, rats, and wallabies as well as diverse birds, snakes, and a number of different lizards. Many species of shellfish as well as crocodiles lived along the rivers and shores, and the sea contained green and hawksbill turtles in addition to many fishes. Thus these people had abundant, diverse, and predictable food resources throughout the year. Jane C. Goodale (1971, 169) reports that the harvesting of terrestrial species, with the possible exception of the wallaby, required comparatively little equipment, skill, or strength and the women provided the major food supply. Crocodiles and turtles, more difficult species to harvest, were hunted by men, but they contributed comparatively little to the daily food supply. Goodale (correspondence) estimates that their diet consisted of about fifty percent wild plant products, twenty-five percent aquatic species including shellfish, and twenty-five percent terrestrial animals including birds. From their island setting the distant coastline of Australia was considered the land of the dead, and they maintained that before the arrival of whites they had very little if any direct contact with the mainlanders. The Tiwi did not make either the throwing-board or boomerang that usually are associated with aboriginal Australians.

The Ingura lived on Groote Eylandt and adjacent islands near the western coast of the Gulf of Carpentaria in northern Australia. They occupied a tropical woodland and lived at camps in sheltered bays, near coastal streams, or on the borders of tidal swamps. It appears that wild plant products formed their primary source of food, and wild roots, fruits, seeds, and shoots probably comprised the bulk of their diet. The most important terrestrial species were opossums, tortoises, and wallabies. From the water they took dugong, fish, sea turtles, and shellfish. They maintained rather close ties with adjacent mainland peoples, from whom they received stone knife blades since local sources of stone were unsuitable for blade production. Metal fishhooks had been obtained from Malay traders for so many years that the aboriginal form was forgotten.

The third group of tropical foragers is the Chenchu, who lived on the Amrabad Plateau in Hyderabad in east-central India. When they were studied in 1940, only about 400 followed an aboriginal life-style, but it appeared to be quite viable at that time. The Chenchu lived in a tropical savanna, with rolling hill country separated by deep and narrow watersheds. These drainages formed streams that ran in torrents during the rainy season but were dry most of the year. However the major river, the Kistna, flowed throughout the year. The countryside was covered with open forests, sometimes broken by grasslands, and higher elevations supported more verdant growth, as did the deep ravines, with their dense jungle foliage. The monsoon rains changed the tinder-dry hillsides into a profusion of greenery. During the rainy season and in cold weather the Chenchu occupied village sites, where they built substantial dwellings, but for three to four months of each year they moved from one camp to the next, searching primarily for fruits, roots, and tubers. The most important wild game included antelope, deer, goats, hares, monkeys, porcupines, and squirrels. Lizards and game birds also were taken, but wild plant products supplied the bulk of their diet. At the time they were studied iron was received in trade, as was thread for attaching feather vanes to arrows.

The Andamanese lived on the Andaman Islands in the Sea of Bengal, a tropical forest habitat, and their more permanent villages consisted of a single large structure occupied by all the inhabitants. The most important accounts of these people are by Alfred R. Radcliffe-Brown (1948) and Edward H. Man (1883). Greater emphasis has been placed on the information provided by Radcliffe-Brown because he attempted to distinguish aboriginal forms from those introduced in early historic times. Considerable diversity occurred in the subsistence round of the Andamanese, and I have attempted to stress the forms used by people on Great Andaman Island, who exploited coastal resources most intensively but also ranged inland for food. It appears that the bulk of their diet, possibly as much as sixty percent, consisted of fauna. Based partially on reports by Man (1883, 343, 417), it is estimated that thirty percent of the meat was from terrestrial species, meaning primarily wild pigs and lizards. The forty percent of meat obtained from aquatic species included crustaceans, dugong, fish, and sea turtles. The balance of their diet consisted of plant products and honey.

The Andamanese and Chenchu searched for food on a daily basis, and the Chenchu sometimes were faced with periods of food stress. The seasonal round was most pronounced among the Chenchu, who exploited more diverse life zones than the others. The food-getting activities of the Ingura and Tiwi varied comparatively little from one season to the next, and they appear never to have had a difficult time finding something to eat.

As a group tropical foragers possessed fewer subsistants with lower part totals than did desert foragers, but the range of technounit averages was much greater for the foragers in the tropics (Table 8-1). A striking contrast exists between the two groups in terms of the use of untended facilities. Among the tropical peoples a single form was identified, the fish-catching platform used at a small waterfall by the Ingura. The explanation for this near-absence is elusive but seemingly must lie in the nature of the habitats of the peoples involved. Perhaps such sets were impractical in many tropical regions because they were destroyed by insects, or because any game taken was consumed quickly by other species or spoiled rapidly. However other people in the tropics depended heavily on untended facilities for food; an example is the Yagua, who hunted and farmed in northeastern Peru (Fejos, 1943).

The simplest subsistant technology by far was that of the Tiwi, who used only eleven forms, of which only one, a four-part ax, consisted of more than a single technounit. The 1.3 technounit average for Tiwi subsistants illustrates that very elementary food-getting technologies existed in early historic times. The bountifulness of their island homeland and its freedom from competition from foreigners provide a partial explanation for the simplicity of their technology. Another consideration that seems important is their isolation from mainland peoples. That the Tiwi obtained about fifty percent of their food by using instruments is not ignored, but the six weapons having one part each illustrate the effectiveness of very simple forms to obtain about half of their food.

The Andamanese technounit average of 4.6 is significantly higher than that of any of the other foragers whose technologies have been analyzed thus far. In stark contrast with the Tiwi, the Andamanese had only two subsistants, out of a total of eleven, with a single part each. The Andamanese made more complicated forms than did any of the other tropical foragers sampled: bow (6 tu), turtle net (7), fish arrow (8), and pig arrow (13). These technological elaborations are compatible with the fact that about sixty percent of their food was harvested with weapons and tended facilities.

The populations of foragers in desert and tropical settings exhibit a great deal of homogeneity in their patterned technological responses for obtaining food. This is especially true when it is taken into account that the Paiute groups stand apart from the others in terms of habitats exploited. However the overall simplicity of the subsistant technologies for all eight peoples, with an average of 2.9 technounits per item, is clear evidence that uncomplicated forms served them well. For all but the Andamanese, what is most impressive about their manufactures is that food was obtained with instruments that included only a few parts. At the dawn of history the subsistant technologies of foragers in the tropics and deserts were dominated by the digging stick, which harvested the bulk of the food supply. Because of the simplicity of the technological forms involved, there is good reason to believe that a similar patterning prevailed in remote human times.

Tropical Root Crop Farmers Farmers in the tropics have been separated on the basis of whether root or cereal crops were among the dominant foods. Four peoples were selected to represent each economic focus in an attempt to distinguish more clearly between the pertinent technologies. First among the root crop farmers are the Jivaro of Ecuador, who lived along the eastern slope of the Andes. They occupied small, dispersed hamlets that averaged nine persons each, and one family usually was separated from the next by a half mile. Shifting cultivation was practiced in a tropical rain forest with gardens abandoned each three or four years. After the soil had been exhausted in a locality, which occurred every five to nine years, they moved elsewhere and built new houses. Their primary staple was sweet manioc, which could be harvested during most of the year; sweet potatoes, a crop that may have been taro, and maize were important foods. The domestic animals and artifacts clearly introduced in recent historic times have not been included in the subsistant inventory. Michael J. Harner (1972, 47, 55, 60, 61) estimated that in terms of bulk their diet consisted of sixty percent cultivated plants, twenty-five percent animals that had been hunted or trapped, ten percent fish, and five percent wild plant foods that had been collected. The most important meat animals were agouti, armadillo, monkeys, peccary, and diverse species of birds.

The second people considered are the Trukese, who lived on an atoll of volcanic origin with an encircling barrier reef, in the Caroline Islands of Micronesia. The mean annual temperature was about 80°F, and the rainfall measured about 120 inches per year. Settlements consisted of large houses owned by lineages but occupied only by lineage women, their husbands, and unmarried children. Lineages owned land, and their members formed cooperative work groups. The most important crops were breadfruit, coconuts, and taro, but fish and shellfish also were very important in the diet. Although the islands were covered with dense vegetation, small land animals and terrestrial wildfowl were relatively unimportant as food. The subsistants and domestic animals clearly introduced in comparatively recent historic times have been excluded from consideration.

Another Oceanian population sampled, the people who lived on the three atolls comprising Pukapuka in Polynesia, occasionally were faced with severe famines following tidal waves and hurricanes. On these tropical islets built of sand and gravel, vegetation was sparse, and to cultivate their primary crop, taro, it was necessary to make beds of vegetable fill and fertilizer. Diverse species of fish were found in the lagoon, along the beaches, and within as well as beyond the reef. Many species of sea birds also frequented the atolls. The most important domestic plants were taro and coconuts, but fish contributed significantly to their diet. They were somewhat unusual because they captured wild animals and raised them as food. It should be noted that it was difficult to distinguish among the forms of fishhooks employed, and some of these have been judged as insignificant varieties, which may not be fully justified.

Last among the cultivators of root crops in the tropics, the Kapauku lived in western New Guinea and were shifting cultivators with gardens on mountain slopes as well as in valley bottoms. Ninety percent of the cultivated land was allocated to growing sweet potatoes, by far the most important crop. They also raised small amounts of bananas, manioc, sugar cane, and taro. Wild game such as boars, cassowaries, marsupials, and rats were relatively unimportant sources of food, and the same was true of wild plant products. However fishing for crayfish, insects, and tadpoles was more important. The only domestic animal of consequence was the pig, an important source of protein; chickens were introduced in comparatively recent times but are not considered. Leopold Pospisil (correspondence) estimates that in terms of bulk the diet consisted of seventy-five percent domestic plant products, five percent wild plants, ten percent aquatic fauna, and ten percent terrestrial fauna.

Among these tropical farmers those on Truk and Pukapuka maintained settlements that appear to have been quite stable, while the Jivaro moved more often than did any of the others. The Kapauku settlements were essentially permanent but did shift from one locality to another over a span of many years. It appears that for all these people at least sixty percent of the diet consisted of cultivated crops, but on Truk breadfruit was far more important in the diet than was taro, the primary root crop.

The overall technounit average for tropical root crop cultivators only ranged from 3.2 to 3.3, which is remarkable irrespective of the manner in which the sample was selected. Furthermore the general patterning is much the same from one taxonomic unit to the next even though the Jivaro used far fewer forms than any of the others. These data suggest that people who depended on root crops and lived in the tropics manifested about the same degree of technological elaboration irrespective of where they might have lived.

Tropical Cereal Crop Farmers   The Sema Naga, as cereal crop cultivators, depended most heavily on rice for food, but Job's tears and millet were eaten when rice was not available. These people occupied a forested tropical area between Assam and Burma along the upper reaches of the Tizu River and along the upper Dayang River. Their villages were built on high ground, and settlements with 100 houses were considered large. The domestic animals raised for meat included cattle, dogs, fowl, goats, and pigs; milk was not a normal part of their diet. Chickens and pigs were kept in houses, but these structures have not been considered as subsistants. Wild game included deer, serow, bears, and pigs. These Naga reworked imported iron hoes into diverse finished metal products.

The Akamba (Kamba) occupied a tropical scrub forest setting along the eastern slope of the East African Highlands in Kenya. On their scattered homesteads they farmed, hunted, and raised domestic animals. For food they depended most heavily on cultivated crops, of which maize, millet, and sorghum were most important; legumes and root crops also contributed to the diet. Their homeland was relatively dry, and when rains failed there were severe food stresses and even famines. Cattle were kept as a form of wealth, never used as draft animals, and were killed only on ceremonial occasions. Most meat from domestic species came from goats, poultry, and sheep, although milk from cows and goats played a significant part in the diet. Poultry apparently were kept in the houses of people, although again these structures have not been analyzed as subsistants. The Akamba obtained iron from local iron-bearing sands and smelted it to produce metal products.

The Tanala occupied the southern sector of the eastern plateau of the Malagasy Republic, which is a mountainous, tropical rain forest area. The subsistant technology of only the Ikongo or southern Tanala is considered. These people were swidden cultivators who planted crops on cleared and burned mountain slopes; they also farmed swampy land. Dry rice was by far the most important crop, but they also raised bananas, beans, maize, manioc, and diverse species of greens. Only a few families terraced land and irrigated plots of wet rice. Domestic animals from the aboriginal period included cattle, chickens, ducks, and goats; other species introduced in comparatively recent times were not important in the diet. Wild guinea fowl eggs were taken from nests to be hatched and raised by chickens. Although the ownership of cattle was important in social terms, cattle were killed only on ceremonial occasions, and their meat contributed little to the diet. Cows were milked, but goats were not, nor were goats important as a source of meat. Chickens, by contrast, were the most important source of fresh meat, and chicken eggs were a favored food. Wild game was hunted primarily as a sport, with birds, fossas, lemurs, and pigs the usual prey. The Ikongo Tanala used four forms of traps to prevent rats from eating stored rice, but these forms are not included because rats were not eaten and the grain already had been harvested. Thus the traps do not fall within the subsistant definition.

The Gwembe Valley Tonga of Zambia occupied a tropical savanna and grassland along the Zambezi River. The river's semiannual floods deposited fertile alluvial soil on the more productive garden plots during years of normal rainfall. These Tonga lived in extended family homesteads clustered in villages and practiced hoe cultivation. Five different types of gardens were identified, and women were the primary cultivators. The most important crops were bulrush millet, maize, and sorghum, which not only were differentially vulnerable to predators but had different soil and water requirements, different planting dates, and different harvest times. In spite of this diversity their crops failed frequently, and they sometimes faced severe famines. Thayer Scudder (correspondence) estimates that the diet for one village in the late 1950s was based on the following percentages: 70, cultivated plants; 27, wild plants from the land; 1, wild plants collected from water; 1, domestic animals; 0.5, wild mobile animals on land, and 0.5 fish.

The overall technounit average for tropical cereal crop farmers ranged from 3.5 to 3.9. Although not as narrow as the average for tropical root crop cultivators (3.2 to 3.3), it is nonetheless quite restrictive. Furthermore both clusters of peoples share a similar patterning in terms of subsistants representing the same taxonomic groups.

Interim conclusions about the complexity of subsistants for the twenty aboriginal foragers and farmers in deserts and the tropics are as follow:

1. Food-getting forms average slightly more than three technounits each (3.2). Thus the technoeconomic forms involved included very few parts and legitimately may be labeled as simple.

2. The subsistant technologies of desert farmers, with a technounit average of 2.4, are more elementary than those of desert foragers, with an average of 3.0. Desert peoples in general depended primarily on plants for food, and the forms used to cultivate, protect, or harvest plants always were uncomplicated.

3. Foragers in the tropics, with an overall technounit average of 2.8, had simpler technologies than root crop farmers in tropical areas (3.2). Root crop farmers had a lower overall average than cereal crop farmers (3.7). These too were simple technologies for obtaining edibles.

4. Since farming technologies in deserts are less developed than are desert foraging ones, there is no lineal progression from foragers to farmers in terms of the complexity of their subsistants. A lineal progression is seen for tropical peoples from foragers to root crop and then to cereal crop farmers.

Further comparisons of these subsistant technologies are presented at the close of Chapter 9, after the sixteen other peoples sampled have been described. All farmers and foragers are presented as a unit in a comparative summary. There too dietary percentages and food-getting technologies are compared in an effort to assess the productivity of subsistants in terms of foods actually consumed.

▲▲▲▲▲▲▲▲

TEMPERATE TO
ARCTIC HABITATS
AND OVERVIEW

Temperate, subarctic, and arctic environments are considered as a unit because of their distinct contrast with desert and tropical settings in terms of seasonal temperature differences. Fluctuations in seasonal temperatures for desert and tropical regions are relatively minor compared with those recorded for temperate to arctic settings. With their relatively uniform climates, desert and tropical areas produced wild food resources that varied far less from one season to the next than did those in cool and cold areas. As a result we expect to find that in deserts and the tropics the same subsistants were used throughout the year, or at least during most of the year. In temperate through arctic areas the warm to hot summers and cold to frigid winters had a profound effect on economic activities. Most subsistants were far more likely to have been used intensively during one particular season because of the changing resource base. We know too that in temperate to arctic regions some important food resources, especially big game and fish, migrated seasonally. These movements are far more dramatic than those common to species in desert and tropical habitats. In sum we would expect the subsistants used in cool and cold areas of the earth to be more varied and more technologically specialized than those found in hot regions.

The potential for obtaining food at any particular time of the year in hot environments contrasts with conditions in cool to cold settings. While there occasionally may be periods of scarcity in desert and tropical areas, obtaining adequate food on a day-to-day basis throughout the year was the norm for foragers. In many tropical areas farmers harvested crops on a year-round basis, but most desert farmers appear to have depended heavily on stored crops during the winter months. In temperate regions farmers obviously could not cultivate crops during cold weather, and during the winter they ate either stored foods or wild species. In the subarctic and arctic all peoples were either foragers or pastoralists. For foragers in these regions the late winter and early spring, after stored foods had been consumed, were periods of potential food scarcity or famine. During extremely cold weather migratory species usually were absent or scarce, while predators and prey alike were less mobile than during warmer months. These remarks about biotic conditions for the major regions of the earth are by necessity very general, yet they are meaningful in terms of subsistants and their uses (Tables 9-1 and 9-2).

Temperate Foragers   Tasmania, one of the larger islands in the world, is ecologically a temperate rain forest, and when the first whites settled there, the indigenous animals were mainly marsupials such as the bandicoot, kangaroo, opossum, platypus, wallaby, and wombat. Fish and shellfish were abundant along the coasts, and freshwater fish also were relatively common. Aboriginal Australians are well known for the comparative simplicity of their manufactures, and indigenous Tasmanians produced even fewer artifact forms. In Australia a spear usually was propelled with the aid of a throwing-board, boomerangs were common, but pitfalls and pole snares were uncommon. Not one of these forms is reported for Tasmania, and the semidomesticated Australian dog, the dingo, was absent. Furthermore, in early historic times these islanders did not eat fish despite the fact that fish was plentiful and had been consumed in prehistoric times. When first encountered, the Tasmanians did not know how to kindle fire, and most important in terms of the present study, they did not make composite instruments or composite weapons.

Most of the ethnographic information about the Tasmanians pertains to a remnant population, although the diaries of George A. Robinson (1966)

Table 9-1 Summary of subsistants used by the sampled foragers in temperate, subarctic, and arctic settings. The first number in each set refers to the subsistant total, and the number in parentheses is the corresponding technounit total

	Simple instruments	Weapons		Facilities				Total	Average
				Tended		Untended			
		Simple	Complex	Simple	Complex	Simple	Complex		
Temperate									
Tasmanians	3 (3)	3 (3)		4 (8)		1 (1)		11 (15)	1.4
Klamath	9 (18)	2 (8)	5 (27)	21 (66)	1 (4)	5 (28)		43 (151)	3.5
Tlingit	4 (7)	2 (6)	6 (19)	8 (34)		2 (14)	6 (41)	28 (121)	4.3
Twana	4 (7)	5 (22)	7 (48)	15 (72)	4 (24)	11 (53)	2 (11)	48 (237)	4.9
								130 (524)	4.0
Subarctic									
Caribou Eskimos	3 (12)	3 (14)	7 (25)	13 (37)		6 (21)	2 (9)	34 (118)	3.5
Nabesna	1 (1)	3 (9)	5 (27)	8 (23)		3 (11)	5 (34)	25 (105)	4.2
Ingalik	6 (14)	3 (9)	10 (55)	15 (61)		14 (93)	7 (64)	55 (296)	5.4
Tanaina	7 (13)	3 (7)	13 (76)	3 (17)		6 (45)	8 (66)	40 (224)	5.6
								154 (743)	4.8
Arctic									
Copper Eskimos	4 (16)	4 (18)	4 (35)	11 (36)		3 (11)	1 (6)	27 (122)	4.5
Iglulik	3 (8)	6 (24)	14 (118)	8 (27)		8 (36)	3 (12)	42 (225)	5.4
Tareumiut	1 (3)	4 (17)	14 (116)	10 (41)		4 (18)	2 (10)	35 (205)	5.9
Angmagsalik	4 (18)	3 (9)	15 (142)	9 (20)		1 (6)	1 (7)	33 (202)	6.1
								137 (754)	5.5

Table 9-2 Summary of subsistants used by sampled farmers in temperate settings. The first number in each set refers to the subsistant total, and the number in parentheses is the corresponding technounit total

	Simple instruments	Weapons		Facilities				Total	Average
				Tended		Untended			
		Simple	Complex	Simple	Complex	Simple	Complex		
Huron									
Foraging	3 (5)	2 (6)	7 (27)	9 (24)		5 (16)	1 (4)	22 (62)	2.8
Farming	3 (7)			2 (2)				5 (9)	1.8
								27 (71)	2.6
Aymara									
Foraging	8 (24)	4 (6)	2 (7)	19 (84)		1 (3)		26 (100)	3.8
Farming			2 (2)	1 (1)	1 (5)	2 (5)		15 (42)	2.8
Animal husbandry	2 (4)			1 (1)		3 (6)	1 (5)	6 (11)	1.8
								47 (153)	3.3
Ojibwa									
Foraging	4 (9)	3 (5)	7 (27)	10 (33)		4 (22)	4 (18)	32 (114)	3.6
Farming	4 (4)					1 (3)		5 (7)	1.4
								37 (121)	3.3
Lepcha									
Foraging	1 (1)	3 (7)	7 (31)	9 (26)	1 (6)	11 (43)	5 (31)	37 (145)	3.9
Farming	10 (29)		2 (11)	1 (1)		5 (11)	2 (15)	21 (67)	3.2
Animal husbandry	2 (2)					5 (16)		7 (18)	2.6
								65 (230)	3.5

contain a wealth of information about aboriginal customs. The Tasmanians must be considered, even though the data are limited, because of their simple technology. It is important to note that the Tasmanian subsistant inventory is a composite of the technoeconomic forms used on the entire island during the early historic period. It would have been far more desirable to consider one band in detail, but given the inexactness of the reports, this was an unattainable goal. Since there clearly were regional differences in Tasmanian culture, the subsistant inventory necessarily suggests the presence of more forms than could have existed for a particular local group.

The western portion of Tasmania received at least sixty inches of precipitation a year and was heavily forested. In most of the eastern portion, with about twenty inches of rainfall, forested areas were scattered, and grasslands predominated. The general impression is that except for the western interior, food resources were quite adequate for peoples with economies based on foraging. Each of the seventy tribes included between forty and seventy persons representing from ten to twenty families (Jones, 1971, 278–9). Although bands of families camped together, few instances have been recorded of cohesive social units beyond the family level. Some men coordinated group hunts and raiding parties, but in general each family was responsible to no other human aggregate.

The Klamath lived on the high plateau of southeastern Oregon, a region that included a great marshy area and a number of large lakes. Water lily seeds from marshlands, which covered about 10,000 acres, were an important staple. Fish appear to have dominated the diet, and waterfowl were comparatively important. Big game included antelope, deer, and elk, yet hunting these animals and other land game apparently did not contribute a great deal to the food supply. During the winter these people lived in earth lodges at established villages near good fishing spots, and they returned to the same sites from one year to the next. During the summer months families scattered widely and lived in long, dome-shaped structures of willow pole frames covered with mats. Theirs was a land of plenty in the summer, but when deep winter snows made subsistence activities difficult at best, starvations apparently were not uncommon.

The subsistant information for the Tlingit is limited to the most northerly group, the Yakutat Tlingit, who lived in a temperate rain forest area along bays fronting the Gulf of Alaska. Their comparatively large and durable plank houses were occupied by the core members of matrilineages. During the late fall and winter the members of each household left their small settlements to occupy a number of different hunting and fishing camps. The most important edibles were aquatic species such as halibut, salmon, seals, sea otters, and shell-fish. Terrestrial game included mainly bears and mountain goats, with deer being introduced in comparatively recent times.

In aboriginal times the Twana lived along the Hood Canal in western Washington in a temperate rain forest setting. They depended most heavily on fish, especially salmon, for food, but sea mammals also were important in the diet, along with mollusks. These edibles were supplemented by waterfowl and land mammals, with elk, bears, beavers, and deer among the most important species. Vegetable foods were confined largely to berries, fern roots, and other roots. In this area of abundant food resources, most edibles were obtained during the warmer seasons by family groups or small work parties. At this time of the year the people lived in small pole-framed dwellings covered with mats. In the winter the Twana villages consisted of two or three large plank houses occupied by multiple-family households.

Temperate Farmers   The peoples representing this group have the least satisfactory data in terms of their aboriginal economies, primarily because few temperate-area farmers were described in detail before their life-styles were disrupted by outsiders. The Aymara, Lepcha, and Ojibwa cannot be considered to represent aboriginal populations to the same extent as most of the other peoples. Yet their inclusion is worthwhile if only to establish subsistant uses in acculturative or at least altered aboriginal contexts.

Prior to 1649, when the Iroquois drove them from their homeland, the Huron occupied western Ontario, Canada, along the southern sector of Georgian Bay. The Huron, who were in fact a confederation of closely related tribes, lived in a temperate, deciduous forest setting. For descriptions of their aboriginal life we must rely heavily on the 1615-6 observations of Samuel de Champlain (1929) and the 1623-4 account by Gabriel Sagard (1939), and supplement these reports with the works of ethnohistorians. Huron villages usually were located on high ground near plots with soil suitable for raising crops. Palisades surrounded the larger settlements, and as many as 2000 residents lived in the encircled longhouses. An average of six nuclear families, probably with close ties to the same matrilineage, lived in a single longhouse, and larger settlements included forty or more of these dwellings. The growing season in this area, although relatively short, was of sufficient length to permit the harvesting of a summer crop during most years. Food percentages in terms of caloric values, calculated by Conrad Heidenreich (1971, 163), are as follow: 65, maize; 13, beans; 2, squash; 9, fish; 6, meat; and 5, collected fruits. In terms of bulk this would mean that the percentages are approximately as follow: 62, crops; 13, fish; 7, meat; and 18, collected fruits.

The Aymara lived in the area draining into Lake Titicaca of Bolivia and Peru, an extremely high basin with short grass as the predominant vegetation. In geographical terms this region is mountainous but has a climate that may be considered temperate given the cool summers and cold winters. The people farmed relatively sheltered valleys, and the basin supported comparatively few terrestrial animals, the most important being foxes, guanaco, rodents, and vicuna. Lake Titicaca was a vast reservoir for fish, and diverse species of birds lived in the region. The descriptions of Aymara subsistants are for the population in southern Peru during the last decade of the nineteenth century and are reported by Harry Tschopik (1946). This source is supplemented cautiously with accounts by David Forbes (1870) and by Weston La Barre (1948). The Aymara of southern Peru derived most of their food from farming; potatoes were the most important crop, followed by quinoa and barley. They also raised small numbers of cows, llamas, pigs, and sheep. In their comparatively small villages were kin-group clusters, and each house was surrounded by a compound. The houses were built of different materials depending on the locality, but usually were rectangular with gabled roofs.

The Ojibwa (Chippewa) lived in a temperate, deciduous forest habitat in northern Minnesota and an adjacent sector of Canada. They first were visited by Europeans in 1642 but did not come under direct federal control until the nineteenth century. Given the 250 years of contact with Europeans before the 1905 to 1925 studies by Frances Densmore (1928, 1929), we are not surprised to find that many customs did not represent the aboriginal pattern. The subsistant data and food-getting network analyzed presumably prevailed during the late 1880s. The common Ojibwa dwelling was pole framed in the shape of a dome with a bark covered roof and siding made of mats. The Ojibwa occupied semi-permanent villages, moving from these on a seasonal basis. In the early spring they used an ax and spile to tap maple trees for sap; this is one of the few examples among the sampled peoples of a wild plant liquid being an important source of food. During the summer they planted gardens of maize and squash, but cultivated plants do not appear to have been of great importance in the diet. The intensive exploitation of a wild aquatic plant was unusual among the peoples analyzed, but the Ojibwa collected wild rice systematically. Canoes were propelled through the fields, and sticks were used to knock the ripe grain from the stalks into the vessels. Bears, deer, and moose were hunted, and the people were able to obtain fish during much of the year.

The Lepcha lived in the Himalayas, but only the Lepcha of Sikkim are considered here. The accounts consulted deal with conditions from the 1930s through the 1950s. During that twenty-year span hunting was decreasing in importance as farming increased. The Lepcha habitat, which ranges from great mountains to deep valleys, supports alpine, temperate, and tropical species. The temperate zone ranged from about 5000 to 13,000 feet in elevation, and Geoffrey Gorer (1938, 51) noted that in the locality in which he worked most of the cultivated land and houses were located between 3500 and 7500 feet in elevation. The Lepcha have been grouped with other peoples who were more clearly temperate-area peoples even though it is recognized that the Lepcha also systematically exploited alpine and tropical zones in their food-getting pursuits. They usually lived in geographically separated households or small hamlets consisting of three to four dwellings. The rectangular houses were built on stone pilings, and the space between the ground and floor provided shelter for domestic animals. Houses had woven bamboo floors, plastered bamboo walls, and roofs framed with wood and covered by bamboo and then reeds. Among the most important crops were diverse varieties of dry rice, maize, millet, and wheat. Domestic animals included fowl, goats, oxen, and pigs; butter was important although cow's milk was not. Fish played a significant part in the diet, but wild game, including bears, birds, deer, hares, and pigs, was less important.

Subarctic Foragers The Caribou Eskimos lived on the tundra to the west of Hudson Bay in the Barren Grounds of central Canada; only the portion of the population that exploited inland resources is considered here. Caribou, which migrated northward across the Barrens in the spring and returned southward in the fall, were by far the most important food resource. Sometimes small herds wintered in the Barrens, but they were not a dependable source of food. The fall migration of caribou provided the bulk of meat for the long winter. These Eskimos fished when they wanted a change of diet or when they failed to intercept migrating caribou. The only game on the Barrens throughout the year consisted of hares, marmots, musk-oxen, ptarmigan, and willow grouse. The Caribou Eskimos lived in cone-shaped dwellings framed with poles and covered with sewn caribou skins. Nuclear-family households were typical, and small numbers of families camped together when caribou were plentiful. Cooperative hunting was reasonably important in the fall at localities likely to be passed by caribou. Famines were not uncommon. When Kaj Birket-Smith made his study of these people in 1922–3, the population of 432 was what remained after a terrible famine in 1919. In all likelihood the Caribou Eskimos numbered about 1000 in the early historic period.

The mountainous northern coniferous forestland exploited by the Nabesna (Upper Tanana) is in east-central Alaska. When they were studied by Robert A. McKennan in 1929–30, they numbered 152, and the largest of the five bands included fifty-nine individuals. The Nabesna were primarily big-game hunters, with caribou the most important species taken. Caribou were followed in importance by moose and mountain sheep and then by black bears, ducks, hares, porcupines, and ptarmigan. Fish were far less important in the diet, the most important species being the whitefish. Wild plant foods were of comparatively minor significance, but among them berries stood out. Their pole-framed, dome-shaped, skin-covered winter houses were occasionally moved during the food quest. The summer houses were built near good fishing grounds and were rectangular, with pole frames covered by bark. The Nabesna had access to native copper, which they processed in the same manner as they did stone to make blades and points.

The Ingalik of western Alaska occupied a riverine setting in the northern coniferous forests. Of the four Ingalik subgroups only the subsistants of the Anvik-Shageluk are considered. These people were primarily fishermen who depended heavily on diverse species of salmon as well as grayling, northern pike, and whitefish. The most important mammals were bears, caribou, hares, lynx, moose, porcupines, and river otters. Migratory waterfowl were present in the spring and fall, but grouse and ptarmigan could be found throughout the year. The Ingalik wintered in wooden semisubterranean houses with tunnel entrances; houses and tunnels were covered with grass and then dirt. They lived in small family units, although a number of families might share a larger house. In the summer they built planksided houses with birch bark and dirt covering the roof; these dwellings were built in small villages near good fishing spots.

Among Northern Athapaskan Indians the Tanaina alone extended to the seacoast. Their habitat was the coniferous forests of south-central Alaska, and the Tanaina who exploited maritime resources most intensively, those of the Kachemak Bay area, are the only subgroup whose subsistants have been analyzed. Kachemak Bay is at the mouth of Cook Inlet, and the drainage includes a number of short streams that flow into the sea. For food these Tanaina probably depended most heavily on beluga, porpoises, sea lions, and seals. Four species of salmon played a major part in their diet, and they depended to a lesser extent on halibut, herring, and other fishes. Land mammals included black bears, beavers, hares, lynx, marmots, and porcupines. The

Kachemak Bay Tanaina built substantial winter houses of horizontal logs covered with grass thatching. The gabled roofs were covered with poles over which were placed tied-down slabs of spruce bark. Summer dwellings, built near good fishing grounds, were similar to winter houses except that they were less substantial. Food resources were far more plentiful among the Kachemak Bay group than among the other Tanaina, and in comparative terms the climate in the area of this subgroup was milder than for any of the other subarctic peoples considered.

Arctic Foragers The first of the four Eskimo populations representing the far north are the Copper Eskimos, who lived in a tundra setting along the coasts of Coronation Gulf in northwestern Canada. In the winter they occupied small settlements of dome-shaped snowhouses near good seal-hunting grounds, and in the summer they lived in oblong skin tents framed with poles. Seals were hunted intensively during much of the year, while the most important secondary staple was either caribou or fish, depending on where a particular subgroup ranged. The general impression is that seals, caribou, and fish were important in that order (Jenness, 1922, 100–5). It appears that before the arrival of whites in the region the Copper Eskimos did not travel to the south, where caribou were plentiful, for fear of meeting Indians; therefore caribou may not have been quite as important in the fully aboriginal hunting round (Jenness, 1922, 124). It should be noted that among these people wood was quite scarce, which meant that pieces often were spliced or otherwise reinforced to fashion a short shaft. Driftwood seldom washed up on the coasts, and usable spruce grew far away in the interior. Native copper was locally available, and it was hammered to make diverse artifacts or their parts.

The Iglulik lived in a tundra habitat of northern Canada, where they exploited terrestrial and aquatic resources. They occupied dome-shaped snowhouses in the winter and skin tents during the summer months. Therkel Mathiassen (1928, 21) did not hesitate to group the Iglulik proper with the Aivilingmiut and Tununermiut as a single tribe; he felt that these divisions were more "geographical than ethnographical." While some individuals spent nearly all their lives in one sector, most persons moved about the entire region. Therefore the Iglulik as defined by Mathiassen has been accepted as an ethnographically valid cluster of subgroups sharing a common material culture heritage. It appears that in the diet of the Iglulik proper, caribou were nearly as important as ringed seals, bearded seals, and walrus combined (Mathiassen, 1928, 35–6, 37, 47, 203–6). As among other arctic Eskimos foxes, wolves, and wolverines—

when present—were eaten only in times of food stress. The subsistants used to take these animals have been included because of their importance in supplying food during famines.

The northern extreme of North America, Point Barrow, was the center for the Tareumiut. They occupied substantial semisubterranean houses built of driftwood and covered with sod. Some settlements were rather large; one included about 350 persons during the early historic period. In the summer they ranged from these villages to live in skin tents at fishing and hunting sites. Comparatively little is known about the relative significance of edible species in the aboriginal diet. Ringed seals were the most important staple, followed by caribou, but during a summer in which many whales were killed, whale meat possibly supplied the bulk of the nourishment. These edibles were followed in importance by other species of seals, walrus, waterfowl, and fish, presumably in that order (Murdoch, 1892, 56, 61, 264–78; Ray, 1885, 39–41; Simpson, 1875, 261–4).

The most detailed account of aboriginal Eskimos is given for the Angmagsalik, who occupied the tundra zone along fjords on the narrow coastal fringe of southeast Greenland. Their large stone houses accommodated numerous small family units, who hunted and fished nearby during the winter. The Angmagsalik had exterminated all the local caribou, hares, and musk-oxen by the time of early historic contact, but these species had been present in the recent past. Plant products were eaten only in times of food stress, and the only wild land-dwelling species included in their diet were ptarmigan and ravens. As was true of most Eskimos, they ate their dogs during famines. All primary foods came from the sea and included capelin, narwhal, polar bears, salmon, seals, sharks, and waterfowl. The metal used for technounits by the Angmagsalik was recovered along the shore from wrecked vessels or found embedded in pieces of driftwood.

SUBSISTANT TECHNOLOGIES: AN OVERVIEW

The forms of the peoples reported in this and in the preceding chapter are compared in general and specific terms. The emphasis is primarily on comparative subsistant complexity and to a lesser extent on the principal food-getting focus. At the close of this chapter the percentages of foods and relevant procurement technologies are discussed in detail.

The nine clusters of four peoples each, representing foragers and farmers by environment, are ranked as follows in terms of their technounit averages:

Habitat	Economy	Tu average
arctic	foraging	5.5
subarctic	foraging	4.8
temperate	foraging	4.0
tropics	farming, cereal crops	3.7
temperate	farming	3.3
tropics	farming, root crops	3.2
desert	foraging	3.0
tropics	foraging	2.8
desert	farming	2.4

These averages, derived by dividing the total number of subsistants into the total number of technounits for each people, ignore many key differences among the technologies involved. In certain contexts instrument and weapon comparisons tell more, and technounit or subsistant totals in combination provide other measures of achievements. Yet the average number of parts per form is the most useful summary figure for broad comparisons.

By far the most complicated subsistants were made by arctic Eskimos, and their technounit average was much higher than for any other four-people cluster. As sophisticated technologists, arctic Eskimos had no serious rivals among aboriginal peoples anywhere. The complexity of arctic Eskimo food-getting forms may be accounted for by a combination of sociocultural and environmental variables. The arctic resource base made it impossible for people there to subsist on wild plant foods or on the meat from relatively immobile animals. It was equally out of the question to raise domestic crops. As a result of these environmental conditions, survival based on the use of instruments, the simplest class of subsistants, could not be realized. Given the achievements of aboriginal Siberians in domesticating reindeer, the potential for herding caribou in the American arctic clearly existed but was never developed, for whatever reasons.

The Eskimo habitat supported comparatively few species of wild animals, but they often were found in very large, or at least sizable, aggregates at one or more times during a year. Examples include caribou, walrus, waterfowl, and whales. Other species, especially seals, often were present in small numbers throughout the year and might at times form large groups. Marked seasonal variability in the resource base typified arctic habitats, and the migration patterns of some species often were dramatic. Furthermore the environmental conditions for taking animals varied widely by season. By far the most important species were aquatic, and as has been demonstrated, subsistants designed for use in water were usually more complicated than those employed on land. In light of all these factors we would anticipate that specialized, even species-specific, forms of relatively elaborate design would prevail among Eskimos.

Throughout this book the distinction between the technology for taking mobile food resources and that for stationary or relatively fixed resources has been stressed. We would expect that the harpoons used to hunt large sea mammals that had been partially immobilized because of ice conditions would be less complicated than those for hunting large sea mammals in open water. The Angmagsalik, Iglulik, and Tareumiut hunted intensively under both sets of conditions. We find that their ice-hunting harpoons had from seven to seventeen parts, whereas forms for hunting in open water had from seventeen to twenty-six parts. Thus we have evidence of highly specialized harpoons used for taking the prey most capable of escaping.

It might be tempting to attribute much of the complexity of Eskimo food-getting technology to the scarcity of raw materials, especially wood, which was available to most other people around the world. Admittedly wood was scarce among the Angmagsalik, Copper Eskimos, and Iglulik, but this had only a slight effect on subsistant complexity. The scarcity or absence of wood meant primarily that spliced shafts and their binders were more often reported among some Eskimos, but these added relatively few technounits to their overall totals of parts.

Among Eskimos, as well as among all other peoples sampled, the Angmagsalik of southeastern Greenland had the highest technounit average, 6.1. They also made the most complicated linked subsistants: a throwing-board that combined eight parts, used with a twenty-five part toggle-headed sealing harpoon and float. Ironically, if the Angmagsalik had not been discovered by Europeans, the population probably would have become extinct before many more decades had passed. They had killed off the most important game on land, caribou, and ice conditions were increasingly adverse for hunting in winter. When ice lodged and froze at the openings to fjords during the early winter, it was impossible for hunters to reach open water in their search for food. When discovered in 1884, the Angmagsalik numbered 413, but during the winters of 1881-2 and 1882-3 at least thirty-eight persons died. They perished from starvation, committed suicide because they were famished, or appear to have died from disease that resulted from famine conditions (Thalbitzer, 1914, 131-3, 202).

If we had dependable population figures for the time of early historic contact for most peoples, their technological complexity could be gauged against the number of persons supported by a given inventory. Yet these data usually are poor. The Copper Eskimos possibly numbered about 750 (Jenness, 1922, 42), the Iglulik group about 500 (Mathiassen, 1928, 15), and my estimate for the Tareumiut is 1500. If these figures are reasonably accurate, the Tareumiut with a 5.9 technounit average appear to have been the most successful. Among them periods of food stresses not directly associated with epidemics of exotic diseases seldom were mentioned. For the Copper Eskimos a severe scarcity of food occurred about once every four years, but starvations occurred only once every fifteen or twenty years (Jenness, 1922, 108, fn). The Iglulik too faced famines, but few specific examples are well documented (Mathiassen, 1928, 21, 54; Rasmussen, 1929, 29, 52). With the exception of the Tareumiut it appears that these Eskimos, in spite of their complicated technologies, could support relatively few persons on a long-term basis, and the Angmagsalik literally were hunting themselves to death.

The manufactures of Northern Athapaskan Indians in the American subarctic often are regarded as poorly developed. Although this may have been true for those living in Canada, the food-getting forms used by the Ingalik, Nabesna, and Tanaina in Alaska had technounit averages that overlap those of arctic Eskimos and were greater than those for the fourth subarctic people, the Caribou Eskimos. Some Ingalik and Tanaina forms clearly were modeled after Western Eskimo subsistants, and a certain amount of their complexity may be explained in this manner. However the same does not appear to be true for the Nabesna, whose technounit average (4.2) was greater than that for the Caribou Eskimos (3.5) and approached that of the Copper Eskimos (4.5). In comparative terms it seems far more important that these Indians had highly developed food-getting technologies; in the context of subsistant ecology, the derivation of particular forms has been considered insignificant throughout this book.

The Ingalik and Tanaina together used more varied subsistants with higher technounit totals than are reported for any other arctic and subarctic foragers sampled. Furthermore only two groups of Eskimos, the Tareumiut and Angmagsalik, had higher technounit averages. The Tanaina, and the Ingalik to a lesser extent, occupied habitats with rich aquatic and terrestrial resources that were seasonally abundant under varied conditions. Their settings appear to have contained more plentiful sources of food than were found in the arctic littoral occupied by Eskimos. Thus we might expect the aboriginal population figures for these Indians to be much greater than for arctic Eskimos. Comparisons of subsistant technologies by population groups must be made for peoples using the same forms in similar ways. Presumably the subsistants were the same throughout each Eskimo population. However for the Tanaina and Ingalik localized groups existed who exploited different species with different combinations of subsistants. While the Tanaina population total was about 3000 persons at the time of historic contact (Osgood, 1937, 19), it is doubtful that the Kachemak Bay group, whose subsistants were analyzed, included as many as 600 individuals. The total Ingalik population in their early history was about 1500 (Osgood, 1940, 481), and for the Anvik-Shageluk group considered here, 800 persons is a reasonable estimate. Thus there is no clear evidence that the superior resource base of these Indians resulted in larger population totals than those of arctic Eskimos subsisting on far more limited resources.

As a food staple Pacific salmon were incredibly plentiful along sectors of the northwest coast of North America and in some Bering Sea drainages of Alaska. Furthermore diverse species of salmon ascended the rivers of these regions from early spring to late fall. Salmon are a highly nutritious source of food, and the arrival time for a particular species is highly predictable. Their number fluctuates from year to year, but the runs never fail completely except as the result of a natural disaster, such as a landslide blocking access to a stream. The cultural elaboration of Northwest Coast Indians stands out as exceptional among foragers of the world. In fact their accomplishments often are compared with those of diverse farmers. The complexity of Northwest Coast Indian life usually has been attributed to the abundance, predictability, and richness of salmon as food.

It is a common belief that the technology for harvesting salmon is relatively simple because these fish were so abundant and often ascended shallow, narrow streams to reach their spawning grounds. Four of the people in the sample depended heavily on salmon for food. They were the Ingalik and Tanaina, representing the subarctic, and the Tlingit and Twana, both temperate area foragers. The most complicated Ingalik weapon was an eight-part toggle-headed harpoon used for taking salmon. Their most complex tended facility was a twelve-part gill net for salmon, and of the three simple untended fish traps with twelve parts each, one was for salmon. The most complicated form used by the Tanaina was a fifteen-part salmon trap. Among the Twana the dip net for salmon with twelve parts was their most complicated simple tended facility, and the salmon basket trap, which possibly included nine technounits, was among the most developed untended facilities. The complexity of Tlingit salmon traps is not quite as impressive, nor are the descriptions as clear as those for the other peoples. Yet one tended Tlingit salmon trap had ten parts, and an untended form appears to have included nine parts. These figures for traps do not include the weirs to which they were linked in use, which add still more to their complexity. Thus the technological forms designed by these peoples to take salmon were among their most developed subsistants. A preliminary analysis of subsistants used in salmon fishing elsewhere along the northwest coast suggests that this pattern prevailed widely.

Complex tended facilities, forms with two or more parts that move in relationship with one another when used by a person, are rare. They were employed by the Klamath (waterfowl-hatchling net) and Twana (deer net, two forms of seal net, and a game-bird enclosure trap), and this distinguishes them from all other foragers in temperate to arctic regions. Among the remaining foragers the Chenchu alone used a complex tended facility (arrow designed to decoy game and shot with a bow). While simple tended facilities were both numerous and widespread, complex tended facilities, as a logical development from simple ones, were uncommon. If aboriginal technological developments had not ended as a result of contact with members of industrial societies, complex tended facilities probably would have been far more important and widespread. If this interpretation is correct for the direction in which lasting innovations could have moved, the Twana stand as extraordinary aboriginal technologists among foragers. Furthermore the Twana had forty-eight different forms, just seven less than the Ingalik, who made the most subsistants. The Ingalik utilized 296 parts in their subsistants, and their nearest rivals were the Twana with 237 subsistant parts. These figures suggest that the Twana were manipulating technology in more varied ways than most other peoples considered.

When compared with other temperate to arctic peoples, the most notable feature of Klamath subsistant technology is the high number of instruments and the numerous simple tended facilities used for taking fish. The stress on these forms as opposed to those for taking big-game animals is instructive. Leslie Spier (1930, 155) wrote, "While game is varied and plentiful in Klamath country, the Klamath are not much given to hunting." Furthermore he reports (Spier, 1930, 156) "larger game animals are abundant. Elk is everywhere ... deer and antelope are plentiful ... and other game abound in the open country...." The Klamath apparently preferred to build their technoeconomic lives on more dependable resources, fish, water lily seed, and wild plant products. These foods clearly formed the bulk of their diet, perhaps even as much as eighty percent. Thus it is reasonable that the Klamath technounit average of 3.5 approaches those of temperate area farmers rather than the averages of foragers in temperate to arctic regions.

Among foragers anywhere the Tasmanians had one of the most elementary subsistant technologies. Their technounit average is 1.4 for eleven forms that included only fifteen parts. Since these figures represent an island-wide composite, it is possible that the subsistants of some Tasmanian tribes averaged one part per form! It is not surprising that Edward B. Tylor (1894) judged Tasmanian manufactures, especially those made from stone, as survivals from Paleolithic times. We might wonder just how much of Tasmanian technology in the early 1800s mirrored achievements in the ancient past, but we cannot dispute the simplicity of their productions compared to those of most other aboriginal peoples. In technological terms the Tasmanians certainly approach "contemporary ancestors." However the Tiwi with a 1.3 technounit average approximate the Tasmanian composite, and other aboriginal Australians used primarily elementary forms with relatively few parts.

The reason most often advanced for the relative simplicity of aboriginal Australian, and especially Tasmanian, technology is that their ancestors began to settle these lands at a time in which worldwide technologies were uncomplicated. With a rise in sea levels the inhabitants became isolated from the mainstream of cultural knowledge, and their simple technologies were perpetuated largely unchanged. This interpretation seems reasonable, and if the food-getting forms of all aboriginal Australians were as underdeveloped as those of the Tasmanians and Tiwi, it would appear to be valid. The difficulty is that other Australians maintained subsistant inventories at complexity levels approaching, or comparable to, those of diverse foragers around the world. Among Australians the average is 2.6 for the Aranda and 2.5 for the Ingura. We know too that some aboriginal Australians had higher averages than the Aranda and Ingura; for example, 3.0 is the average for the Pitapita of northern Queensland, a group not considered in this sample. The complexity levels recorded within Australia cannot be explained in terms of long-term cultural isolation. Nor does the low technounit average of the Tasmanians and Tiwi result from a stress on instruments, which usually have few parts and were used primarily to obtain plant products or immobile animals. The Tasmanians and Tiwi obtained about half of their food with very elementary weapons and facilities. The answer probably lies in a combination of environmental and cultural factors that cannot be isolated because of the size of the sample for Australians. However it should be stressed that some aboriginal Australians had rather complex technologies compared to those of many foragers elsewhere.

The technounit average for all sampled temperate area farmers is 3.3., and for farmers in the tropics, both cereal and root crop cultivators, the average is 3.4. Desert farmers stand apart with an average of 2.4. Farmers in general had food-getting technologies that were far less developed than those of foragers in temperate (4.0), subarctic (4.8), and arctic (5.5) regions, but not strikingly different from those of foragers in the tropics (2.8) and deserts (3.0). When only subsistants used primarily in farming are considered, the range of the average is narrow: deserts, 2.0; tropical cereal crops, 2.5; tropical root crops, 2.7; and temperate, 2.7. The patterning seems clear and the conclusion obvious. When plants were raised for food, the pertinent technology, as measured by techno-unit averages, is more elementary than when wild animals formed the bulk of the diet. The reason is that animals usually are mobile whereas plants are not, and the difference is reflected in the instrument versus weapon-facility distinctions.

When the technounit averages for farming subsistants were higher than usual, it was because a particular people employed complicated traps designed to take predators at garden plots rather than because the planting, cultivating, and harvesting forms were more elaborate. For example, on Pukapuka three farming subsistants had one technounit each (a coconut shell to excavate a taro plot, digging stick, and knife to extract plant cuttings as well as harvest crops). The fourth form, a rat trap used only to protect crops, had eleven parts and leads to the high average (3.2). The Kapauku technounit total for farming forms was forty-six, but nearly half of these (22) are in a boar trap built at a section of garden fencing and a trap set for garden rats. The same is true for the Lepcha to a lesser degree; fourteen of their sixty-seven technounits in farming forms were accounted for by predator sets associated with cultivated lands.

There was a tendency for cultivators who received metal tools in trade or who made farming implements from metal to have more diverse farming subsistants than other peoples. The Akamba, Aymara, Lepcha, and Tonga are examples. The overall complexity of their forms does not stand in striking contrast with those of other nondesert farmers, and yet these peoples maintained rather large populations. The Lepcha of Sikkim numbered about 13,000 (Gorer, 1938, 35), and the Gwembe Tonga 54,500 (Reynolds, 1968, 5). The Aymara population was 600,000 (La Barre, 1948, 36), and the Akamba 230,000 (Lindblom, 1920, 11), but these figures are not comparable because the number for the Aymara represents the total population, not the portion whose subsistants were sampled, as probably was true also for the Akamba. As stone-age farmers the Kapauku were able to support a large population, about 45,000 persons (Pospisil, 1963, 15), and therefore it appears that the use of metal in farming equipment had no clear and direct influence on productivity as measured by population figures.

Throughout Part 3 technounit averages have been cited as an overall measure of comparative subsistant complexity. Now that the data for the sampled peoples have been presented, we may consider subsistant and technounit totals in combination for all. It generally is assumed that people who made few forms were not likely to make very complicated ones. Conversely people who made many things are thought to have a more diverse body of technological knowledge to draw on, and thus were likely to have made comparatively elaborate forms. Cast in terms of the present study, it would be presumed that

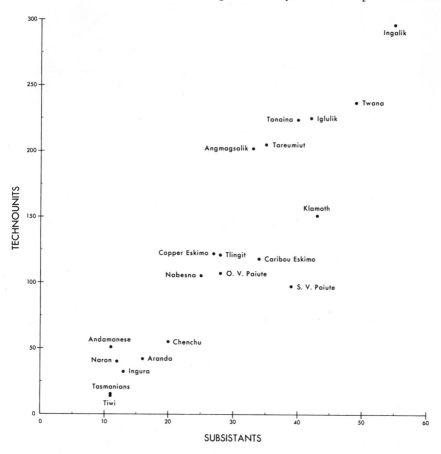

Figure 9-1 Subsistant and technounit totals plotted for the foragers sampled.

the more subsistants a people utilized the greater likelihood that the forms would embody larger numbers of technounits. Subsistant and technounit totals are plotted for foragers (Fig. 9-1) and farmers (Fig. 9-2). For both techno-economic networks, when people had few forms the subsistants included few parts, but when many forms were made they had many parts. None of the peoples sampled had many subsistants with few technounits. The Tiwi, with eleven subsistants that included fourteen parts, represent the technological baseline for early historic contact among foragers. The Pima, with seventeen subsistants that included thirty-six parts, hold the same position among farmers. The Ingalik represent the greatest degree of subsistant-technounit

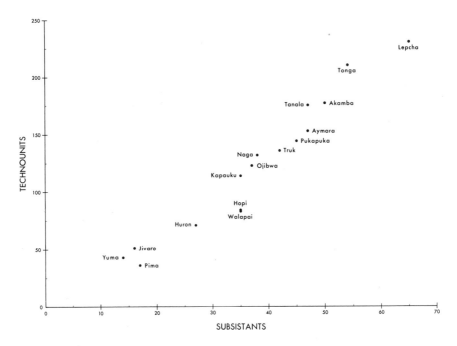

Figure 9-2   Subsistant and technounit totals plotted for the farmers sampled.

diversity among foragers, and the Lepcha occupy the same position among farmers.

The increase of subsistants and technounits is lineal for foragers and farmers alike, but the progression is more orderly for farmers. One important reason probably is that fewer exploitative alternatives were open to farmers. The ways in which plants could be handled in a productive manner were comparatively few, and exploitations were confined to a limited number of habitats. Foragers, by contrast, utilized far more diverse settings and did so in more different ways.

Technology and Diet   Dietary percentage estimates are offered for the foragers (Table 9-3) and farmers (Table 9-4) sampled. These data are organized in terms of whether the species consumed were immobile and thus associated with instruments, or mobile and involved weapons or facilities. For farmers a distinction is drawn between wild and domestic species. The percentages are in terms of dietary bulk and are most trustworthy for the Andamanese, Huron, Jivaro, Kapauku, Tiwi, and Tonga. The estimates for subarctic foragers and Eskimos are relatively reliable, but for the other peoples the percentages are reasonable guesses.

Table 9-3　Percentage estimates for immobile and mobile species in the diets of foragers sampled

		Mobile	
	Immobile	Land	Water
S. V. Paiute	65	30	5
Aranda	60	39	1
Naron	60	40	—
O. V. Paiute	70	20	10
Tiwi	50	25	25
Ingura	70	10	20
Chenchu	70	25	5
Andamanese	40	30	30
Tasmanians	40	50	10
Klamath	40	10	50
Tlingit	10	25	65
Twana	5	10	85
Caribou Eskimos	3	82	15
Nabesna	5	75	20
Ingalik	5	35	60
Tanaina	5	20	75
Copper Eskimos	6	20	74
Iglulik	3	45	52
Tareumiut	3	25	72
Angmagsalik	7	5	88

In Figure 9-3 dietary percentages are plotted against technounits for the weapons and facilities used by the foragers sampled. Technounit totals are used to represent the complexity of subsistant technology since, in this context, they are a more sensitive indicator than averages, which have a comparatively narrow range. Instruments have been excluded in spite of the fact that they sometimes were used to actually kill animals immobilized by weapons or facilities. For foragers two distinct clusters of weapons and facilities are identified on the basis of whether a particular people lived in desert-tropical habitats or temperate-arctic settings. The Tasmanians stand somewhat apart because of their small number of forms with few parts. The Andamanese, who depended heavily on meat, were unusual among desert and tropical peoples, and

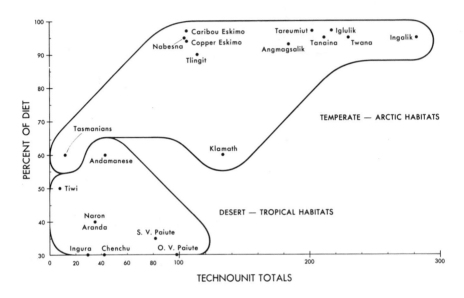

Figure 9-3 Technounit totals for weapons and facilities used by foragers plotted against dietary percentage estimates.

seemingly as a partial result, Andamanese weapons and facilities were comparatively complicated. From the summary data in Figure 9-3, we find that most foragers in temperate to arctic regions had over sixty percent meat in their diet, and to obtain it their weapons and facilities were both complicated and specialized. Presumably specialization in weapons and facilities emerged as a result of successful efforts to take animals under highly specific conditions produced by seasonal changes. Furthermore many species were aquatic, and the forms used to take them often had more parts than comparable land-use forms. The net result was the development of subsistants having more complicated design than would be expected in deserts and tropical regions where there was less seasonal variability in the resource base and therefore less diversification among the pertinent forms. The Owens Valley Paiute and Surprise

Valley Paiute, because of the seasonal variability in their habitats classed as deserts, might more properly be considered with temperate area peoples; if so then the desert-tropics cluster is even more cohesive.

Table 9-4 Percentage estimates for wild and domestic, mobile and immobile, species in the diets of the farmers sampled

| | Wild | | | Domestic (or captive) | |
| | | Mobile | | | |
	Immobile	Land	Water	Immobile	Mobile
Pima	30	20		50	
Walapai	60	30		10	
Hopi	10	5		75	10
Yuma	20	15	10	55	
Jivaro	5	25	10	60	
Trukese		10	20	70	
Pukapuka		5	33	60	2
Kapauku	5	10	10	75	
Naga		10	20	50	20
Akamba		20		60	20
Tanala	15	10		60	15
Tonga	28	0.5	0.5	70	1
Huron	18	7	13	62	
Aymara		5	30	60	5
Ojibwa	10	25	40	25	
Lepcha		10	10	60	20

The technounit totals for instruments used by farmers and foragers to obtain food are plotted against dietary percentage estimates in Figure 9-4. The sample has been restricted to peoples who obtained at least thirty percent of their food by using instruments. This eliminates arctic and subarctic foragers as well as the Tlingit and Twana, all of whom used instruments to obtain ten percent or less of their food. The reason for setting aside these peoples and their instruments is that their instruments most often served to kill mobile animals originally brought to hand with weapons or facilities. It is apparent from Figure 9-4 that no clear correlation prevails between technounit totals for instruments and the importance of nonmobile edibles, meaning primarily wild and domestic plants, in the diet of a people. The most cohesive cluster is for foragers, merging into those of farmers for each of the habitats. When an instrument technology was reasonably well developed, as among the Aymara, Kapauku, Lepcha, and Tonga, different habitat groups are represented. In over-all terms instrument technology was underdeveloped when compared with that of weapons and facilities, because there were far fewer ways conceived or apparently necessary to manipulate immobile species of edibles.

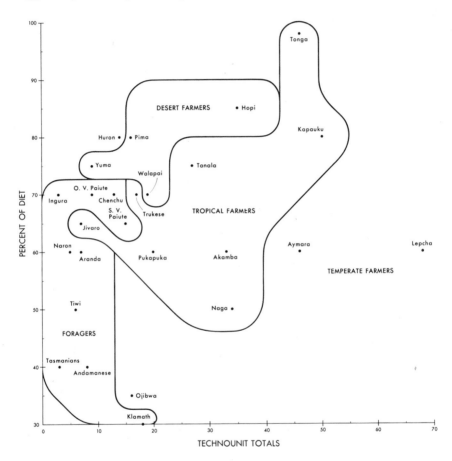

Figure 9-4   Technounit totals for instruments used to obtain at least thirty percent of their food by farmers and foragers plotted against dietary percentage estimates.

Little purpose would be served by systematic comparisons between dietary percentages and the use of weapons and facilities for obtaining wild species by farmers. This is because no clear correlation has been identified. Farmers some-times used complicated weapons or facilities to obtain wild animals or fish that contributed very little to their diet. The situation is well illustrated by data for the Gwembe Tonga. For fishing they used twelve subsistants with fifty-five parts in order to obtain about one half of one percent of their food! (This estimate of the amount that fish contributed to their diet was provided by correspondence of Thayer Scudder.) Although these Tonga were anxious to fish for recreation and to obtain food, a full day's fishing typically provided only a single meal. During each year there was a comparatively brief span in which fishing was a profitable enterprise. As Scudder (1960, 42) has written, "The Valley Tonga fish because they desire and occasionally crave fish as an adjunct to a highly carbohydrate diet." A similar explanation may account for the comparatively large number of fishing devices used by the Tanala. The overtly recreational aspect of hunting is illustrated by the Aymara, who employed unusual facilities, musical instruments, with a comparatively large number of technounits to drive wild game, which contributed little to their overall diet. The dietary need for protein was demonstrably important among the Gwembe Tonga, and this explains the number of forms for fishing. They also had a comparatively large number of forms with numerous parts used in association with domestic animals, which contributed about one percent to their diet (Scudder, correspondence).

Because of the limitations about dietary information for most peoples sampled, it appears that foragers who depended heavily on weapons and facilities for a high percentage of their food made diverse, complicated, and specialized forms, especially those peoples in temperate to arctic regions. Some cultivators, such as the Ojibwa, Pukapukans, and Trukese, developed elaborate forms that provided important amounts of food from wild animals. Farmers in general had cultivating equipment that was much the same, although there was a great deal of variability in the importance or complexity of weapons and facilities.

PART 4

CONCLUSIONS

CHAPTER 10

PRODUCTION
PRINCIPLES

Countless numbers of artifacts have been recovered from archaeological sites or are in current use, and a vast amount has been written about material culture past and present. From these data one summary conclusion is inescapable: Technological change is cumulative. No one denies that the earliest known artifacts are elementary in technological terms or that with the passage of time increasingly complicated forms have been made. It also is quite clear that for the last 30,000 years the forms produced have been more likely to change in structure than to remain the same for long periods. The direction of technological change has been from simplicity to complexity and from the manufacture of a few similar forms to many that are highly diverse. Nowhere has the change from homogeneity to heterogeneity seemed more apparent than in material culture. However few persons have attempted to explain technological heterogeneity in terms of the processes involved. Thus it is a compelling challenge to identify the production principles that have led to major changes in material culture.

Great moments in the evolution of technology often are identified in terms of particular artifacts. The bow and arrow, firearms, mechanical clocks, and pottery are examples. Each archetype anticipated major changes in technology and had a profound effect on cultural life. Yet from my perspective the most important advance occurred before people made even the simplest artifacts. The removal and use of free naturefacts was an experiment in handling objects that led to future technological accomplishments. Motivation, foresight, intelligence, and manipulative skill stand as prerequisites to the earliest production of artifacts, and these first were exhibited when people learned to use free naturefacts. Although it may seem presumptive, these qualities are, for the time being, accepted as essentially constant for human populations through time. The reason is that we know comparatively little about the evolution of human thinking and the development of craft skills. With variables such as these beyond the scope of thorough inquiry, we begin by identifying expectable preconditions for artifact production on a different basis.

The obtaining of food by hand and the use of free naturefacts have been isolated as preliminary steps toward making things. These activities collectively are labeled as the *contextual removal* of natural forms for food and for use. Presumably, when free naturefacts came to serve diverse purposes, the adaptive advantages that they provided led to even more intense involvements with objects. If we accept the contextual removal and use of forms as an anticipation of things to come in technology, the next step was to make things by changing the mass of a raw material. In studying this step it seems far more important to isolate the manufacturing procedures involved than to speculate about what the earliest artifacts were. Through evaluating the ways in which nonhumans make artifacts, the manner in which forms were produced by aboriginal peoples in the recent past, and the means by which things are made today, four *production principles* are identified. In this context a production principle is an underlying plan for the expenditure of energy to make something. Production principles are not particular ways in which to make things but the comprehensive procedures by which things come to be made. The principles are applied through *production methods*, or the manner of working particular materials. Flint is flaked, slate is ground, bone is fractured and abraded, wood is hewn, and metal is forged or cast. Materials are modified physically by the application of *production techniques* achieved with particular tools. As examples, flint may be chipped with a hammerstone or a flaking tool of bone, slate polished on a grindstone, bone fractured with a hammerstone and abraded with a grindstone, and wood hewn with an ax and finished with a plane. Methods and techniques are culture specific, but all lead to the production of artifacts.

Given the amount of recorded information about artifacts, we might expect that establishing the emergence of major technological changes in material culture would not be an especially difficult enterprise. Yet efforts by anthropologists to deal with the question have not been very rewarding. In writings about technological change the words accident, borrowing, chance, diffusion, discovery, distribution, invention, and purpose occur frequently. As general descriptive labels none of these terms comes to grips with the universal basis for material changes. A single word is required to include all that is implied in each of the origins of technological change cited above. Such a word must be both particularistic and applicable to principles of artifact production. Such a word is *innovation*. H. G. Barnett (1953, 7) defined innovation as "any thought, behavior, or thing that is new because it is qualitatively different from existing forms." In terms of "culture," as conceived by Cornelius Osgood and outlined in the Introduction, the "thoughts" are mental culture, the "behavior" is social culture, and the "things" are material culture. The essence of Barnett's seldom-appreciated approach to culture change is that it places stress on the *qualitatively new* as opposed to the *quantitatively different*. Innovations, irrespective of the end product, represent a new combination of ideas. All innovations originate from either the existing techniculture or ideas derived from the natural world. Techniculture includes all knowledge of the methods, principles, and techniques for making, repairing, or using things, as well as ideas about the things themselves. The persons in a society are a part of the natural world as are all the things that would exist in the absence of people. Our concern is not with the cultural contexts giving rise to innovations (Barnett, 1953, 39–95)—as important as they are—but with how technological knowledge was reorganized to produce the innovations.

A survey of select technological forms produced in the recent past suggests that after a new device or system is originated its pattern of growth and development follows a sigmoid curve. A plot of performance against time shows that a period of rapid growth is succeeded by performance improvements during a period of consolidation, which is followed by a leveling off of development (Fig. 10-1). The leveling off may represent either social constraints or the approach of physical growth limits. However growth for an artifact cluster representing a "field" of forms may be exponential because of the wide range of forms involved. For example, along particular lines of development in basic machines a sigmoid curve is approximated, yet when all basic machines are considered, the curve is exponential (Starr and Rudman, 1973).

It seems reasonable to view all artifacts as a single field of forms with exponential growth potential. For buildings, conveyances, facilities, instruments, weapons, and so on, as subfields, the growth may be represented by a sigmoid curve. When a people's perceptions about technology were elementary, it is likely that the body of information would expand and diversify at a relatively slow rate because their artifacts were made in a few simple ways. Conversely, when people knew a great deal about different ways to produce artifacts, more diverse forms of complicated design would emerge, with innovations occurring at a more rapid pace. Thus interest focuses on innovation as a technological process leading to change.

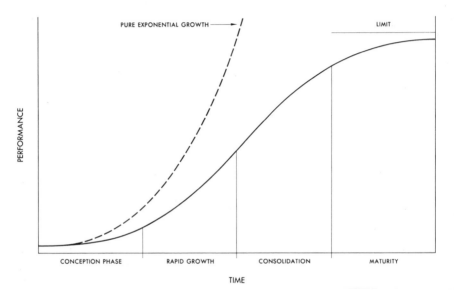

Figure 10-1   The form of a sigmoid curve with reference to the development of a techno-logical device or system (Courtesy of Chauncey Starr and Richard Rudman; Copyright 1973 by the American Association for the Advancement of Science).

Barnett (1953, 181) states that the *innovative process,* as it begins, is "an intimate linkage or fusion of two or more elements that have not been previously joined in just this fashion, so that the result is a qualitatively distinct whole." The process occurs in the mind and produces a synthesis that has properties different from those of its antecedents. A fundamental precept is that all innovations are derived from previously known ideas: they do not and cannot spring from nothing. It is equally necessary to acknowledge that while techno-logical innovation is identified as a qualitative concept, it is based on the proper-ties of things and the shapes of forms which are quantifiable.

Those things called artifacts are important because of the ideas entertained about them, or as Barnett (1953, 182) states, "Ideas define the nature and extent of things." In all instances they are unified and organized patterns of experience, termed *configurations*, which may be very specific or highly general. They are conceived through mental activity but are expressed in terms as particularistic as atoms or parts, at a broader level by sizes and weights, or even by purely subjective terms such as *good* or *bad*. The qualities of a configuration at one level are different from those at another level. In these terms, attention does *not* focus on the innovation of specific artifacts in terms of particular methods and techniques of production but rather on the different ways in which their production has been conceived.

The most basic principle of artifact production is termed *reduction*, which means to reduce the mass, whether natural or man-made, to produce a functioning form. A one-part artifact is made by taking material away from a larger mass. The physical operation is that of subtraction, withdrawing from, or diminishing in size. As the simplest principle involved in artifact manufacture, reduction justly may be viewed as the oldest way to make things. Seemingly the most elementary application would be to diminish a natural material by anatomical means and then to use the resultant product. Examples include breaking a limb from a tree to serve as a club, snapping a twig off a bush to use as an earpick, and pulling a quill out of a porcupine skin to use as an awl. Reduction also occurs when grass is detached from a clump, wadded up, and used as a sponge, and when a handful of sand is picked up to smooth a wooden shaft. Aboriginal Australians in northern Queensland sometimes carried water in a leaf that had been removed from a tree and then rolled into the shape of a cone (Roth, 1904, 31). In each of these instances the act of withdrawal or physical separation from a greater mass resulted in the production of an artifact. Although examples similar to the one reported from Queensland are unusual, they illustrate the possibility of reduction without the taking away of any part or piece of the material used. In most cases, however, to reduce means to decrease the volume of a material by removing some of its physical mass with the aid of a tool. Such artifacts are technologically more complicated. Examples include producing a flint scraper by removing flakes with a hammerstone, carving a doll from a block of wood with a knife, and shaping a missile stick with an adz. As the most basic principle of production, reduction not only results in one-unit artifacts but is essential in making the parts for composite forms.

The second production principle could only have prevailed following the habitual manufacture of artifacts by reduction. Technounits could then be combined in order to create finished forms by the *conjunction* principle. Conjunction simply means joining technounits, by any means, to fashion composite forms. A gouge consisting of a tooth blade, bone haft, and fiber cord to bind the blade and handle is an example. Each part is a distinct physical and structural entity, a technounit, and each makes a unique contribution to the whole. The same would apply to a breechclout of skin with a leather thong attached as a belt, and to a fruit-picking pole with a bone hook tied at one end. The technounits comprising conjuncted artifacts may or may not be created by people. Water is a technounit when it is mixed with shredded leaves to make a medicine, and a dead bird as bait for a trap serves a similar purposes. An intact naturefact may form a technounit, such as a tree used to support a pole that serves as a ladder. These examples are accommodated fully in the concept of a technounit, but they do not often occur. Technounits more commonly are fashioned by people.

After forms had been made by a combination of reduction and conjunction, a third principle of production was utilized. Termed *replication*, it refers to two or more similar structural elements that are crafted and used to function as one part of a form. A cluster of such components represents only one technounit and most often is combined with other technounits that are dissimilar. For example, a typical leister includes a shaft and lashings, which are dissimilar, bound to be similar, multiple impaling prongs. Other artifacts with replicative technounits include funnel-shaped fish traps with similar splints, metal scissors with similar blades, and like pistons in a six-cylinder gasoline engine. In these examples the blades, pistons, and splints represent one technounit each because of their similar contributions to the whole. Unlike the other production principles, replication does not result in increased technounit totals.

Linkage, the final production principle, is applied to the manufacture of forms that are discrete physically but must be combined to perform a particular purpose. Linked forms always are joined in a technicized manner during their primary usage. Examples include a mano and metate, bow and arrow, spear and throwing-board, and tractor and plow. Linked artifacts may or may not serve other purposes when used alone. A spear could be used without a throwing-board or a tractor without a plow, but in technological terms these usages would not be as complicated as those resulting from their combination.

In terms of technological evolution two very basic and universal production principles have been identified: reduction, followed by conjunction. Expansions on these construction principles are replication and linkage, which presumably were subsequent developments. It has been indicated that the technological knowledge necessary for fashioning one-part forms would be uncomplicated compared with that required to produce compound artifacts.

The conjunction principle of production can be applied only after several intermediary steps have taken place following the development of forms made by reduction alone. Fashioning forms by the conjunction principle requires (*a*) a distinct mental template for each part, (*b*) raw materials which may differ greatly in their physical qualities, (*c*) the skill to fashion technounits into different shapes and often from different materials, (*d*) an ability to conceive of the finished product as a whole, (*e*) the knowledge to join the parts by using still other forms, and (*f*) sufficient precision to arrive at a harmonious fit among the technounits of the finished form. These integrated concepts suggest that only after the conjunction principle of artifact production was well developed could people conceive of many new forms of artifacts.

Now is the time to consider the earliest-known examples of diverse portable artifacts in terms of production principles. It is not especially difficult to establish when a new manufacturing principle was applied to lithic materials because paleoethnographers usually describe and illustrate their finds well. However excavators and interpreters alike often are hesitant to attribute function to particular forms, and for very good reason; they may not know how an artifact or surviving parts were used. Then too, in an effort to give substance to their accounts, some anthropologists speculate freely about the early appearance of such forms as bolas, fish weirs, pitfalls, snares, and so on, with absolutely no supporting evidence; these references have been ignored. It often was difficult to date the appearance of a form with precision, which is frustrating but understandable. Another major limitation is the preservation of organic materials. The older an organic form or technounit, the greater is the likelihood that it will have disintegrated. Finally, a limited number of key sources were consulted, and the search was confined to the Old World.

No one is prepared to state when people began to make artifacts, but it is clear that they were being produced 2.6 million years ago. Stone tools of approximately this age have been recovered from the Koobi Fora site, near the eastern shore of Lake Rudolf in Kenya. Choppers, flaked and battered cobbles, and flakes have been found in association with hippopotamus tusk fragments and antelope teeth. Unmodified cobbles of lava are included and appear to have been carried to the site from an outcrop a few miles distant. Nearly all of the stone forms recovered were made of lava. The boldest interpretation of these finds is that the location was occupied briefly by hominids who used it as a base camp. It was here that they apparently brought meat to eat and lava to use as a raw material in making tools (*see* Table 10-1 for references).

The earliest known wooden artifact, presumed to have been a spear, is from Clacton, England, and may have been made as long ago as 500,000 years. It is the tip of a yew-wood shaft and has a sharpened, fire-hardened point. The first form that unquestionably is a one-piece spear is from Lehringen, Germany, and dates from the last interglacial period. Made of yew, it is some eight feet in length, and it too has a fire-hardened point. This spear was found between the

Table 10-1   The earliest known occurrence of artifacts, listed by production principle

Artifact	Age	Area	Reference
Linkage (codependent artifacts joined in a technicized manner)			
Spear & throwing-board	13,000 B.C.	France	Bordes, 1968, 164
Bow & arrow	ca. 15,000 B.C.	North Africa	Clark, 1970, 157
Replication (compound forms with some structurally similar parts)			
Wood fish weir & trap	2600 B.C.	Yug R., U.S.S.R.	Dolukhanov et al., 1970, 135
Fishnet	3000 B.C.	Shilka R., Siberia	Treistman, 1972, 30–1
Bark-lined storage pit	Neolithic	Lena area, Siberia	Okladnikov, 1970, 84
Sled and skis	Mesolithic	Northern Europe	Clark and Piggott, 1970, 259
Seine	7000 B.C.	Northern Europe	Clark and Piggott, 1970, 136–7
Arctic clothing	7000 B.C.	Buret, Siberia	Michael, 1958, 33; Okladnikov, 1970, 30–1
Trident spear	12,000 B.C.	France	Bordes, 1968, 164
Microliths for knives and spears	13,000 B.C.	Africa	Clark, 1970, 154
Poles for dwelling	300,000 B.P.	Nice, France	De Lumley, 1969, 42–50
Conjunction (compound forms with structurally different parts)			
Bone spearpoints with cleft tangs	27,000 B.C.	France	Bordes, 1968, 155
Hafted scrapers	28,000 B.C.	Ordos region, China	Treistman, 1972, 18–9
Hafted end blades	30,000 B.C.	Aterian, North Africa	Clark, 1970, 126–8, 142
Reduction (one-part artifacts)			
Missile stick	70,000 B.P.	Kalambo Falls Zambia	Clark, 1970, 142
Shaft spear	last interglacial	Lehringen, Germany	Clark and Piggott, 1970, 42
Shaft spear head	500,000 B.P.	Clacton, England	Clark and Piggott, 1970, 42
Choppers, flaked cobbles	2.6 million years	Koobi Fora, Kenya	Isaac et al., 1971; Leakey, 1970

ribs of an extinct species of elephant. Another one-part weapon of respectable antiquity is a missile stick from Kalambo Falls in Zambia, dating from about 70,000 years ago. These data suggest that reduction was indeed the earliest production principle for artifacts made of stone or wood. Since organic materials rarely are preserved for tens of thousands of years, this does not mean very much in terms of any firm conclusions. However current evidence supports the supposition that the first forms were made by reducing the mass of natural materials to derive one-part artifacts.

The preservation of organic materials is reasonably good at numerous sites dating from about 30,000 B.C., and it is at this point that the conjunction principle of artifact production seems to appear first. The Aterian period begins around 30,000 B.C., and at Aterian sites in northern Africa diverse forms of chipped stone end blades with distinct tangs have been recovered. These almost certainly were attached to handles or shafts. Hafted scrapers are reported from China, and hafted bone spearpoints occur in France, all at about the same time. These are the oldest clear examples of composite and portable artifacts of which I am aware. Notably, they are from widely separated regions, but they occur in nearly the same temporal context.

The earliest clear instance of crafted replicative parts used in a form is reported from a site in Nice, France, dating from some 300,000 years ago. Poles similar to one another formed the sidewalls of a dwelling, and presumably they were cut to nearly the same length prior to construction. The use of multiple poles to contribute one technounit in making this house is a much older example of replication than any others reported. The use of multiple, similar parts for *nonportable* artifacts appears to have a technohistory distinct from that of portable forms with replicative components. For portable artifacts replicative units do not seem to appear until about 13,000 B.C. The 17,000 years that separate the first portable forms produced by conjunction and those made by replication may prove to be shorter, but a sizable gap still is expected. The earliest examples to date of replication are microliths set into knife handles and into the sides of spearpoints. Examples of other forms dating from more recent times are included in Table 10-1. Each is self-explanatory except that for the seine and net it is assumed that weights were attached or that the forms included floats.

The linkage production principle, identified by codependent artifacts joined in a technicized manner, clearly had been applied by 13,000 B.C. The earliest known example, from this time period, is the spear and throwing-board combination found in France. No one is certain when and where the bow and arrow originated, but northern Africa is a likely possibility. It appears that the bow and arrow had a single point of origin from which it spread over most of the world by early historic times. The earliest uncontested evidence is from a find in Germany that dates from before 9000 B.C. However in the latter part of the Aterian, ca. 10,000 to 20,000 B.C., are found small tanged and barbed points, presumed to have been arrowpoints (Clark, 1970, 156–7). If bows and arrows were being made in the Aterian at about 15,000 B.C., it would seem that the replication and linkage principles of production appeared at about the same time. If this is true, the division between replication and linkage has comparatively little chronological importance in the general evolution of technology. Even so the distinction seems important in technological terms for assessing forms produced in industrial societies.

In addition to identifying the earliest applications of each production principle in the paleoethnographic record, we also may seek the earliest examples of complex artifacts. Those with parts retaining the same relationship with one another when the artifact was in use are *simple*, or *nonmechanical*; artifacts with parts that changed their physical relationship with one another during use are *mechanical*, or *complex*. Among the earliest forms hesitantly identified as complex are the bow and arrow and the spear used with a throwing-board. In a sense the movement involved when a bow is used with an arrow is more technologically complex than that of the spear and throwing-board. The bow and bowstring change form when an arrow is shot, but the throwing-board does not change its form when a spear is propelled. The harpoon dart with a detachable head linked to the shaft by a thong is the earliest fully acceptable complex form; one of the earliest harpoon darts is from France and dates from about 7000 B.C. (Bordes, 1968, 165–6). Other examples of complex manufactures by aboriginal peoples include the bow drill, as well as certain forms of deadfalls and snares, but the archaeological evidence for their first appearance is unclear.

The difference between tended and untended facilities was important in the presentation of subsistant classes. It would appear that throughout most of time the presence of one or more persons was required for the functioning of most artifacts. Exceptions do exist, but it appears that these are limited to nonportable forms. Artifactual storage facilities functioned whether or not the makers were present, and the same was true for their natural counterparts. When a Tasmanian cached a kangaroo in a tree (Robinson, 1966, 402–3, 412–3), the tree "worked" for him in his absence. The same applies to any dam, granary, or irrigation ditch. Yet greater elaboration of parts was required for portable artifacts operating in the absence of people than for similar forms functioning as a result of direct human manipulation. Of the portable artifacts cited in Table 10-1, those that functioned in man's absence all are presumably of very recent origins. Included are set nets for fish, and weirs and traps which date from around 2800 B.C.

The paleoethnographic record suggests that the earliest artifacts were made by reduction. Furthermore this appears to have been the only production principle known until about 30,000 B.C. If some people were primarily hunters by 300,000 B.C., if not much earlier, then we would infer that the simple shaft spear was the primary weapon and that it served them well, as is suggested by what we know about Tasmanian hunting in early historic times. If reduction alone were the principle of artifact production from 2.6 million years ago until 30,000 B.C., and if people in the interim became increasingly efficient food-getters, then major improvements of a technological nature could not be evoked as a primary explanation. Instead, an expansion of human intelligence and exploitative skills seems most reasonable.

It even appears that once people learned to join two technounits to make an artifact the accomplishment did not lead to any marked increase in the number of forms produced. Only when three or more parts were combined and replicative technounits were embodied in portable artifacts did the diversity of forms increase abruptly, and these were processes that do not appear to have begun until about 13,000 B.C. *It would appear that most of the forms produced by aboriginal peoples in early historic times did not originate until about 10,000 B.C. or even later.* I am quite aware that the paleoethnographic record may seem compatible with the proposed sequence only because we know so little about the distant past. Most artifacts and their parts were made from organic materials that have disintegrated. However, at the moment at least, the sequence of production principles does appear to be valid, artifacts did increase in number of techno-units through time, forms with moving parts do appear late in the sequence, and the independent functioning of some portable artifacts is very recent in technohistory.

The outline to follow represents an effort to establish a sequence of major advances in the evolution of technology. The numbered items are of greater importance, and presumably are more reliable, than are the lettered entries.

1. The physical form of a material must be changed from its natural state or condition before any truly technological accomplishment is realized.

   a. The first forms produced probably were used for purposes that had little or nothing to do with subsistence welfare.

2. The most elementary means for changing a material to produce an artifact is decreasing its physical mass, thereby applying the principle of reduction.

   a. The earliest one-part forms were reduced by breaking, tearing, or twisting them from their natural context. Artifacts simply "detached" and used without further modification are the most elementary forms.

   b. Next one-part forms were produced with the use of natural tools.

c. One-part productions created with man-made tools represent a further progression.

3. Through application of the conjunction principle, artifacts consisting of two previously prepared, different technounits were combined physically to operate as a combination.

a. The most common means for joining two parts was by wedging or twisting them together.

b. Two-part artifacts, as a group, were relatively ineffective as techno-economic forms because they tended to come apart during use.

4. When two technounits, each different in form, were joined by a separate binder, a significant advance occurred, but the number of different forms produced did not increase abruptly.

5. Further elaborations were achieved when two or more worked techno-units of very similar design were used to serve a single function in an artifact; the manufacturing principle involved is identified as replication.

a. An abrupt increase in the number of different forms produced followed the application of this principle to portable forms.

6. Finally, the production of coordinated artifacts combined in a techni-cized manner is the most advanced manufacturing principle developed by aboriginal peoples; the principle involved is termed linkage. This view of technological change finds little accord with traditionally accepted stages. The Stone Age, Bronze Age, and Iron Age differences carry little weight. The Paleo-lithic, Mesolithic, and Neolithic distinctions likewise are of minimal importance. Preindustrial and industrial periods make more sense but still fall short of the mark. Neither does the concept of technological "traditions" find its place in this approach. A distinction is not drawn between core and blade traditions in working stone, nor are bone-, horn-, or woodworking traditions significant in this analysis. In fact, on a technological basis there is no reason to separate the manufactures of farmers from those of foragers or, among foragers, to isolate collectors from hunters and fishermen. These hallowed distinctions undeniably are significant in the histories of cultures, yet are not critical for plotting evolution in technology or for assessing the comparative complexities of technologies.

This chapter offers a novel means for the analysis of technological change. The thesis is that the production principles identified are in themselves sufficient to identify the most important ways in which artifacts have been made in the past and will be fashioned in the future. Specific production methods and techniques are secondary results of the application of the principles, and materials are significant only in terms of such methods and techniques. By isolating the principles involved in the manufacture of artifacts and by offering technounits as production units, we establish a universal means for analyzing technologies and technological innovations, regardless of their time or place of origin and their development or spread.

CHAPTER 11

TECHNOLOGICAL
PERSPECTIVES

My general perspective is that the detailed analysis of material culture on a worldwide and temporally expansive basis is a worthwhile endeavor. The establishment of the different ways in which artifacts are produced or used and the resolving of questions about the origin, development, or distribution of forms clearly are important goals. Yet I seek an even broader comparison, a ranking of all artifacts within a single analytical system in terms of comparative complexity. The idea of comparisons along a single scale is fundamental not only in the evaluation of artifacts produced within one society but, more importantly, on a cross-cultural basis. Among anthropologists the "comparative method" long has been a dominant approach to data analyses. In the recent past, and at present to a lesser degree, a great deal of energy has been devoted to comparative studies in order to generate a broad base for understanding variability in human behavior. Generations of anthropologists have compared and derived generalizations about kinship terminologies, marriage residence and settlement patterns, economic and political networks, and religious behavior. We seek in vain, however, to identify contemporary ethnologists who have analyzed material culture in detail for the purpose of generalizing about technology. Nor can we identify individuals who have broad conceptual approaches to the study of aboriginal technology and who have considered specific bodies of data thoroughly in support of their positions. Not even contemporary ethnologists termed *cultural materialists* have classified, measured, and then plotted the technological accomplishments of diverse peoples against one another within a coherent framework and along a single scale. My position is obviously that material culture should be accorded a more thoughtful evaluation than that currently prevailing among anthropologists. This point of view was raised in the Introduction and at the opening of the second chapter, but further elaboration is required to place my goals in perspective.

As a clearly recognized core ingredient in culture, technology should not be dismissed without, at least, first demonstrating its lack of pertinence. My contention is that this is precisely what has been done; technology is recognized as being essential in culture and then is largely ignored. It is instructive to document the role accorded technology and material culture in modern comparative studies. The purpose is not to discourse on the failings of ethnologists, because there can be no failing when a topic has not been identified as deserving studied attention. I seek instead to convey how infrequent and inadequate the analysis of material culture has been in modern anthropological works about aboriginal peoples.

Introductory cultural anthropology textbooks are a ready guide to the topics stressed in the teaching of any particular generation of students, and texts change their emphasis rather rapidly to reflect shifting anthropological interests. A systematic review of college texts is not attempted, but certain trends seem reasonably clear. Every textbook that includes a discussion of the beginnings of culture and prehistory stresses material culture because artifacts provide the bulk of evidence about the distant past. An emphasis on material remains as a means of interpreting prehistory characterizes most old, as well as new, textbooks. Discussion of the archaeological record usually is separated from the presentation of manufactures by aboriginal peoples both at the time of historic contact and more recently. Through the early 1950s the tendency was to devote a number of substantive chapters to material culture in order to introduce the varied life-styles of aboriginal peoples. Clothing, containers, conveyances, housing, and tools usually were considered, with examples drawn from diverse peoples around the world. Worldwide differences in material culture were attributed to environmental contrasts, differences in economic foci, the availability of materials, and cultural isolation. Similarities in material culture often were ascribed to the likeness of habitats and subsistence patterns as well as to shared cultural traditions and specific borrowings. By the 1960s aboriginal material culture had begun to receive far less attention than it had previously. An exception is a text by Philip K. Bock (1969) in which one part, a quarter of the text, is devoted to ethnographic material culture. A more recent and successful text, by Carol R. and Melvin Ember (1973), includes nearly 550 pages of text, but only two pages are explicitly allotted to "Tools and Technology" in a nonarchaeological context. Even the textbook by Marvin Harris (1975), who accords technology a prominent position in the study of culture, lacks any detailed discussion of artifacts in the approach to aboriginal peoples. For example, artifacts in the food-production and energy flow equation formulated by Harris (1975, 233–4) are accounted for only by the heading "technological inventory," without further consideration of the forms involved. In all their varied configurations, artifacts simply are reported as being present.

A clear indication that the study of material culture finds few supporters among ethnologists is the fact that few books deal exclusively with the subject. One early work, *The Origins of Invention*, by Otis T. Mason, was published first in 1895 and reissued in 1966. A more recent volume of note is *Primitive Arts and Crafts*, by R. U. Sayce, published in 1933 and again in 1965. Probably the most influential volume in which material culture has been considered at length is *Habitat, Economy and Society*, by C. Daryll Forde, published first in 1934 and frequently reprinted since. This book provides the most detail about material culture in the formulation of a comprehensive statement about cultural diversity. Thus far in the 1970s each single-author book about technology has been very short and has had limited appeal. These include volumes by Vera Lustig-Arecco (1975), Robert F. G. Spier (1970, 1973), and Wendell H. Oswalt (1973). A book edited by Miles Richardson (1974), *The Human Mirror*, is one of the rare multiauthored studies of material culture to appear recently.

In the structural analysis of material culture a single bold and innovative discussion has appeared recently. It is in the book *Invitation to Archaeology*, by James Deetz (1967, 83–94). He emphasized the importance of artifact parts in a formal analysis and turned to linguistics for an analogue. Two basic units in the structure of language are the phoneme and morpheme. Phonemes are classes of sounds that *affect* the meaning of words, and morphemes are classes of sounds that *carry* meaning. These concepts make it possible to analyze different languages in terms of their structures. Deetz stressed that artifacts and words have much more in common than generally is recognized. A word is made up of phonemes the way an artifact is made up of parts, and in each the configuration has structural and meaningful morphology. Deetz (1967, 86) asked, "Could it be that both words and artifacts are in fact different expressions of the same system?" His response was positive in an admittedly conjectural manner. Both are products of mind and muscle coordination which in proper attribute combinations yields meaningful forms. He proposed that an artifact attribute equivalent to a phoneme be designated a *facteme*, and he defined it as "the minimal class of attributes which affects the functional significance of the artifact" (Deetz, 1967, 89). A notch on the side of a stone arrowpoint was cited as a facteme. These notches may vary in shape, such as from round to triangular, but this is unimportant unless it affects the purpose of the haft. Deetz (1967, 89) also coined the term *allofact* to accommodate the differences among notches that serve the same structural goal. An allofact is thus a variable that does not influence meaning, paralleling an allophone in linguistics. He proposed also that the unit comparable to a morpheme is the *formeme*, defined as "the minimal class of objects which has functional significance" (Deetz, 1967, 90). As formemes, a stone point, a wood shaft, feathers, and binders are combined to create an arrow, and each formeme can be used in other contexts as well. Deetz suggested that to carry this approach further it would be logical to interview living peoples about the structure of their artifacts and to observe the behaviors involved in making them. He also recognized that the purpose served by a form such as an arrowhead is functionally inherent in the attributes of the form, which facilitates a factemic and formemic analysis. The Deetz approach is very inviting because it seeks first to isolate universal structural attributes of artifacts and then to distinguish levels of significance among them.

We might expect that reference books devoted to method and theory in anthropology would discuss technology at some length, if only to explain its lack of importance. The Introduction noted that technology is virtually ignored in *Man the Hunter*, edited by Richard B. Lee and Irven DeVore (1968), implying that it was not really very important among aboriginal foragers. In the weighty volume edited by Raoul Naroll and Ronald Cohen (1970), *A Handbook of Method in Cultural Anthropology*, we would search in vain for a reasonably comprehensive commentary about technology and material culture. This is neither to ignore nor disparage the chapter by Harold E. Driver (620–39) about the geographical distribution of cultural objects and behaviors. The point is that manufactures as such are not really considered. In *Main Currents in Cultural Anthropology* (1973), edited by Raoul and Frada Naroll, technology merits a single index entry. It refers to a section in the chapter authored by Robert L. Carneiro (57–121) entitled "Classical Evolution," a review of evolutionary thinking in cultural anthropology. This is probably the best statement on the subject that has appeared, but the focus is historical and does not address the present or future. The only reference work that deals with material culture in a comprehensive manner is *Notes and Queries on Anthropology*. The first edition, which appeared in 1874, was edited by Lane-Fox Pitt-Rivers; the sixth edition, prepared by a select committee of British anthropologists, was published in 1951. From its origin *Notes and Queries*, as it usually is known, was designed as a handbook for professional and amateur fieldworkers. In early, as well as late, editions a major portion of the text is devoted to topics to be considered when collecting information about technology, but this stress is understandable because of the purpose of the volume.

In broad-spectrum comparative studies, items of material culture usually are included in an inventory of variables considered. It was material culture that L. T. Hobhouse, G. C. Wheeler, and M. Ginsberg (1915) used as a primary means for ordering their sample of peoples for a detailed analysis of social institutions. Technology also was considered at some length in the follow-up study by Alvin W. Gouldner and Richard A. Peterson (1962). Material culture was important in the Culture Element Survey organized by Alfred L. Kroeber in 1933 (Kroeber, 1939, 435). A vast amount of information was assembled about diverse aspects of Indian culture in western North America, but the goals of the project never were fully realized. With the exception of Driver most of the persons who collected information for the survey were not really interested in the project and did not make follow-up studies as professional anthropologists (Driver, 1962, 17-8). One of the worthwhile results was that, when working on the surveys, Julian H. Steward began to formulate his ecological approach to the study of foragers. In his concept of "cultural core", material culture was accorded an important role (Steward, 1955, 89). At the present time, when technology is considered in a thoughtful manner it is most likely to be in an ecological context (e.g., Damas, 1969). *Ethnographic Atlas* (1967), by George P. Murdock, includes information about material culture for boat building, housing, leather- and metalworking, pottery, and weaving. The diverse studies that have drawn on Murdock's data base may have considered material culture, but only in a secondary manner as was inherent in the categories chosen for inclusion. Article-length studies of material culture have appeared from time to time, but in proportion to the amount written about other anthropological subjects the volume is small. I do not mean to slight the significant contribution of H. S. Harrison (1930), cited in the Introduction, or those of N. C. Nelson (1932), Clellan S. Ford (1937), and J. H. Hutton (1944), but the publication dates for these articles are sufficient to suggest that material-culture studies command little contemporary interest.

The case rests for the treatment of material culture and technology in texts, reference works, and comparative studies. In a nonarchaeological context anthropologists traditionally have dealt with material culture most thoroughly in accounts about particular peoples. Descriptions of clothing, houses, tools, utensils, and so on, provided a data base about worldwide technology. However we find that currently this information is less likely to be included in an ethnography, especially for peoples who used a large number of forms imported from industrial societies. When diverse objects of exotic origins were used, the tendency has been to slight or ignore all but those that made a dramatic impact on the lives of the peoples involved. This means above all else that the cumulative data base about the cultures of aboriginal peoples, or of those undergoing the process of westernization, is more likely to exclude than include any reasonably systematic treatment of material culture. It is frustrating to know that fieldworkers usually are very familiar with the artifacts of a people among whom they lived and that the collecting of data about material culture is less difficult than that for any other block of ethnographic information. There are of course some excellent descriptions of ethnographic material culture by contemporary fieldworkers, but the trend seems to be for manufactures to be reported in increasingly superficial terms.

The remaining text summarizes the technounit approach to the study of material culture and reviews the methodological difficulties encountered when artifacts are analyzed. Then it is demonstrated that a technounit analysis may be applied to the artifacts produced by industrial societies. This section also includes a discussion of the problems encountered when making comparisons of artifacts produced by machines and those crafted with hand tools.

In the formulation of a measure of technological complexity, the first concern was to isolate a primary unit for analysis that would have broad spatiotemporal applicability. The most reasonable point of departure seemed to be to recognize that every artifact is a physical object. By acknowledging further that all artifacts must be made from one or more materials, form or structure in itself is identified as a universal attribute of artifacts. The materials used to make things may be ignored in a basic formulation since everything must be fashioned from something. To assume this perspective is contrary to the manner in which material objects traditionally have been assessed for comparison. The distinction between stone versus metal products long has been considered important, and the same is true for the difference between flaked and ground stone tool industries or between working bamboo as opposed to grass or wood. By not considering specific materials or their differential availability as crucial, comparisons of a different relevance were facilitated.

It was felt that for the unit for analysis to be of universal scope, preeminence could not be accorded to specific production methods or techniques. Furthermore production tools have been ignored because they tend to be culture specific along with the motor habits and skills involved in their use. The purpose behind each exclusion was to negate the impact of particulars for each specific technological tradition in order to evaluate technology within culture rather than for particular cultures. In the basic formulation questions concerning the origin of forms, their spread, and geographical distribution must be ignored. As the approach has been conceived, it does not matter a great deal whether an "aboriginal" technology included only local manufactures or some additional forms received in trade from other indigenous peoples or industrial societies. Once again the traditional comparative framework for evaluating material culture has been set aside as unimportant in the context of the primary evaluative goals.

The crafted configuration resulting in an artifact part has been identified as the most acceptable unit for analysis. Since all artifacts include one or more parts, it seemed logical to consider these as the building blocks of technology. In essence each part manifests specific structural attributes and serves a purpose in an artifact's overall design. For all compound forms the end product, or artifact, represents a configuration that is more than a sum of the parts. The question of what constitutes a part has been central to the entire presentation. I am satisfied that a part defined as a "technounit" is operational in the sense that it may be applied in a reasonably consistent manner in the analysis of diverse manufactures, especially those of aboriginal populations. The definition proposed in Chapter 2 is as follows: a technounit is an integrated, physically distinct, and unique structural configuration that contributes to the form of a finished artifact. When each physical part of an artifact is structurally and functionally distinct, as in a typical spear, one technounit readily may be distinguished from the next. In some artifacts two or more parts may be virtually identical and share a similar purpose; the barbed points of a leister or the rocks of a weir are examples. Each barbed point or rock is a separate part yet with its replicative or duplicative counterparts makes a single structural contribution to the whole. One or more leister points or weir rocks might be removed, and the form still could function, which indicates the unity of structural purpose for the parts. In this context the structural qualities of a leister prong are quite precise while those of weir rocks are not.

When assessing as technounits two identical binders that join different parts, each has been evaluated as distinct. An example is a thong serving as a binder of shaft to vane as opposed to a similar thong joining arrowpoint to shaft. The logic behind the separate nature of these thongs is that each joins a unique structural configuration with respect to the other technounits involved. One might elect to count them as equivalents, but to do so violates the technounit definition.

When parts are totalled for an artifact or for an inventory, all technounits are presumed to be of equal value. The equality is based on the individual contribution of each technounit to a particular form. From this perspective it is presumed further that each technounit was necessary for the form to operate. One alternative to treating each artifact technounit as unique, or regarding all the technounits in an inventory of artifacts as different, is to group technounits. We may, for example, identify categories of technounits on a structural basis depending on whether parts are thick or thin, rigid or pliable, long or short. Alternative distinctions may be drawn on a functional basis, depending on whether a part serves as an anchor, barrier, binder, grip, link, or piercer. The difficulty encountered in attempting to establish structural or functional groups lies in determining degrees of similarity and difference on a consistent and equal basis. Thus far efforts to isolate qualities such as these have not been successful, and as a result each technounit has been judged different from all others.

Even virtually identical technounits that occurred repeatedly in different subsistants for a given inventory are regarded as distinct. A people might have made three different styles of arrows distinguished on the basis of structural differences among the arrowpoints. If each arrow included a shaft, feather vanes, and binders, they were counted as separate technounits every time they occurred. Thus proportionally higher technounit numbers prevail for inventories that included many broadly similar artifacts. Styles of toggle-headed harpoons and fish traps represent forms whose similar parts were counted repeatedly in particular inventories. The net effect was to make the technounit total for a people who used a small number of contrasting forms seem disproportionately low. A people who used many subsistants with diverse parts and produced forms that were structurally similar but functionally distinct had the highest totals. Yet these judgments were consistent, and therefore low versus high technounit numbers represent relative development along a single scale.

When natural materials alone were used to make artifacts, the greater the number of technounits per form for a field of forms or for an inventory, the greater the complexity represented. The discovery of a new material might have made it possible to reduce technounit numbers while increasing the artifact's effectiveness, but the human capacity for this to happen seemingly would be comparable among all peoples. The substitution of antler for a bone and stone combination in a spearpoint might be an example. Yet it would seem that an increase in the number of parts would be a far greater possibility. A one-piece shaft spear of comparatively soft wood could come to include a hard-wood point bound to the end of the softwood shaft. The reason for the greater probability of increasing the numbers of technounits with the use of new materials is that any particular material is inherently limited in its number of possible uses. The perspective is that there were indeed decreases and increases in technounit numbers after compound forms were fashioned in new materials by the conjunction and replication principles, but more important, the trend has been toward greater and greater diversity not only for technological productions but for culture in general.

The introduction of Western manufactures among aboriginal peoples usually produced rapid changes in certain material forms. Metal-bladed tools and metal-pointed weapons usually were accepted rapidly because of their superiority as sharp and durable cutters. Technounit numbers for traditional forms then might be reduced, as apparently was the case for the Tongan hippopotamus harpoon with a barbed point and foreshaft made from a single piece of metal (Reynolds, 1968, Fig. 26). A metal part for a subsistant was taken to represent a single technounit, irrespective of the source of metal or the manner in which it was worked. It was also felt that each metal part of an artifact produced in industrial societies could be "counted" as one unit even when different materials were combined to create a single part. The logic behind this decision is that the number of technounits combined to make artifacts in industrial societies was so much greater than those produced in aboriginal societies that to count the separate materials making up the part would be difficult and not very meaningful. It is notable that when metal replaced another material on already existing forms, its impact on the complexity of a particular inventory appears to have been relatively slight.

Applying a technounit analysis to industrial manufactures raises essentially the same classificatory questions as were posed by aboriginal forms. The problem most often encountered for mass-produced artifacts is how to evaluate parts that are structurally similar but clearly not identical. Each part of an aboriginal form was regarded as distinct if the structural purpose served was different, and the same judgment is reasonable for industrial manufactures. Numerous bolts might be included in a machine, and they might be of identical length and diameter, as well as of similar thread pattern. Yet the bolt heads might be countersunk, hexagonal, rounded, or square. The structural distinctions among these bolt heads are clear, and if each style served a different purpose—as presumably was the case—it must be regarded as unique. The same would apply to an analysis of nails, screws, springs, plates, and so on. However when identical parts, such as the bearings, pistons, rods, and valves in an engine, served essentially the same function, each represented a single technounit. Forms with less exact size and shape continuity, as represented by gradations in the lengths and diameters of nails, collectively represent a single technounit if they served one structural purpose. In each of these analytical decisions the pattern followed for industrial manufactures is the same as that applied to aboriginal manufactures. The greatest contrasts between artifacts produced in aboriginal contexts and those of industrial ones appear to be in the relative number of different forms, technounits per form, and replicative parts within an inventory. With respect to the production principles involved, the distinction between aboriginal and industrial technologies is a quantitative rather than a qualitative one. They employed the same principles but utilized different methods and techniques of production.

Frequently it has been asserted that artifacts produced in industrial societies are likely to include many more parts than those made by aboriginal peoples. For the thirty-six peoples sampled 1175 subsistants were represented, and nearly all the forms were handcrafted by nonspecialists from locally available materials. The greatest number of technounits in a single form was twenty-six for an Iglulik toggle-headed harpoon. Among linked subsistants the highest total was thirty-three for an Angmagsalik toggle-headed harpoon and throwing-board combination. The average number of parts for all the subsistants involved in the study was 3.8.

To illustrate the relative complexity of modern material culture I have most often turned to statements about parts and part inventories. Parts lists for rifles are readily available, and since each part usually is distinctive, each inventory approximates a technounit analysis. We find that a typical Pennsylvania flintlock rifle includes forty-five parts and that the model 1886 Winchester rifle part total is seventy-four (Amber, 1972, 326–7). A model 1881 Marlin has forty-four parts, and the Stevens model 44 has thirty-nine parts (Amber, 1965, 286–7). Compared with aboriginal manufactures the number of parts in a complicated machine is enormous. We find for example that the rear axle assembly of an early Triumph automobile, model 3, has sixty-one technounits (*Service Instruction Manual, TR 2*, n.d., Section F, Fig. 13). One of the difficulties in determining technounit numbers for complicated manufactures from parts books or service manuals is that some parts listed are in fact assemblages of many technounits such as in bearings, compressors, motors, and switches.

For a machine as complicated as a John Deere model 7700 combine, we find that the index to the *Parts Catalog* (John Deere, 7700 Combine, 1973), includes 250 major entry categories for different kinds of units such as auger, brake, control, or housing assemblages. A technounit analysis of this combine might reasonably yield a total of over 5000 parts. We find too that the operation of a typical modern 300 acre vegetable farm in Ventura County, California, requires seventeen different pieces of equipment for tillage and planting, in addition to four tractors and the forms used to harvest particular crops (Brendler and Rock, 1973, 6).

The modern vegetable seed planter is immensely complicated in comparison to its counterpart, the aboriginal digging stick. The planters currently used in Ventura County, California, for such seeds as broccoli, carrot, and tomato have been analyzed in terms of technounits in order to assess the magnitude of their difference from a typical digging stick. The analysis is for the planter units only; not considered are the sled or wheel mountings and carrier bar to which a gang of planters is attached behind a tractor. A planter is designed to dig a shallow furrow, drop seeds, and cover them in a single operation. The most exacting planters deposit one seed at a time at predetermined and highly regular intervals. For the most precise planters two different design principles are involved for dropping the seeds. One form utilizes a continuous belt with holes punched through it at intervals. Seeds drop onto the belt from a hopper, and soon after an individual seed falls into a belt hole, it is pressed out with a repeller belt. The second form has a plate onto which seeds fall from the hopper. Individual seeds drop through notches at the sides of a plate and then onto the ground. The belts have hole sizes gauged to seed size, and the plate notches also are sized to conform with seed sizes. The John Deere vegetable planter number 33 (*Parts Catalog, John Deere, Planter, Vegetable-33*, 1969) is a plate planter with seventy-two technounits. The Stanhay planter (*Stanhay Ltd.*, n.d.) dispenses seeds through holes in a continuous belt; model S766 has seventy-eight technounits and model S870, which is nearly identical, includes eighty-one technounits. For many years the most important crop in Ventura County was lima beans, which because of their shape were most successfully planted with a specialized unit, the Ventura planter (*Ventura Planter*, n.d.). The key to its design is a cupped pickup wheel that revolves through a loose pile of seeds in the hopper and picks up seeds individually, releases them into a boot as the wheel rotates, and then drops them onto the soil. This is not a precision planter, but it is and was the most popular means to plant lima beans. The Ventura planter, model E-1, has thirty-one technounits. The most notable characteristic of the plate and belt planters is that they include nearly the same number of techno-units despite significant differences in the manner in which seeds actually are released. The lima bean planter, which appears to have remained unchanged in basic design for more than forty years, is by far the least complicated but is nonetheless quite specialized. The John Deere and Stanhay planters are each far more versatile and specialized because of the changeable belts and plates for different seed sizes. As the most precise planters the John Deere number 33 and Stanhay S870 have an average of seventy-seven technounits compared with an average of 1.0 for the digging sticks used in farming by the aboriginal peoples sampled.

To count the parts of a hunting rifle, combine, or vegetable seed planter and to compare these forms with a spear, sickle, or digging stick yields a crude but reasonably satisfactory index to the relative complexity of each form. This is so regardless of the differences between industrial and aboriginal cultures in the use of specialized tools and techniques by modern industry as opposed to the use of far more generalized hand tools by aboriginal peoples. It might be felt that for industrial productions recognition must be accorded to casting, forging, lathing, and using machine tools in general. However in the technounit approach manufacturing tools are important only in terms of the artifacts produced. For the same reason an aboriginal awl, drill, or knife used to produce other forms is not taken into account. It is the finished, usable product, not the manner in which it came into being, that commands attention.

So long as aboriginal artifacts are compared only with one another, and modern industrially produced forms are compared only with each other, technounit numbers are a fruitful means for establishing the comparative complexity of an artifact style or for summarizing an inventory at a given point in time. Cross-comparisons are not as satisfactory because of the quantitative differences, and other factors must be considered that affect manufactures, especially industrial productions, over long periods of time. Technounit totals alone do not always reflect complexity for specific styles of forms at different points in time. Examples exist in aboriginal inventories but are far more common for industrial manufactures. For instance, a contemporary automobile includes about 15,000 parts, whereas those made in 1940 had about half as many parts and presumably were simpler. Efforts currently are being made by some manufacturers to decrease the number of parts in automobiles to be produced in the near future (McGuire, 1975, 4). The reduction of part numbers presumably can be achieved only by redefining what is necessary for the functioning of an automobile and by consolidating the structures of previously discrete parts. When new sources of energy are tapped or novel design principles are conceived and applied, the number of parts for a form or assembly may decrease abruptly. Presumably this is what happened in the change from reciprocating to jet aircraft engines, in the shift from vacuum tubes to early transistors, and from the standard piston engine for automobiles to the experimental Wankel engine. A Wankel engine, which has nearly the same horsepower as a piston engine, is less than half as large, weighs about thirty percent less, and has about forty percent fewer parts (Salpukas, 1972, 6). In each instance application of new design principles led to reductions in the number of parts. Thus the number of technounits in industrially produced items clearly may be reduced, indicating technological advances, and the reduction may occur for any field of forms. Similar technounit number decreases for aboriginal forms have occurred repeatedly but never as much as for industrially made artifacts.

Reductions in technounit numbers seldom were identified in the subsistants for the peoples sampled, which is to be expected since a single point in time was represented for the inventories. It would appear that one form usually prevailed for a given purpose at any particular time. There were, however, instances of apparently competing forms with different technounit totals. The Klamath made certain arrows that appear to have been designed to skip across water to kill waterfowl. Typically the arrowpoint was made from wood with a pitch and sinew binder near the tip. However a bulge sometimes was carved as a collar beneath the point, and this served as an alternative to the sinew and pitch combination. Only the three-part form was entered in the Klamath inventory since it appears to have been the dominant form. The wood bulge may represent an integrative design principle resulting in a reduction of technounits. From these data we know only that the three-technounit form was most typical, but the potential clearly existed for the one-technounit arrowpoint to replace the three-part form. At the same time it also is possible that the one-part arrowpoint was found to be inadequate, which led to the use of sinew and pitch as a replacement for the bulge. In this and similar cases it is essential to know the cultural history of a particular form before any meaningful judgment can be offered about the direction of change.

An example of an increase in structural complexity for a single technounit is found in an Angmagsalik harpoon for hunting seals at breathing holes in ice. A shaft might be smooth or have raised rings as finger rests; both forms appear to have been acceptable (Thalbitzer, 1914, 419). In terms of technounit number each shaft is represented by a single unit, but there is a refinement of structure for the one with rings, presumably for greater efficiency. This is what I term *design amplification*, meaning that the basic structure of a technounit is elaborated without the addition of a separate technounit. For instance, the structure of an awl changed when it became an eyed needle. Perhaps a better example is the spear made by the Tiwi from a single piece of wood. Hunting spears appear to have been pointed only at one end, but the spears used in warfare had elaborate arrangements of barbs at the head of the shaft (Basedow, 1913, 302–3; Spencer, 1914, 368–75).

Counting the number of technounits for aboriginal manufactures is a rather exacting gauge to relative technological complexity, and this is true even when metals were used in comparatively small numbers of forms. If industrial technologies are assessed in terms of technounits, the totals again yield a measure of comparative complexity. When a style of artifact is considered over time, it is apparent that technounit number may shift from low to high or from high to low. Smaller numbers indicate either a more basic configuration or improvements within a single technological tradition. The same is true for all similar forms compared on a cross-cultural basis. To acknowledge that technounit number may decrease for a style or field of forms over time does no violence to the thesis that the overall and long-term trend in material culture has been toward ever-increasing numbers of technounits.

A decrease in the number of technounits that results in increased complexity is largely attributable to the contrast between the use of natural materials as they are found and materials whose molecular structure is changed prior to or during artifact production. Natural materials, such as bone, grass, wood, and stone, are simply reduced in size by aboriginal peoples to create technounits. Materials whose structures are changed by chemical means form a second cluster; bronze, plastic, pottery, and steel products are representative. The basic process involved was known both in aboriginal and modern societies; the difference is one of degree. With the physical amalgamation of diverse materials a technounit of a different order is produced. When more different materials are combined as technounits in a form, the complexity is increased, and greater industrial development is represented. Modern technologies are built on the ever-increasing utilization of innovative materials that are in and of themselves more complicated than natural materials. The net result is greater change through diversity and recombination. Thus it is the difference in types of materials used to make things that most clearly separates aboriginal from modern technologies.

A technounit analysis of food-getting artifacts calls attention to the simplicity of the subsistants used by aboriginal peoples, whereas even a brief review of the parts of forms used in modern agricultural technology indicates that it is extraordinarily complex by comparison. I have suggested that the production principles identified prevail for all manufactures, industrial and nonindustrial alike, and that no novel production principle has been developed within the last 10,000 years. Admittedly no effort has been made to detail these production principles for industrially produced artifacts, but to do so does not seem necessary given the focus of the study. It does seem clear that technounits are important for the evaluation of artifacts produced by reduction, conjunction, and replication, or those produced by these principles and then joined by linkage. Even if other production principles are identified, it is likely that they would be amenable to a technounit analysis. In the designing of modern artifacts it seems that increased attention will be devoted to lowering technounit numbers while at the same time increasing effectiveness. This endeavor will require design amplifications that integrate the separate functions and structures of discrete technounits. What appears to be necessary in these productions is to acknowledge the distinctions among reduction, conjunction, and replication principles while at the same time integrating them in the creation of a given technounit or form. Perhaps it is plastics as deformable materials that hold the greatest potential for achieving a new level of integration. Time and again it has been demonstrated that highly complex modern machinery cannot be maintained in the absence of elaborate support systems, which is why Western exports often have failed among peoples who welcomed the advantages that the artifacts provided. To reduce the number of parts for forms while preserving their purpose and effectiveness would surely be a great service to all of mankind. This is what I meant by stating that technology today is underdeveloped in terms of our future needs and desires.

The goal of this book, the measurement of technological complexity on a cross-cultural basis, has been set forth repeatedly in general terms. It is now appropriate to identify the specific origins of the approach and then to define its limitations. In the initial formulation the concepts of culture core and cultural ecology as developed by Julian H. Steward were of critical importance. In order to study cultural ecology Steward (1955, 40) stated, "First the interrelationship of exploitative or productive technology and environment must be analyzed." He wrote that all material culture may not be of equal importance, and he accorded primacy to subsistence-related devices. I have interpreted his position narrowly and have focused on subsistants as the technological forms most crucial in obtaining food. From my perspective subsistants are more important than the clothing and housing, containers, and transportation devices which Steward would include. Steward's second procedure in the study of cultural ecology was to consider "the behavior patterns involved in the exploitation of a particular area by means of a particular technology," and finally "to ascertain the extent to which the behavior patterns entailed in exploiting the environment affect other aspects of culture" (Steward, 1955, 40–1). The present study is addressed solely to Steward's first procedure, determining food-getting technologies, narrowly defined, in environmental contexts. To set this restrictive goal is justified on the basis of reasonable priorities. It was essential to develop a means of measuring similarities and differences for a given set of manufactures before detailed comparisons could be made; the technounit concept was originated for this purpose. Although the social patterns of subsistence activities have not been considered, a technounit analysis of the artifacts involved may be extended to include the social contexts of use. For example, all the tended sets used by a sample of peoples may be analyzed by technounits. Those forms employed by a lone individual may be separated from those managed by two or more persons. This comparison would provide an index to cooperative effort and its correlation with technological complexity as reflected in the artifacts involved. Technounit comparisons for clothing, tools, utensils, vehicles, and so on, may be made, focused on such variables as comparative community mobility, craft specialization, and social status. It is clear that counting the number of parts constituting artifacts other than subsistants can be profitable when answers are sought to questions about the integration of material, mental, and social culture.

The subsistant taxonomy and technounit concept, as classificatory devices, are neutral with reference to the uses of material culture. Therefore the data about food-getting forms were ordered in terms of the foraging or farming economy of the peoples represented and by the type of habitat they occupied. This arrangement was made in order to determine whether differential complexity was a reflection of the technoeconomic adaptations of the peoples sampled. As summarized at the close of Chapter 9, there were indeed major differences. The forms used by intensive hunters were much more likely to be complex than those used by intensive farmers. Peoples in desert and tropical areas were likely to use less complex forms than those who occupied temperate to arctic regions. Intensive hunters tended to have far more complex food-getting technologies than did intensive gatherers; foragers in deserts reflected greater complexity than did farmers in deserts. On a more particular basis the Tiwi had the simplest subsistants, and the Angmagsalik the most complicated in terms of average numbers of technounits. Thus this analysis does yield quantitative differences among the forms used by given populations. It remains to be demonstrated whether the nearly identical technounit averages for the sample of tropical root crop cultivators prevails for other peoples with the same economic focus. It also remains to be established whether the biased nature of the sample of desert farmers, all of whom are from the southwestern United States, was one reason for a technounit average lower than that reported for foragers in desert settings. Any detailed study of subsistant ecology would require consideration of factors such as the specific characteristics of a habitat exploited, trophic levels of food products, biomass represented, and species diversity, preferably for different peoples in similar settings.

Subsistants, as food-getting forms, have been identified exclusively on a functional basis. Before any artifact can be analyzed as a subsistant, its purpose in an ethnographic context must be either known or presumed. A hunting spear is a subsistant, but a spear used exclusively for warfare is not unless the victims were eaten. Therefore one of the greatest limitations of the technounit approach to the study of subsistants as such is inadequate documentation about the uses of artifacts. Fortunately most ethnographers discuss the functions of the forms that they describe. Ethnographies are unsatisfactory when they do not include all of the forms in customary use and all of the parts for these forms. Unfortunately a typical account often is deficient in one or the other of these requirements, and the same is true for most musuem collections and their accompanying field notes. As a result the potential data base is more restrictive than might be envisioned despite the vast amount of ethnographic information that has been collected. Yet there are enough good to excellent material-culture inventories to analyze all of the major technoeconomic adaptations by habitat around the world. Within most geographical areas the systematic comparison of subsistants by population is difficult except for well-studied peoples such as aboriginal Australians, California Indians, and Eskimos. For other peoples documentation often is expansive for particular clusters of forms such as bows and arrows, fishhooks, and harpoons, which makes additional comparative studies possible on a regional or localized basis. Nonsubsistants may of course be analyzed in terms of their technounits. Comparisons of ceremonial objects, garments, musical instruments, and so on, are feasible. When questions about developmental sequences or comparative complexity are involved, a consideration of technounits fosters far greater insights than may be realized by most other means of comparison.

Artifacts whose uses are unknown cannot be analyzed in the manner of subsistants but still can be studied profitably in terms of their form alone. Evaluations of technounits could produce more precise statements about structural configurations and production principles than those currently prevailing. For archaeological materials the technounit approach is limited in applicability because the purposes served by diverse forms cannot be established with certainty and because most finds consist of artifact technounits rather than complete forms. Yet structural trends may be established by technounit numbers for clusters of similar forms through time or at a given point in time. Thus in the evaluation of items of material culture whose different kinds of parts are an important consideration, the technounit approach may be useful. The greatest barrier to this or any other innovative analysis of material culture is curatorial and ethnological tradition.

Given the material basis of all human lifeways and the scope of anthropological research, this book has attempted to establish a culture-wide basis for the analysis of technology. The concept of a technounit has been offered as a common denominator for the analysis of all artifacts in terms of their comparative complexity. A technounit assessment of forms not only provides a cross-cultural measure of accomplishments for given points in time but also is a gauge to evolutionary trends. The approach is novel and clearly apart from most contemporary anthropological concerns. Ethnologists have tended to evaluate the manufactures of aboriginal peoples as adaptive and with rare exceptions uncomplicated. For the peoples sampled herein, a technounit analysis of food-getting forms clearly demonstrates that they were simple but far from homogeneous. The difference in complexity between Angmagsalik and Aranda artifacts or between those of the Lepcha and Pima are of sufficient magnitude to encourage further studies of subsistants, especially with reference to ecological and social factors. The technounit approach, imperfect though it may be, makes it more difficult to ignore, in good conscience, the artifacts of aboriginal peoples in the detailed study of culture on a comparative basis.

Not so many years ago anthropologists contended that one rationale for studying aboriginal peoples, with their comparatively simple life-styles, was to better understand the basis for the complexities of life in modern industrial societies. This position has lost favor, possibly because it promised so much and produced so little, yet it has special merit with reference to technology. This is so if only because of the clear continuity from primeval to modern developments. To identify measurable units in technology that crosscut all cultures and accommodate change through time becomes a basis for diverse comprehensive, comparative studies of material culture.

The intellectual thrust of anthropology has expanded and diversified immensely since the discipline emerged in the midnineteenth century. About 100 years ago, in 1875, Lane-Fox Pitt-Rivers detailed his approach to the comparative analysis of material culture, but ethnologists have neither pursued the leads he provided nor made broad-scale studies of material culture from other perspectives having comparable breadth. No one doubts that man is a tool-making animal and that there is a material basis for much of human behavior. Our collective tomorrows surely are destined to be molded by the things that we make, and we would do well to become more conscious of the parts of artifacts as they help identify the complexity of our material heritage.

▲▲▲▲▲▲▲▲

SUBSISTANTS
AND THEIR
TECHNOUNITS

The lists to follow are subsistant inventories for the thirty-six peoples sampled. In Part 2 these subsistants are classified as instruments, weapons, tended facilities, or untended facilities, and their uses are reported. Part 3 is devoted to comparisons of these same subsistant inventories in terms of habitat groupings. It would be ideal to describe the technounits for each form reported in Parts 2 and 3; however to do so is not practical since the inventories alone span about 200 manuscript pages. Therefore a complete inventory, with each technounit itemized, is presented for one people in each of the nine ecological and technoeconomic clusters. Thus for desert foragers the complete Aranda inventory has been included, while the full Yuma inventory represents desert farmers, and so on. The particular inventories described in detail were selected for a number of reasons. The Tiwi were chosen because they were one of the peoples with the fewest forms, and the Ingalik because they had the highest number of technounits. The Aymara and Yuma subsistants have been detailed to illustrate the quality of inventories that are not as complete as might be hoped. The Tasmanians have been included because of the general interest in them and because of the simplicity of their technology. The Aranda, Iglulik, Kapauku, and Sema Naga were selected to represent further variability among subsistants. For the other twenty-seven peoples, subsistants have been listed with only the number of technounits for each form.

An effort has been made to maintain reasonably consistent subsistant and technounit designations despite the varied descriptions in ethnographies. When this goal could not be achieved, the ethnographer's terminology usually was followed. For example, most descriptions of arrows focused on the species taken, but in some accounts arrows are described primarily or exclusively in terms of their structure. When these two styles of presentation could not be reconciled, the arrow descriptions are inconsistent; traps and their parts often posed a similar problem.

In the inventories the name of a form appears first, and this is sometimes followed by an alternative designation in parentheses. A form's use is not specified when it seems obvious from the descriptive designation. However a primary use is entered when appropriate, and secondary uses may be added in parentheses. In the descriptions an ampersand indicates the combined use of two forms, for example, emu guide & poison; however *each is counted as a separate subsistant*. Any use combination that is quite obvious, such as bows and arrows, is not identified. To distinguish use combinations that are more secondary, forms often are listed as "used with" other forms, for example, brush blind used with weapons.

Abbreviation Key

   tu   technounit(s)
   N   naturefact
   A   assumed technounit, function, material, structure, or subsistant
   AA   all technounits assumed
   ah   animal husbandry
   fa   farming
   &   separates subsistants

1   *Surprise Valley Paiute*
Numbers in parentheses refer to pages in Kelly (1932).

Instruments

Simple

1 tu: long stick, dislodge pinecones N (99); stick, impale (remove) rat in (from) burrow N (89); straight stick twisted in skin, remove squirrel from hiding place (remove skunk suffocated by smoke) N (87); stick, kill deer in pitfall N (82)

2 tu: digging stick (101)

3 tu: tool used as ice pick for fishing *AA* (96)

6 tu: seed beater (fish scoop), 1 tu*A* (95, 129–30)

Weapons

Simple

1 tu: stick, kill young geese (mud hens) N (90); short stick, kill sage hens, used with antelope disguise N (89); club, kill fish, used with basket trap (96)

3 tu: leister, used at hole in ice, 1 tu*A* (96)

Complex

5 tu: sinew-backed bow (142–3)

6 tu: toggle-headed *A* fish harpoon, may be used with blind, 1 tu*A* (96)

10 tu: arrow total: fish, 1 tu; bird (small game), 3 tu; big game, 6 tu, 1 tu*A* (96, 143–5)

Tended facilities

Simple

1 tu: straight stick, drive groundhog from burrow N (87); hooked stick, remove groundhog from burrow N (87); torch, encircle deer, used with bow & arrow (attract porcupine; smoke to suffocate skunk in burrow, removed with stick) (82, 87); dry tree thrust into cave, impede movement of bear, used with bow & arrow (86–7); tule blind, used with fish harpoon (96)

2 tu: antelope brush guide, 1 tu, & surround, 1 tu, used with bow & arrow (83–4); deer blind pit, 1 tu, & guides, 1 tu, used with bow & arrow (82); pit blind for sage hens, captured by hand (89)

3 tu: rope surround for antelope, used with bow & arrow (84–5; 86); rabbit spread net, 2 tu*A* (88)

4 tu: pitfall for deer, used with deer-killing stick, 1 tu*A* (81–2); duck blind, 1 tu, & lures, 3 tu, used with bow & arrow (90); basket fish trap, used with club *AA* (95–6, 125)

5 tu: antelope disguise, used with bow & arrow (mud hen-killing stick) (82–3, 116)

7 tu: spread net for sage hens, 6 tu, 1 tu*A*, & pit blind, 1 tu (89)

Untended facilities

Simple

2 tu: rabbit snare (88)

3 tu: weir-trap (96)

Complex

3 tu: spring-pole snare, sage hens (89)

6 tu: squirrel deadfall (87–8)

	Subsistants	Technounits	Average
Foraging total	39	97	2.5

2 *Aranda (Arunta)*

Instruments

Simple

1 tu: seed-removal stick N (Albrecht, n.d.)
       digging stick (Spencer and Gillen, 1927, v.1, 23–4; Stirling, 1896, 96)
       grub hook (Albrecht, n.d.)

4 tu: ax, remove animals (eggs, honey): stone blade + wood handle + sinew, handle binder + resin, blade-handle binder (Spencer and Gillen, 1927, v.2, 548–50)

Weapons

Simple

1 tu: missile stick (boomerang) (Spencer and Gillen, 1927, v.1, 17, v.2, 530–4; Stirling, 1896, 92–3)

5 tu: leister: wood point + reed shaft + resin, point-shaft binder + sinew, point-shaft binder + sinew binding on butt of shaft (National Museum of Victoria; Chewings, 1936, 28)

Complex

6 tu: throwing-board, used with spear: wood shaft + wood peg + sinew, shaft-peg binder + resin, shaft-peg binder + stone flake + resin, shaft-flake binder (Spencer and Gillen, 1927, v.2, 525–7)

9 tu: spear, used with throwing-board: wood point + wood barb + sinew, point-barb binder + wood foreshaft + wood shaft + sinew, point-foreshaft binder + resin, point-foreshaft binder + sinew, foreshaft-shaft binder + resin, foreshaft-shaft binder (National Museum of Victoria; Spencer and Gillen, 1927, v.2, 523–4; Stirling, 1896, 87)

Tended facilities

Simple

1 tu: torch, drive game, killed with weapons (Stirling, 1896, 51)
brush (branch) fish sweep (Albrecht, n.d.)
brush kangaroo guide, used with spear (Albrecht, n.d.)
stone blind at water hole for emu, used with weapons (Stirling, 1896, 52)

3 tu: emu guide & poison: brush guide fence + mud A dam ; + crushed poisonous leaves (Stirling, 1896, 52)
emu lure, used with weapons: head + neck + binders AA (Spencer and Gillen, 1927, v.1, 16–7)

Untended facility

Simple

4 tu: emu pitfall: pit + upright spear in pit + brush cover + earth cover (Spencer and Gillen, 1927, v.1, 17)

	Subsistants	Technounits	Average
Foraging total	16	42	2.6

3 *Naron Bushmen*

Numbers in parentheses refer to pages in Bleek (1928).

Instruments

Simple

1 tu: digging stick (7, 14, 49)
4 tu: game-removal hook, might be used with missile stick (15, 16)

Weapons

  Simple

    1 tu: missile stick (digger, club) (14, 16)
    3 tu: spear (14)

  Complex

    5 tu: self bow (13)
    10 tu: arrow total: bone point, 5 tu; iron point, 5 tu (13–4)

Tended facilities

  Simple

    1 tu: termite trap hole (16–7); torch, burn area for game (17)
    3 tu: pit blind, hunting (16)

Untended facilities

  Simple

    4 tu: baited bird snare (15)

  Complex

    7 tu: small mammal spring-pole snare (15)

	Subsistants	Technounits	Average
Foraging total	12	40	3.3

4 *Owens Valley Paiute*
Numbers in parentheses refer to pages in Steward (1933).

Instruments

  Simple

    1 tu: digging stick (239, 244, 245, 255); irrigation ditch-clearing pole (247)
    3 tu: pinecone-removal pole (241)
    4 tu: seed beater (239, 244–5, 272)

Weapons

  Simple

    1 tu: club, kill game, used with rabbit net (253–4)
    3 tu: leister, may be used at weir, 1 tuA (251)

Complex

  2 tu: self bow (259)
  4 tu: sinew-backed bow (259–60)
34 tu: arrow total: fish, 3 tu, 1 tu*A*; rabbit, 6 tu; duck, 7 tu; bird, 8 tu; game, 10 tu, 2 tu*A* (251, 260–3)

Tended facilities

Simple

  1 tu: torch, smoke out burrowing animal (bring down caterpillar from tree, taken in pitfall; drive deer, killed with arrow) (253, 255, 256); brush, mountain sheep surround, presumably used with bow & arrow (253)
  2 tu: weir, used with poison (arrow; leister; carrying basket trap) (251)
  3 tu: deer disguise, used with bow & arrow, 1 tu*A* (252)
  4 tu: fishhook assembly, 2 tu*A* (251); rabbit spread net, used with club, 3 tu*A* (253–4); seine, 3 tu*A* (252)
  5 tu: hunting blind, used with weapons (255, 265)
  6 tu: fish poison, 1 tu, & container, 5 tu, used with weir (arrow; leister) (251)

Untended facilities

Simple

  1 tu: caterpillar pitfall, used with torch (256)
  8 tu: conical carrying basket (open twined basket as fish scoop trap), used as fish trap at weir, 1 tu*A* (251, 272)

Complex

  4 tu: deer (mountain sheep) trap *AA* (252); rabbit (wildcat) spring-pole snare (254)
  7 tu: small-game deadfall (254)

	Subsistants	Technounits	Average
Foraging total	28	107	3.8

5 *Pima*

Numbers in parentheses refer to pages in Russell (1908).

Instruments

Simple

1 tu: digging stick, clear plot (dig irrigation canal; work soil; plant crop; collect plants) *fa* (70, 88, 97); wood shovel, dig irrigation canal *fa* (88, 97); wood hoe, cultivate crop (cut weeds) *fa* (88, 97); tongs, collect cactus fruit (71, 103); stick *A*, remove thorns from prickly pear to collect fruit (75)

3 tu: ax, clear plot *fa* (88, 110); saguaro fruit-dislodging pole (103)

Weapons

Simple

1 tu: club, used with bow & arrow, take squirrel driven from burrow with water (81)

Complex

3 tu: self bow (95, Pl. 13)

9 tu: arrow total: small game, pointed shaft, 4 tu; big game, stone point, 5 tu, 1 tu*A* (82, 95, 96, 111)

Tended facilities

Simple

1 tu: stick, prod gopher from burrow (beat down thorny bush containing edible berries) N (76, 82); water poured down squirrel burrow, used with club (bow & arrow) (81)

Complex

5 tu: bird deadfall (81, 101)

Untended facilities

Simple

1 tu: cholla ring, protect individual plants from predators at night *fa* (92)

2 tu: plot fence #1, stakes and withes *AA fa* (88); plot fence #2, mesquite and brush *fa* (88)

	Subsistants	Technounits	Average
Foraging	10	25	2.5
Farming	7	11	1.6
Total	17	36	2.1

6 *Walapai*
Numbers in parentheses refer to pages in Kroeber (1935).

Instruments

Simple

1 tu: forked-stick seed beater (pick cactus fruit) N (51, 55); stick, knock squawberries into basket N (55); barbed stick, pull chuckwalla from crevice N (64, 68, 94); hammerstone, used with mescal chisel N (48, 52); pole, knock fruit from Spanish dagger N (52); crooked stick, dislodge pinecones (49, 54); tongs, retrieve cactus fruit (48, 49, 50, 51); branch, brush spines from cactus fruit (48, 50, 51); mescal chisel, used with hammerstone (48, 49, 52, 57); digging stick, planting (cultivating) *fa* (57, 58, 98); hand shovel, dig irrigation ditch (remove fox from burrow) *fa* (58, 60, 63)

2 tu: rabbit(rat)-removal stick twisted in animal's fur (63, 64, 67, 94, 96); seed beater (48, 49, 55–6, 80–1)

3 tu: retrieval hook, obtain fruit from cactus (48, 49, 56, 97)

Weapons

Simple

1 tu: stick, club small game N (63;) stone, kill rabbit N (63, 67)

Complex

2 tu: self bow (92)

32 tu: arrow total: bird, 5 tu, 2 tu*A*; wood point, small game *A*, 5 tu, 1 tu*A*; stone point, big game $\sharp$1 *A*, 10 tu, 5 tu*A*; stone point, big game $\sharp$2, 12 tu, 6 tu*A* (64, 68, 92–4)

Tended facilities

Simple

1 tu: stick, prod rat from burrow, killed with bow & arrow N (67); long pole, remove fox from burrow, used with club (bow & arrow) (63); crook, remove rat (rabbit) from burrow, killed with club (stick; bow & arrow) (61, 64, 67, 94, 97); torch, drive fox (rat) from burrow, used with hand shovel or club (drive rat from burrow, killed with bow & arrow) (63, 64, 68); stone blind for antelope (deer, mountain sheep), used with bow & arrow (61, 62, 65); brush *A* plug in hole of

fox, used with club (bow & arrow) (63); deerskin disguise, used with
bow & arrow (61, 65); doeskin disguise, used with bow & arrow (65)

3 tu : rabbit spread net, 1 tuA (63–4, 82)

6 tu : antelope disguise, used with bow & arrow, 1 tuA (62, 65)

Untended facilities

Simple

1 tu : brush plot fence *fa* (58, 60)

2 tu : pigeon snare (64, 69)

Complex

9 tu : small-animal guide, 1 tu, & deadfall, 8 tu (62–3, 64; Spier, 1928, 113)

	Subsistants	Technounits	Average
Foraging	32	80	2.5
Farming	3	3	1.0
Total	35	83	2.4

7 *Hopi*

Instruments

Simple

1 tu : digging stick, planting (retrieve burrowing animals) *fa* (Hough,
1919, 236; Stephen, 1936, 732, 983, 1035–6); wood hand trowel, tend
plants *fa* (Hough, 1919, 236); split wood tongs, pick prickly pear fruit
(Hough, 1919, 237); wood weed cutter *fa* (Forde, 1931b, 389; Hough,
1919, 236)

2 tu : hoe, weed plot (*A* make irrigation ditch; form rivulet to drive
prairie dog from burrow, killed with stick) *fa* (Forde, 1931b, 389;
Hough, 1919, 236, 271)

3 tu : rake, clear brush from plot *fa* (Hough, 1919, 237); knife, slaughter
domestic animals *AA ah* (Titiev, 1944, 194)

Weapons

Simple

1 tu : club, kill game N (Titiev, 1944, 191); missile stone, game N (Hough,

1919, 285); prairie dog-killing stick, used with hoe to form rivulet N (Hough, 1919, 285); missile stick, small game (Beaglehole, 1936, 12; Hough, 1919, 276, 285, 287)

Complex

3 tu: self bow, 1 tu*A* (Hough, 1919, 287–8)
5 tu: arrow, 1 tu*A* (Hough, 1919, 271, 288)

Tended facilities

Simple

1 tu: antelope-head hunting disguise (Hough, 1919, 285); crook, herd sheep *ah* (Hough, 1919, 239); lasso, capture domestic animals *A* (obtain mountain sheep driven to rock ledges) *ah* (Beaglehole, 1936, 11); water, rivulet made with hoe to drive prairie dog from burrow, killed with stick (Hough, 1919, 285); natural enclosure & man-made gate for taking antelope, killed with bow & arrow *A* (Stephen, 1936, 149); torch, drive antelope, used with man-made guides and natural enclosure (Stephen, 1936, 278)

5 tu: antelope guides, 2 tu, & surround, 3 tu, 1 tu*A*, used with torch to drive animals and bow & arrow (Hough, 1919, 285; Stephen, 1936, 278)

Untended facilities

Simple

1 tu: stone terraces for irrigated plots *fa* (Forde, 1931b, 391); brush dam in gullies, build level of cultivated plots (prevent erosion) *fa* (Hough, 1898, 147); windbreak, brush piles to protect crop *fa* (Forde, 1931b, 389, 391; Hough, 1898, 147; Stephen, 1936, 389); stone cairn scare, protect crop from prairie dogs (protect sheep from wildcats) *fa* (Stephen, 1936, 390); hobbles for horses (burros), leather strap *A ah* (Hough, 1919, 238; Titiev, 1944, 194–5)

2 tu: barrier, 1 tu, & wrappings, 1 tu, protect peach trees from sheep (burros) *fa* (Forde, 1931b, 394); corral for livestock, 1 tu*A ah* (Hough, 1919, 239)

3 tu: bell, grazing animals, 1 tu*A ah* (Hough, 1919, 238, 278)

4 tu: bird snare (Beaglehole, 1936, 17; Hough, 1919, 285)

7 tu: scare, protect crop, 2 tu*A fa* (Hough, 1919, 237)

13 tu: scarecrow, 6 tu*A fa* (Stephen, 1936, 390)

Complex

5 tu: deadfall #1 (Beaglehole, 1936, 17–8, Fig. 2; Hough, 1919, 286)
8 tu: deadfall #2 (Beaglehole, 1936, 17–8, Fig. 1; Stephen, 1936, 188)

	Subsistants	Technounits	Average
Foraging	16	39	2.4
Farming	13	34	2.6
Animal husbandry	6	11	1.8
Total	35	84	2.4

8 Yuma

Numbers in parentheses refer to pages in Forde (1931a).

Instruments

Simple

1 tu: stone knife, fell trees to clear plot *fa* (110, 123)
digging stick, plant seeds *fa* (97, 110, 112)
wood weed cutter *fa* (112)

Weapons

Simple

2 tu: hunting knife: stone blade + sinew wrapped handle (170)

Complex

2 tu: self bow: wood shaft + sinew bowstring (170–1)
14 tu: arrow total (171–2)
fish, 3 tu: wood point *A* + shaft + point-shaft binder *A*
animal #1, 5 tu: wood point + cane shaft + feather vanes + gum,
vane-shaft binder + sinew, vane-shaft binder
animal #2, 6 tu: stone point + arrowweed shaft + sinew, point-shaft
binder + feather vanes + gum, vane-shaft binder + sinew, vane-
shaft binder

Tended facilities

Simple

1 tu: torch, clear plot *fa* (110, 123)

4 tu : fishhook assembly: cactus spine hook + bait A + line + sinker A
(119)

fish scoop net: netting + crossed stick frame + frame binder +
frame-net binder (119–20)

5 tu : seine: netting + vertical net support rods + rod-net binders +
poles at net ends + pole-rod-net binder A (119–20)

Untended facilities

Simple

3 tu : fish trap: vertical rods arranged in semicircle with opening + brush
fencing A + seeds as bait (119–20)

5 tu : scarecrow, protect crop *fa*: vertical A poles + reeds as pole wrapping + sherds, noisemakers + stones, noisemakers + noisemaker-
pole-reed binders A (113)

	Subsistants	Technounits	Average
Foraging	9	34	3.8
Farming	5	9	1.8
Total	14	43	3.1

9 Tiwi

Instruments

Simple

1 tu : honey-removal stick (Basedow, 1913, 300)
digging stick (Goodale, 1971, 168, 189)

4 tu : ax, remove animals: stone blade + withe handle + bark string,
blade-handle binder + resin, blade-handle binder (Goodale, 1971,
154–6, 162–8; Spencer, 1914, 355–6)

Weapons

Simple

1 tu : missile stick (club) N (Goodale, 1957, 30, 32)
missile stone N (Goodale, 1957, 30)
missile stick (club) (Basedow, 1913, 300–1; Spencer, 1914, 368–75)
fish club (Spencer, 1914, 372–3)

shaft spear (Basedow, 1913, 302–3; Spencer, 1914, 359–66)
long, straight goose-killing missile stick (Goodale, 1957, 24–5)

Tended facilities

Simple

  1 tu: animal-probing stick (Goodale, 1957, 11, 30; 1971, 162)
        torch, smoke out opossum (Goodale, 1957, 31)

	Subsistants	Technounits	Average
Foraging total	11	14	1.3

10 *Ingura*
Numbers in parentheses refer to pages in Tindale (1925–8).

Instruments

Simple

  1 tu: honey-removal stick N (82); digging stick (77); stone knife, remove
        honeycomb (82, 95, 98, 131)

Weapons

Simple

  1 tu: missile stone, birds N (80)

Complex

  1 tu: wood shaft spear, used with throwing-board (93)
  3 tu: multipronged leister #1, used with throwing-board (93); multi-
        pronged leister #2, used with throwing-board (93)
  5 tu: throwing-board, used with leisters (spears) (98)
  6 tu: dugong (turtle) harpoon dart (78–9, 93)

Tended facilities

Simple

  1 tu: torch, drive game (80)
  3 tu: weir (81)
  4 tu: fishhook assembly (81–2)

Untended facility

Simple

2 tu: fish-catching platform below waterfall (81)

	Subsistants	Technounits	Average
Foraging total	13	32	2.5

11 *Chenchu*
Numbers in parentheses refer to pages in Fürer-Haimendorf (1943).

Instruments

Simple

1 tu: pole, dislodge fruit N (64); wood spatula, honey retrieval (34, 66–7); string (tied to arrow), honey retrieval (66)

2 tu: line and toggle, honey retrieval (34, 66–7); ax, chop down trees (branches) for fruit (game) (33, 58)

3 tu: digging stick, roots (tubers) #1 (29); digging stick, roots (tubers) #2 (29)

Weapons

Simple

1 tu: stick as club N (69); missile stones N (69)

Complex

4 tu: composite bow (30–1)

20 tu: arrow total: sharp bamboo point, 4 tu; blunt bamboo point, small bird, 4 tu; metal, leaf-shaped point, 6 tu; metal, spike point, 6 tu (31–2)

Tended facilities

Simple

1 tu: stones, drive game, killed with bow & arrow N (67–8); sticks, drive game, killed with bow & arrow N (67–8)

2 tu: fish poison (71)

3 tu: leaf blind, used with bow & arrow, 2 tu*A* (68); torch, smoke bees from nest, used with honey-removal spatula, 1 tu*A* (66)

Complex

6 tu: metal blunted point arrow, decoy game (31–2)

	Subsistants	Techounits	Average
Foraging total	20	55	2.8

12 *Andamanese*

Numbers in parentheses without an author name refer to pages in Radcliffe-Brown (1948).

Instruments

Simple

1 tu: digging stick (418, 476); hook-ended crabbing stick (476)
3 tu: fruit-picking hook (418, 476; Man, 1883, 398); adz, remove mollusks (obtain honeycomb) (418, 449–50)

Weapons

Simple

4 tu: multipronged leister (444)

Complex

6 tu: self bow (423–6)
21 tu: arrow total: fish, 8 tu; detachable-pointed, pig, 13 tu (435–9)

Tended facilities

Simple

5 tu: dip net, 4 tu, 1 tu*A*, & poison, 1 tu (417–8, 471–2; Man, 1883, 366, 399)
7 tu: turtle (fish) net (442–3)

	Subsistants	Technounits	Average
Foraging total	11	51	4.6

13 *Jivaro*

Numbers in parentheses are to Harner (1972), Karsten (1935), or Stirling (1938).

Instruments

Simple

1 tu: digging stick, planting (harvesting) tubers or corms (retrieve agouties) *fa* (Harner, 50, 59); planting pole, plant seed crop *fa* (Harner, 50; Karsten, 127, 129, 139); wood knife, clear (weed) plot *fa* (Harner, 65; Karsten, 127)

3 tu: stone ax, clear plot (obtain wild plant products or insects), 2 tu*A fa* (Harner, 62; Karsten, 127)

Weapons

Simple

1 tu: barbed, wood shaft leister (Harner, 61; Karsten, 176)

Complex

4 tu: fish harpoon dart (Karsten, 175–6)
5 tu: blowgun (Harner, 57–8; Karsten, 156–7)
9 tu: poisoned blowgun dart (Karsten, 153, 157; Stirling, 84)

Tended facilities

Simple

1 tu: torch, clear plot *fa* (Harner, 49)
4 tu: fishhook assembly (Harner, 60; Karsten, 175)
5 tu: fishnet, thrown, 2 tu*A* (Harner, 60; Karsten, 176–7)
6 tu: fish trap, 3 tu, 2 tu*A*, & weir, 2 tu, & poison, 1 tu (Harner, 61; Karsten, 178–9)

Untended facilities

Complex

4 tu: game-bird snare (Karsten, 169)
6 tu: bird (small-animal) deadfall (Karsten, 168–9)

	Subsistants	Technounits	Average
Foraging	11	44	4.0
Farming	5	7	1.4
Total	16	51	3.2

14   *Trukese*

Numbers in parentheses refer to pages in LeBar (1964).

Instruments

Simple

1 tu: digging stick, domestic roots (tubers) N *fa* (66); digging stick, plant-
        ing (shoot prying) *fa* (19, 60, 61); land-clearing stick *fa* (59); fish-
        groping stick (67); octopus-probing stick (66–7); shell knife *A*, sever
        plant cuttings *fa* (10, 60)

3 tu: breadfruit-picking pole *fa* (21); tree-felling blade *fa* (9)

Weapons

Simple

1 tu: wood leister, kill (drive) fish at sweep or weirs, may be used with
        branch lobster lure (68, 70–1, 79–80)

4 tu: composite leister (73–6)

Complex

1 tu: fish arrow, sharpened wood shaft-point (67–8)

2 tu: self bow (67–8)

Tended facilities

Simple

1 tu: fish-driving stick, fish driven into hand nets N (66); missile stone,
        fish driven into weir (nets) N (68, 88, 90); coconut bundle, fish
        poison container (67); fish poison, pounded plant (67); branch
        lobster lure, used with one-piece leister (71)

3 tu: torch, clear plot (fish lure, *A* used with composite leister or circu-
        lar hand net) *fa* (59, 68–9, 73, 88–9); basket fish trap, used with rock
        pile lure *AA* (67); fish sweep, used with one-piece leister (net), 1 tu*A*
        (68, 88); weir #1 (79–80); land crab trap (62)

4 tu: land crab snare (62); deep-water fishhook assembly, 1 tu*A* (77);
        shore fishhook assembly (77–8); weir #2 (79–80); weir #3 (79–80)

5 tu: surface fishhook assembly, 1 tu*A* (77); float fishhook assembly, 1
        tu*A* (77); trolling fishhook assembly (78–9); woman's triangular
        hand net (86–7); sea turtle (fish) net (89)

6 tu: circular hand net, fish (flying fish, used with torch) (87–9)

7 tu: kite fishing rig, 3 tu*A* (79)

Untended facilities

Simple

1 tu: rock pile, attract fish, used with basket fish trap (67)
2 tu: plant-shoot protective wrap *fa* (60); lime trap, birds (62)
4 tu: double-entrance fish trap, 1 tu*A* (84)
6 tu: basket snare, bird (62); coconut shell bird snare (62)
8 tu: small-fish basket trap (81–3)

Complex

9 tu: spring-pole bird snare, 1 tu*A* (62, 64)

	Subsistants	Technounits	Average
Foraging	34	121	3.6
Farming	8	15	1.9
Total	42	136	3.2

15 *Pukapuka*
Numbers in parentheses refer to pages in Beaglehole and Beaglehole (1938).

Instruments

Simple

1 tu: stone, kill fish (birds) N (54, 75); stick, kill fish (birds) N (54, 75); bird-striking pole (74); coconut shell, excavate taro plot *fa* (40); crab-probing stick (73); digging stick, planting (harvesting) *fa* (40, 88, 125); shellfish-dislodging knife, wood(71); plant-cutting extraction (harvesting) knife, bone *fa* (88, 125); fish-killing club (55, 189)

Weapons

Simple

3 tu: leister (55, 190)
4 tu: ray leister (56)

Complex

3 tu: sea-bird bola, used on land (76)

Tended facilities

Simple

1 tu: torch, fishing (crabbing) (55, 56, 58, 73); loose bait, fish lure (62); coconut leaf butts, drive fish to seine (57, 58); fish sweep, tied coconut leaves (57); stone weir, used with basket trap (scoop net) (56, 159); handheld bird snare (75)

2 tu: bird pole snare (75)

3 tu: jig-fishing rig (55); fish gorge #1 (66, 190–1); fish gorge #2 (190–1)

4 tu: fish snare, 2 tu, & lure bait, 2 tu (69, 188); seine, used with coconut leaf sweep, 3 tu*A* (58); fishing basket, used at stone weir (56); coconut leaf weirs, used with basket trap (scoop net) (57)

5 tu: fishing basket, 3 tu, & coconut leaf mat weir, 2 tu, used with rock pile fish trap (55, 135, 136); bag net, fish (58); U-shaped (circular) shell fishhook assembly, beach (lagoon) fishing (194–7)

6 tu: bird snare, 4 tu, & guides, 2 tu (75, 211); fish scoop net, used at weir (canoe outside reef) (58–9, 206); bird pole net, used on land *A* (206–7)

14 tu: bonito fishhook assembly (small composite trolling hook), used from canoe (187–8, 197–8, 203–4)

15: V-shaped (U-shaped) wood fishhook assembly, deep-sea fishing from canoe (64–5, 186, 191)

Untended facilities

Simple

1 tu: toasted coconut crab lure, collector returns, picks up crabs by hand (73)

2 tu: crab pen *AA* (72)

3 tu: hatchling sea turtle pen (209–10); bird cage (73, 140); baited coconut bird snare (75, 211); rock pile fish trap, used with fishing basket and leaf mat (55)

4 tu: bird gorge (75–6)

Complex

11 tu: spring-pole snare rat trap, crop protection *fa* (107, 209–10)

	Subsistants	Technounits	Average
Foraging	41	130	3.2
Farming	4	14	3.5
Total	45	144	3.2

16 *Kapauku*
Numbers in parentheses refer to pages in Pospisil (1963).

Instruments

Simple

1 tu: domestic (wild) animal-killing club N *ah* (208, 237, 238)
domestic boar-branding (gelding) knife, bamboo *ah* (204, 207)
forked pole, lift lake-bottom weeds to which insects were attached
and in which crayfish were entangled (223, 227)
digging stick, planting (harvesting) *fa* (96–7, 101, 108–10, 119)
plant-cutting extraction (harvesting) knife, stone *fa* (109, 112, 116,
118, 278, 279)
stone "machete," clear plot (obtain banana cutting) *fa* (91, 104, 127)
spatula-shaped weeding stick *fa* (98–9)
wood shovel, harvest sweet potatoes (dig plot drainage ditch) *fa*
(105, 124–5)
wood *A* spadelike tool, cultivate soil *fa* (103, 122)

3 tu: crayfish leister, used with torch: wood prongs + reed shaft + rattan,
prong-shaft binder (228)

4 tu: stone ax, clear small trees from plot *fa*: stone blade + wood, blade
support loops + rattan, blade-support binders + wood handle
(91–2, 278)

Weapons

Simple

1 tu: missile stone, kill snake N (238)

Complex

2 tu: self bow: wood shaft + split vine bowstring (232–3)
20 tu: arrow total (233–8)
marsupial (rodent), 4 tu: wood point + reed shaft + rattan line,
point-shaft binder + braided rattan ring, point-shaft binder
small game, 4 tu: multiple points + string, point binders + reed
shaft + rattan, point-shaft binder
wild boar ♯1, 6 tu: bamboo point + wood foreshaft + reed shaft +
string, point-foreshaft-shaft binder + beeswax, secure string +
braided rattan, point-foreshaft binder

wild boar (other large game) ♯2, 6 tu: wood point + wood foreshaft + reed shaft + string, point-foreshaft-shaft binder + beeswax, secure string + braided rattan, point-foreshaft binder

Tended facilities

Simple

1 tu: reed torch, clear plot (kill game; blind crayfish or frogs, used with crayfish leister; burn wasp nest for insects) *fa* (82, 95, 228, 238, 246, 247–8)

weir, used with dip net, reeds stuck in stream bottom (226)

3 tu: crayfish lure, used with dip net from canoe (shore): forked stick + bait + stick-bait binder (227)

piglet-carrying bag *ah*: netting string + rim string + handle string (205, 268)

4 tu: dip net, crayfish (frogs), used with crayfish lure from canoe (shore): bent branch frame handle + netting + netting-frame binder + handle binder (227)

5 tu: oval dip (drag) net for water insects, tadpoles, etc. in open water: netting fiber + circular wood frame + grass, netting-frame binder + pole handle + handle-frame binder (224)

bird-hunting blind, used with bow & arrow: vertical support poles + horizontal support pole + bent reed cover + branch cover + grass cover (239)

6 tu: bird-hunting platform blind, used with bow & arrow: trees as support posts + horizontal platform support poles + cross poles on supports + tree-platform binder + tree branch-tree binder for roof frame + fern leaf thatch (239)

Untended facilities

Simple

1 tu: dirt smeared on edible plant cutting to prevent rot *fa* (112–3)

soil from drainage ditch, kill weeds *fa* (123)

2 tu: waterfowl fence & snare: fencing; + rattan snare suspended from fencing (242)

4 tu: wild boar pitfall, crop protection (meat) *fa*: pit + logs across each end of pit top + reed cover + grass cover (100, 240, 241)

7 tu: mountain plot fence *fa*: logs on ground + pairs of vertical bundles of posts + vines, post side binders + horizontal poles between

posts + vine, pole binders + vine, post top binders + forked sticks, support posts and poles (93–4)

10 tu: crayfish set net: netting fiber + circular wood frame + grass, netting-frame binder + bait + cane sliver to skewer bait to net + wood pole across net frame + pole-frame binder + forked stick at right angles to pole + anchor stake on bank + forked stick-anchor stake binder (226–7)

11 tu: boar trap, crop protection (meat) at valley plot fence *fa*: bundled saplings as vertical fence supports + rattan, bundle binders + diagonal forked stick supports + horizontal fence crosspieces + rattan, primary support-forked stick support-crosspiece binders + vertical pole fencing + rattan, horizontal-vertical fencing binders + lowered pole fencing for boar to jump over + bamboo impaling spikes driven in ground + vines to cover spikes + leaves to cover spikes (100, 106, 240, 241)

Complex

11 tu: rat spring-pole snare & house, crop protection (meat) *fa*: triangular frame of poles + arched frame support pole + frame pole and arched frame support pole binders + rattan noose tied to frame + diagonal spring pole + sapling trigger sticks + rattan, spring pole-trigger stick tension line; + twig, house elements + reed, house elements + grass, house elements + bait (100, 239–41)

	Subsistants	Technounits	Average
Foraging	17	63	3.7
Farming	15	46	3.1
Animal husbandry	3	5	1.7
Total	35	114	3.3

17 *Sema Naga*
Numbers in parentheses refer to pages in Hutton (1968).

Instruments

Simple

1 tu: piglet(cattle, dog)-killing stick N *ah* (72, 229)
hoe, forked stick, clear (plant) plot *fa* (66)

bamboo *A* knife, castrate pigs (mark ears of cattle; kill cattle) *ah* (71–72, 229) wood club, break dirt clods *fa* (67)

2 tu: semicircular weeding hoe *fa*: bent piece of bamboo + cane binder where handles cross (67)

ax, clear plot *fa*: iron blade + bamboo root handle into which blade was wedged (66)

3 tu: rake, clear plot *fa*: stick split at one end and bent to form tines + crosspiece to hold tines in place + cane, crosspiece-handle binder (62, 67)

metal knife (dao), clear (cultivate) plot *fa*: iron blade + bamboo handle + cane, blade-handle binder (20, 21, 66)

Weapons

Simple

5 tu: hunting (fishing; crop protection) spear: iron point + wood shaft + gum, point-shaft binder + iron spike at butt + shaft-spike binder (19, 74–5, 83)

Complex

9 tu: arrow total (23)

locally made, 4 tu: pointed wood shaft + leaf vanes + shaft-vane binder + nock end binder

imported point, 5 tu: metal point + wood shaft + leaf vanes + shaft-vane binder + nock end binder

10 tu: crossbow: wood stock + horn, string lock + cane, lock-stock binder + trigger + trigger pin + wood bow shaft + fiber bowstring + cane, nock-bowstring reinforcement piece + cane, bowstring center reinforcement piece + leaf, bowstring waterproofing (21–2)

Tended facilities

Simple

1 tu: cane tied around bull's horns to lead it *ah* (229)

torch, clear plot *fa* (60)

whistle, scare predators from crop, 1 tu*A* bamboo *fa* (57)

clapper bird scare, protect crop, split piece of bamboo *fa* (58)

fish poison, used with fish dam, crushed poisonous plant (83–7)

2 tu: water diversion fish dam: stones + earth (83)

fish snare: noose line + line-holding stick (82)

fish dam, used with plant poison: felled trees as dam + stones (83–7)

3 tu: hand dip net: wood frame-handle + netting + frame-mesh binder *AA* (82–3)

4 tu: fishhook assembly: bamboo rod + fiber line + wire hook + bait (81–2)

5 tu: large drag net for fish: netting + net end poles *A* + net-pole binders *A* + stone sinkers + net-sinker binders (82)
small drag net for fish: netting + net end poles *A* + net-pole binders *A* + stone sinkers + net-sinker binders (82)

7 tu: cattle-slaughter post assembly *ah*: 3 tu*A* slaughter post + cane, leg-tripping ropes + poles, fallen cattle weight + leg binders + lever pole inserted between hind legs to prevent movement (229)

Untended facilities

Simple

1 tu: spiked deer path, pointed bamboo spikes placed in trail (24, 78)

2 tu: bitter substances sown with crop seeds, protection from squirrels (lizards) *fa*: bitter leaves + bitter seeds (66)

3 tu: fish tunnel-trap, fish removed by hand: stone tunnel sides + stone tunnel top + stones to block one end (88)
weir, used with basket trap: stones + sticks + mud (81)
basket trap, used with weir *AA* (81)

4 tu: automatic clapper, scare birds from crop *fa*: bamboo, noisemaker tube + string tied to tube ends + wood clapper tied to string + support pole (58)

5 tu: spiked fence-trap, protect crop from deer (pigs) *fa*: 3 tu*A* fence + lowered section of fence + vertical pointed bamboo spikes inside lowered fencing (78)

6 tu: deer pitfall: pit + vertical pointed bamboo impalers + brush cover + reed cover + earth cover + leaf cover (24, 78)

Complex

6 tu: monkey deadfall, protect crop *fa*: bamboo shelf + shelf binders *A* + trigger + stone, deadfall weights + bait + trigger-bait binder *A* (78)

8 tu: spring-pole pheasant snare: hooped stick to hold trigger stick + spring pole + fiber noose line tied at one end to spring pole + vertical noose-spreading sticks + trigger stick + bamboo trigger loop + vertical loop-securing stick + bait (79–80)

9 tu: bird fence & spring-pole snare: vertical fencing + horizontal fencing + fence binders *A*; + arched support stick + horizontal support

stick + vertical noose-holding trip stick + fiber noose line + vertical noose-spreading sticks + bent sapling tied to noose line (80) spring-pole deer snare: bent sapling as spring pole + fiber noose line + hooped stick to hold trigger stick + noose holding trigger stick + vertical noose-trigger support sticks + horizontal trigger support stick + diagonal trip sticks + horizontal trip support, ground log + leaf covering (78–9)

	Subsistants	Technounits	Average
Foraging	21	90	4.3
Farming	13	32	2.5
Animal husbandry	4	10	2.5
Total	38	132	3.5

18 *Akamba*

Numbers in parentheses without an author name refer to pages in Lindblom (1920).

Instruments

Simple

1 tu: digging stick, planting (harvesting; dig up mole, A used with mole-taking pole) *fa* (474, 502, 503); wood shovel A, dig irrigation ditch *fa* (502, 506); awl, castrate bulls *ah* (480); earth-breaking pole *fa* (502)

2 tu: ax, A clear trees from plot *fa* (501, 534–6); "chopper," clear plot *AA fa* (502)

3 tu: knife, clear plot (A harvest grain; A remove honeycomb), 1 tu*A fa* (497, 498, 502, 505)

Complex

4 tu: cattle-bleeding arrow, used with bow and lines to hold cow *ah* (480)

Weapons

Complex

4 tu: self bow (449, 450); sling, 3 tu, 2 tu*A*, & missile, 1 tu stone A, protect crop from birds *fa* (421, 504)

33 tu: arrow total: barbed point, bird, 6 tu; barbless point, bird #1, 7 tu; barbless point, bird #2, 7 tu; iron point, game, 13 tu (452–8)

Tended facilities

Simple

1 tu: missile stone, protect crop N *fa* (504); torch, clear plot (smoke out bees to retrieve honey) *fa* (494, 502); leather strap, lead cattle *ah* (480); mole-taking pole, *A* protect crop *fa* (474); wood crook, catch calves *ah* (480)

2 tu: lines to hold cattle, used with cattle-bleeding arrow *ah* (480)

3 tu: stuffed calf skin placed near cow with a dead calf in order to milk cow *ah* (479); blind, hunt elephants with bow & arrow, 1 tu*A* (468)

4 tu: cow-milking stand for unruly animals, 3 tu*A ah* (479)

6 tu: watchtower for predators with scares attached, protect crop, 3 tu*A fa* (504)

18 tu: cattle (goat) medicine total *ah*: 8 with 2 tu, 2 with 1 tu, 2 tu*A* (490–3)

Complex

4 tu: deadfall, monkey (bird) (472–3)

Untended facilities

Simple

2 tu: bird of prey scare strings, protect young chickens, 1 tu*A ah* (Hobley, 1910, 58); temporary corral for cattle *AA ah* (478)

3 tu: cowbell, 1 tu*A ah* (480); scare, crop protection, 2 tu*A fa* (504)

5 tu: cattle corral *AA ah* (432, 478); snare, small animal *A*, 1 tu*A* (Hobley, 1910, 30)

6 tu: beehive (494–5)

Complex

6 tu: baited pitfall, 4 tu, & spring-pole snare, 2 tu (471)

7 tu: spring-pole mole snare, protect crop *fa* (473–4); small game spring-pole snare (471–2)

9 tu: deadfall, small game (470)

10 tu: cage trap, birds (472)

11 tu: drop spear-trap, large game, 2 tu*A* (470)

	Subsistants	Technounits	Average
Foraging	15	98	6.5
farming	14	33	2.4
Animal husbandry	21	46	2.2
Total	50	177	3.5

19 *Tanala, Ikongo group*
Numbers in parentheses refer to pages in Linton (1933).

Instruments

   Simple

      1 tu: sticks as tongs, retrieve crayfish N (59); digging stick, harvest sweet
               potatoes *fa* (47); iron knife, harvest rice and bananas (*A* castrate or
               mark ears of cattle and wild lemurs) *fa* (38, 43, 46, 48, 53); maize-
               planting pole *fa* (39, 42)
      2 tu: spade, prepare soil (construct terraces) *fa* (42, 46)
      5 tu: ax, clear plot, 2 tu*A fa* (37, 83, 84, 241)

Weapons

   Simple

      2 tu: game (fish) spear (53, 241, 243)
      3 tu: multipronged leister (56)

   Complex

      2 tu: self bow, used by adolescent boys to hunt small game (247, 258);
               arrow, 1 tu*A* (247); blowgun ♯1 (53, 244)
      3 tu: blowgun ♯2 (53, 244); blowgun dart (246)
      4 tu: eel hook (56)
      5 tu: sling, 4 tu, 3 tu*A*, & pebble missile, 1 tu, protect crop from birds *fa*
               (43,'242)

Tended facilities

   Simple

      1 tu: fish poison, root juice in stream (58–9)
      2 tu: torch, clear plot (obtain honey; used with improvised tongs for
               crayfish or leister for fish) *fa* (38, 39, 56, 59, 115)
      3 tu: bull-roarer, scare birds from crop *fa* (43, 253); woven conical fish
               scoop (58, 95); crayfish lure, used with improvised tongs, 1 tu*A* (59);
               half-cylinder fish scoop (58, 94)
      4 tu: fishhook assembly (untended for eel), 1 tu*A* (58)
      6 tu: seine, 3 tu*A* (58)
      7 tu: dip net, 1 tu*A* (58)

Untended facilities

Simple

2 tu: wild pig snare (53): small bird snare, 1 tu*A* (56)

3 tu: bird lime trap ♯1 (56); plot fence *fa* (43); scare, protect crop from birds, 1 tu*A fa* (43); hen nest, breeding (protection from predators)*ah* (51, 55)

4 tu: small-animal pitfall (53–4); bird lime trap ♯2 (56); beehive (59); bird cage trap, 3 tu*A* (55–6); cattle corral *ah* (48)

5 tu: wild pig pitfall (53); hawk snare, protect poultry *ah* (54); heart-shaped fish trap, 2 tu*A* (58, 94)

6 tu: guinea fowl pit snare, 1 tu*A* (54)

10 tu: cylinder eel trap, 5 tu*A* (58, 95)

11 tu: bottle-shaped eel trap, 5 tu*A* (58, 94–5)

Complex

5 tu: spring-pole snare, 4 tu, & guide fence, 1 tu, guinea fowl (54)

6 tu: bird cage trap with fall door, 4 tu*A* (55–6)

8 tu: spring-pole lemur snare (53)

9 tu: wild pig cage trap, 4 tu*A* (53)

	Subsistants	Technounits	Average
Foraging	33	137	4.2
Farming	11	26	2.4
Animal husbandry	3	12	4.0
Total	47	175	3.7

20 *Gwembe Valley Tonga*

Numbers in parentheses without an author name refer to pages in Reynolds (1968).

Instruments

Simple

1 tu: wood hunting club (140); threshing stick, harvest beans *fa* (77–8)

2 tu: ax, clear plot *fa* (106–8, 109); planting hoe, weeding (harvesting) *fa* (78, 94; Scudder, 1962, 103)

3 tu: knife, *A* harvest millet (butcher livestock) *fa* (69, 103; Scudder, 1962, 103)

Weapons

Simple

1 tu: stick, kill game N (57)
5 tu: hunting (fishing) spear (42, 56–7, 100–1, 103, 105)

Complex

3 tu: hippopotamus harpoon dart, used from boat (58, 104)

Tended facilities

Simple

1 tu: fish dam (43); torch, clear plot (drive game; take termites, used with pitfall) *fa* (58, 67, 71–3, 79)
2 tu: fish poison in pond (53); fish sweep, 1 tu*A* (50–1); xylophone, scare birds from crop *fa* (65, 220)
3 tu: leaf scare, protect crop from birds *fa* (65); rattle, protect crop from birds *fa* (65, 214)
4 tu: rope-rattle scare, protect crop from predators, 1 tu*A fa* (Scudder, 1962, 102)
5 tu: plunge fish trap (47)
7 tu: drum, 6 tu, & stick, 1 tu, elephant scare, crop protection *fa* (120–6; Scudder, 1962, 110)
9 tu: scoop fish trap (47–50, 164–7)

Untended facilities

Simple

1 tu: fuel for fire, protect garden from predators *fa* (79); termite pitfall, used with torch (67); ashes spread on young plants for protection *fa* (Scudder, 1962, 101–2)
2 tu: cattle corral *ah* (21); lime trap for birds, used with caged wild bird lure (63–4); weir, used with funnel-shaped fish trap in slow water (43); small-bird snare (61)
3 tu: goat (sheep) corral *ah* (21); plot fence *fa* (64–79); insecticide *fa* (79); bag net at hole of burrowing animal (63); funnel-shaped fish trap, used with weir in slow (fast) water (46–7); hippopotamus scare, crop protection *fa* (Scudder, 1962, 109–10); spring-pole scare, protect livestock from hyenas *ah* (65)
4 tu: pyramidal goat house *ah* (21, 40); bird snare, 1 tu*A* (61); fishhook assembly (may also be tended) (42–3); bird snare line (60–1)

5 tu: weir, used with funnel-shaped fish trap in fast water (46); caged wild birds as lure, used with lime trap (63–4)

6 tu: pitfall for big game, crop protection *fa* (63; Scudder, 1962, 191)

7 tu: gill net, 4 tu*A* (51); funnel-shaped fish trap with single (double) inner funnel, used with weir in slow (fast) water, 1 tu*A* (46–7)

8 tu: scoop fish net, 1 tu*A* (51)

10 tu: chicken coop, platform type, 2 tu*A* *ah* (21)

11 tu: chicken coop, ground level, 2 tu*A* *ah* (21–3)

13 tu: pigeon coop, 11 tu, 2 tu*A*, & nesting cones, 2 tu *ah* (21–3, 36)

Complex

7 tu: samson-post deadfall, 4 tu*A* (61); unbaited spring-pole snare, 6 tu, & fence, 1 tu (59–61)

9 tu: baited spring-pole snare, 8 tu, & fence, 1 tu (59–61)

10 tu: small animal deadfall, 1 tu*A* (61–3)

	Subsistants	Technounits	Average
Foraging	29	119	4.1
Farming	17	45	2.6
Animal husbandry	8	46	5.8
Total	54	210	3.9

21 *Tasmanians*

Numbers in parentheses refer to pages in Robinson (1966) or Roth (1890).

Instruments

Simple

1 tu: tree-chopping stone, fell tree for edible leaves N (Robinson, 188)
digging stick N (Robinson, 273, 543–4)
shellfish-dislodging stick (Robinson, 63; Roth, 115)

Weapons

Simple

1 tu: missile stone N (Robinson, 58, 220, 310, 379, 557)
shaft spear (Robinson, 220; Roth, 79–81)
missile stick (Robinson, 58, 533; Roth, 81–2)

Tended facilities

Simple

1 tu: torch, drive (smoke out) game (hunt wombats at night) (Robinson, 162, 837, 840, 903)
        kangaroo-tripping device, tied grass (Robinson, 218)
2 tu: hunting blind: deadwood + tree branches (Robinson, 559)
4 tu: baited bird blind: pole A blind frame + grass blind cover + bait + stone anchor (Robinson, 722, 752, 810)

Untended facility

Simple

1 tu: crossed spears in game trail (Robinson, 626, 690, 875)

	Subsistants	Technounits	Average
Foraging total	11	15	1.4

22 *Klamath*
Numbers in parentheses refer to Barrett (1910), Spier (1930), or Voegelin (1942).

Instruments

Simple

1 tu: stick as a club, used with weapon or facility N (Spier, 153, 159, 196); fish-braining stone, used with weapon or facility N (Voegelin, 56); paddle, scrape ground for moth chrysalids (Spier, 160); bone knife, remove inner bark from pine (Barrett, 258; Spier, 165–6, 173); seed-beating stick (Spier, 162, 163)
3 tu: ice pick, fish through ice AA (Spier, 148, 153); water lily seed-collection basket, used in shallow water, 1 tuA (Barrett, 255); seed beater (Barrett, 255, 257; Spier, 187–8)
4 tu: digging stick (Spier, 163–4, 171, 176; Voegelin, 57)

Weapons

Simple

3 tu: barbed leister, used with multipronged barbless leister (Barrett, 251; Spier, 153)

5 tu: multipronged barbless leister, used with barbed leister, 1 tu*A* (Barrett, 251; Spier, 153; Voegelin, 56)

Complex

3 tu: self bow (Barrett, 247; Spier, 194)

5 tu: 2-headed toggle-headed fish harpoon, may be used in ice fishing (Barrett, 251; Spier, 153; Voeglein, 56)

19 tu: arrow total: small game, 4 tu; large game *A*, 6 tu; waterfowl, 9 tu (Barrett, 247, 253, Pl. 20; Spier, 159, 195; Voegelin, 71)

Tended facilities

Simple

1 tu: poles, pounded on ice to drive fish, used with scoop net and ice pick N (Voegelin, 174); torch, drive deer, killed with weapons (antelope taken with net) (Voegelin, 51, 169); pit blind, hunting (Voegelin, 53); brush blind, used with bow & arrow (Voegelin, 52); leaf (grass) deer call, used with weapons, 1 tu*A* (Voegelin, 53, 170); crossed poles, subdue bear emerging from den, used with bow & arrow (Voegelin, 53, 170); sticks, beat on side of canoe to drive fish into large triangular dip net (Barrett, 249); fuel, fire built in canoe to attract birds at night into triangular fish net in canoe bow (Barrett, 247; Spier, 159); stone weir to create eddies, used with leister (dip and gill nets) (Spier, 149; Voegelin, 55, 173)

2 tu: tule mat blind around ice-fishing hole, prevent light from entering, used with toggle-headed harpoon (Spier, 153); animal headdress disguise, used with weapons, 1 tu*A* (Voegelin, 53)

3 tu: basket used as minnow scoop *AA* (Spier, 153)

4 tu: conical drag net, 1 tu*A* (Spier, 151); willow, scoop fish trap (Spier, 152); minnow fishhook assembly, 2 tu*A* (Spier, 154)

5 tu: open-ended basket fish trap, 1 tu*A* (Spier, 152); gorge, small fish (Barrett, 250–1)

6 tu: scoop net, may be used with fish-driving poles on ice (ice pick to make holes) (Barrett, 250; Spier, 151; Voegelin, 55, 174); spread net for antelope, used with bow & arrow (torch to drive animals), 2 tu*A* (Voegelin, 52, 169)

7 tu: fishhook assembly, large fish (Barrett, 250–1; Spier, 154)

9 tu: large triangular dip net, fish (waterfowl), 1 tu*A* (Barrett, 247, 249–50; Spier, 150–1)

Complex

4 tu: waterfowl-hatchling net (Spier, 159–60)

Untended facilities

Simple

3 tu: antelope (deer) pitfall (Voegelin, 52, 170)
4 tu: set (hand-held) waterfowl net, marshy margins of lakes, 1 tu$A$ (Barrett, 247; Spier, 159)
6 tu: fish trap, 3 tu$A$ (Barrett, 257, Pl. 19, 1; Voegelin, 55, 173)
7 tu: trout set line (Spier, 154)
8 tu: gill net, 4 tu$A$ (Barrett, 250; Spier, 151–2)

	Subsistants	Technounits	Average
Foraging total	43	151	3.5

23 *Tlingit, Yakutat group*
Numbers in parentheses refer to pages in de Laguna (1972).

Instruments

Simple

1 tu: digging stick, roots (shellfish, crabs) (393); sea mammal wood club, used with weapon (376)
2 tu: herring rake (388)
3 tu: ice pick, fishing AA (386)

Weapons

Simple

3 tu: bear spear, 1 tu$A$ (367–8); fish gaff, 1 tu$A$ (386)

Complex

2 tu: self bow (368)
3 tu: salmon harpoon dart, might be used with salmon weir (384)
4 tu: arrow, land animals (large birds), 1 tu$A$ (368–9)
5 tu: deer sling, 2 tu, & missile, 3 tu, 1 tu$A$ (369); sea mammal harpoon dart, 1 tu$A$ (376–7)

Tended facilities

Simple

1 tu: salmon weir, stones, used with basket salmon (candlefish) trap (387); salmon weir, vertical poles, used with splint salmon (candlefish) trap *A* (harpoon dart) (384, 386, 387)

3 tu: salmon weir, V-shaped vertical poles, 1 tu, & gate, 2 tu, 1 tu*A* (384, 387)

5 tu: dip net, 2 tu*A* (388)

12 tu: halibut fishhook assembly, 1 tu*A* (388–91); splint salmon trap, 10 tu, 1 tu*A*, & gate, close trap (drive fish), 2 tu *AA*, used with pole *A* salmon weir (386)

Untended facilities

Simple

5 tu: waterfowl gorge, water set, 1 tu*A* (373)

9 tu: basket trap, salmon (candlefish), used with stone weir, 3 tu*A* (387)

Complex

5 tu: fall-log tether snare, bear (372)

6 tu: small-game deadfall, 1 tu*A* (370)

7 tu: bear tether snare, 2 tu*A* (372)

10 tu: tossing-pole snare, 9 tu, 1 tu*A*, & brush guides, fox (bear), 1 tu (371–2)

13 tu: overhung deadfall, fox (lynx, wolverine, bear), 1 tu*A* (370–1)

	Subsistants	Technounits	Average
Foraging total	28	121	4.3

24 *Twana*

Numbers in parentheses refer to pages in Elmendorf (1960).

Instruments

Simple

1 tu: digging stick, roots (clams) (123, 125–6); wood club, deer (sea mammals; fish, used with dip net and double weir for stranding fish) (71, 74, 83, 93, 105, 106)

2 tu: herring rake (81)

3 tu: knife, kill deer, used with bow & arrow (*A* war dagger form), 1 tu*A* (92, 471)

Weapons

Simple

3 tu: sea mammal (deer) spear, used with harpoon for sea mammals, 1 tu*A* (92, 105, 471); 2-pronged unbarbed leister, 1 tu*A* (79); 3-pronged leister, 1 tu*A* (79)

5 tu: 2-pronged barbed leister (79)

8 tu: duck spear, water usage (79, 109–10)

Complex

4 tu: sinew-backed bow (87–8); detachable-headed salmon gaff (80)

9 tu: 2-headed toggle fish harpoon, 1 tu*A* (76–9)

14 tu: single (double) toggle-headed seal (porpoise) harpoon, 1 tu*A* (103–4)

17 tu: arrow total: multipointed, bird, 3 tu, 1 tu*A*; bone (stone) point, large game, 7 tu; duck (small game), 7 tu, 1 tu*A* (79, 88–90)

Tended facilities

Simple

1 tu: brush *A* as blind, used with game bird enclosure trap (114); seal-impaling sticks, sharpened sticks set in shallow water with points upward, seals frightened into water (106); deer call, grass blades blown (92); deer-driving torch, burning stick waved from canoe at night to cast shadows, used with bow & arrow (93); fuel for fire to drive waterfowl at night, used with bird spear (pole net) (112)

3 tu: makeshift herring basket trap *AA* (81)

4 tu: duck (herring) set spread net, 2 tu*A* (113–4)

5 tu: double weir for stranding fish, killed with club (73–4); fishhook assembly (80–1, 83)

6 tu: herring dip net *AA* (81); pole net, geese, water use *A* (110)

7 tu: oval tide-impounding weir, 2 tu*A* (76); waterfowl hunting head-dress, used with fuel and pole net (waterfowl spear), 5 tu*A* (111–2)

12 tu: dip net, used at single weir (68–71); single weir and dip net platform (63–8)

Complex

   4 tu: deer net, 2 tu*A* (92)
   6 tu: seal net ♯1, 2 tu*A* (106)
   7 tu: seal net ♯2 (106); game-bird enclosure trap, used with artificial (natural) blind, 7 tu*A* (114)

Untended facilities

Simple

   2 tu: waterfowl snare, 1 tu*A* (114)
   3 tu: gorgelike set, gulls, 1 tu*A* (114); deer (small mammal, possibly elk) pitfall (92, 94); grouse (hare) snare, 1 tu*A*, & guide fence, 2 tu*A* (94, 114)
   5 tu: roe-collecting bundle, 4 tu*A* (57, 83, 122)
   6 tu: cage for wild bear to be eaten, 2 tu*A* (115)
   7 tu: offshore herring (seal) weir-trap, 2 tu*A* (76)
   9 tu: conical basket trap with end pocket, used with offshore herring weir *AA* (75)
  15 tu: salmon basket trap, 7 tu, 2 tu*A*, & double parallel weir, 8 tu, 4 tu*A* (74–5)

Complex

   4 tu: spring-pole snare, deer (bear, possibly beaver), 1 tu*A* (92, 94)
   7 tu: deadfall, bear (possibly marmot), 4 tu*A* (94)

	Subsistants	Technounits	Average
Foraging total	48	237	4.9

25 *Huron*

Numbers in parentheses refer to pages in Champlain (1929), Heidenreich (1971), Sagard (1939), Tooker (1964), or Trigger (1969).

Instruments

Simple

   1 tu: stick as club *A*, kill game (fish), used with weapon or facility N (e.g., Sagard, 234); digging stick, planting *fa* (Heidenreich, 185; Sagard, 103); sharpened pole, kill deer driven into water (Trigger, 31)

3 tu: stone ax, clear trees from plot, 1 tu*A fa* (Heidenreich, 175; Sagard, 103, 108); ice pick *A*, break in beaver lodge (set nets beneath ice) *AA* (Champlain, 167; Sagard, 98, 231, 233); hoe, cultivate plot, 1 tu*A fa* (Heidenreich, 176, 178, 184, 185; Sagard, 104; Tooker, 61)

Weapons

Simple

3 tu: deer spear, 1 tu*A* (Champlain, 61); leister, 1 tu*A* (Trigger, 30)

Complex

2 tu: self bow (Champlain, Pl. 3; Sagard, 98)
5 tu: arrow, kill game (protect crop from predators), 1 tu*A* (Champlain, Pl. 3; Sagard, 98, 220)

Tended facilities

Simple

1 tu: missile stones *A*, scare birds from crop N *fa* (Heidenreich, 178, 217; Trigger, 29); stick, beat on ice to capture beaver by hand, used with ice pick (brush plug) N (Sagard, 233); pole, set net beneath ice (Champlain, 167); brush *A* plug, block beaver passage, used with driving stick (Sagard, 233); sticks (bones) beat together, drive deer to guide fence & enclosure, killed with bow & arrow (Champlain, Pl. 5, 84); torch, clear plot *fa* (Champlain, 156; Heidenreich, 175; Sagard, 103)
4 tu: beaver net, 2 tu*A* (Sagard, 234)
5 tu: fishhook assembly, used with ice pick *A* for ice fishing, 1 tu*A* (Champlain, 167; Sagard, 98, 189); seine, used in winter with ice pick *A* and net-setting pole, 1 tu*A* (Champlain, 167–8; Heidenreich, 211; Sagard, 98, 231)
6 tu: deer guide fence, 3 tu, 1 tu*A*, & enclosure, 3 tu, used with sticks to drive deer and bow & arrow (Champlain, 83–5)

Untended facilities

Simple

1 tu: bear enclosure, vertical stakes inside lodge as cage in which to fatten captive wild bear (Champlain, 130; Sagard, 220)
2 tu: snare, bird (hare) as food (protect crop), 1 tu*A* (Sagard, 101, 220–1, 223)

5 tu: weir, 2 tu, 1 tu$A$ & net, 3 tu, 2 tu$A$, set in narrows between lakes (Champlain, 56–7; Heidenreich, 211)

8 tu: gill net, set AA (Sagard, 186)

Complex

4 tu: spring-pole snare, large game, 2 tu$A$ (Champlain, Pl. 5, 84)

	Subsistants	Technounits	Average
Foraging	22	62	2.8
Farming	5	9	1.8
Total	27	71	2.6

26 Aymara

Numbers in parentheses refer to pages in Forbes (1870), La Barre (1948), or Tschopik (1946).

Instruments

Simple

1 tu: needle, kill llamas as food *ah* (Tschopik, 521); plow harness ♯1, rawhide line *fa* (Forbes, 262–3; La Barre, 80–1)

2 tu: plow harness ♯2 *fa*: yoke bar + yoke-plow line (La Barre, 80–1); clod crusher ♯1 *fa*: stone ring + handle, one end wedged in ring (Tschopik, 515)

3 tu: knife, kill domestic animals (earmark; castrate) AA *ah* (Tschopik, 521); clod crusher ♯2 *fa*: stone head + handle + head-handle binder (Tschopik, 515); adzlike hoe *fa*: iron blade + handle + blade-handle binder (Tschopik, 515); sickle, harvest barley *fa*: iron blade + cleft stick + blade-stick binder (Tschopik, 515)

4 tu: spade *fa*: iron blade + handle + footrest + blade-handle-rest binder (Tschopik, 517)

6 tu: plow, used with bull plow harnesses *fa*: wood beam + wood blade + wood stanchion + rawhide, stanchion-beam binder + iron share + blade-share binder A (Forbes, 262–3; La Barre, 80; Tschopik, 515)

Weapons

Simple

1 tu: stick, kill viscacha (fox) driven from holes with smoke N (Tschopik,

520); pole, kill ducks N (Tschopik, 520); club, kill game driven with drums and wind instruments (Tschopik, 519)

3 tu: leister: wood prongs + wood shaft + prong-shaft binder (Tschopik, 522)

Complex

2 tu: sling & missile, protect crop from predators (hunting) *fa*: woolen sling; + missile stone (Tschopik, 517, 519)

3 tu: bird bola: large cord + stone bola balls + large cord tied to small cords attached to balls (La Barre, 79)

4 tu: large-game bola: pair of bola balls + bifurcated suspension cord + wrapping at juncture + wrapping for finger grip (La Barre, 79; Tschopik, 520)

Tended facilities

Simple

1 tu: pebbles, drive fish into stationary bag net N (Tschopik, 522); balsa pole, drive fish into stationary bag net N (Tschopik, 522); water, drive wild guinea pig (coney) from burrow to be taken in baskets or nets (La Barre, 78; Tschopik, 520); notched cane end flute, drive game killed with clubs (Tschopik, 519, 556); rawhide lasso, presumably used for animal control *ah* (Tschopik, 534–5); torch, clear plot (attract fish, used with scoop net; produce smoke to drive game, killed with sticks) *fa* (Tschopik, 525)

2 tu: duct flute, drive game killed with clubs: wood tube + mouthpiece (Tschopik, 519, 556)

3 tu: surround for vicuna, used with large-game bolas: upright forked poles + cord suspended between poles + alpaca-wool tassels suspended from cord; the bolas were hung on forked poles to entangle animals as they attempted to jump from the surround (Tschopik, 519)

panpipes, drive game, killed with clubs: cane tubes + split cane binders + plugs in tubes *A* (Tschopik, 519, 556)

5 tu: dip net #1: handle + frame crosspieces + handle-crosspiece binder + netting + net-crosspiece connecting line (Tschopik, 522)

dip net #2: handle + wood hoop frame + handle-hoop binder + netting + net-frame connecting line (Tschopik, 522)

basket trap, viscacha (coney) driven from burrow: warp splints +

weft splints + warp-weft binder + support hoop A + support-basket binder A (Tschopik, 534)

7 tu: two-man drag fish net, pulled by men in two balsas: netting + backing lines A + reed bundles as floats + float-backing binder + stone sinkers + sinker-backing binder + tow ropes (Tschopik, 522) one-man drag fish net: netting + end binders + pole + pole-net connecting lines + sinkers + sinker-net binder + tow line (Tschopik, 522)

scoop fish net: handles + support hoop frame + handle-frame binders + netting + net-frame connecting line + sinker + net-sinker line (Tschopik, 525)

8 tu: stationary bag net, tended by men in two balsas as others drive fish by tossing pebbles and hitting water with poles: netting + backing lines A + floats + float-backing binder + backing line A for fish removal at apex + stone sinkers + backing-sinker binder + net-balsa lines A (Tschopik, 525)

basketry drag net, used in pairs from balsa: weft splints + warp splints + weft-warp binder + hoop support + basket-hoop binder + balsa attachment cord + stone sinkers + basket-sinker lines (Tschopik, 524)

10 tu: fish weir & scoop net: reed weir + grass rope reed binder + anchor for rope; + net hoop + netting + hoop-netting binder + stick frame + binder at frame apex + hoop-stick binders + net-frame binder A (Tschopik, 525)

drum & stick, drive game, killed with clubs: wood cylinder + rawhide heads, top and bottom + thongs, cylinder-head binders + transverse body thong + short sticks + sticks, attachment thong (sticks strike bottom head); + beating stick + rawhide stick head + stick head stuffing + stick-head binder A (Tschopik, 519, 556)

Complex

5 tu: pitfall trap for birds, crop protection (food) *fa*: flat fall stone + pit + support stick + string + bait (Tschopik, 520)

Untended facilities

Simple

1 tu: rope, tether animals *ah* (Tschopik, 535); stone terraces *fa* (Tschopik, 515)

2 tu: dry-stone (sod-block, adobe) corral *ah*: stones & gate poles *A* (Tschopik, 521)

3 tu: waterfowl snare line: grass (reed) clumps + cord tied between clumps + nooses suspended from cord (Tschopik, 520); temporary corral *ah*: support posts + cross-poles *A* + rope binder (Tschopik, 521)

4 tu: scarecrow *fa*: vertical pole + crosspiece *A* + pole-crosspiece binder *A* + clothing (Tschopik, 517)

Complex

5 tu: deadfall, protect crop from wild guinea pigs (mice) *fa*: fall + trigger support pole + trigger catch + trigger stick + bait (Tschopik, 517, 519)

	Subsistants	Technounits	Average
Foraging	26	100	3.8
Farming	15	42	2.8
Animal husbandry	6	11	1.8
Total	47	153	3.3

27 *Ojibwa*

Numbers alone in parentheses refer to pages in Densmore (1929).

Instruments

Simple

1 tu: wood hoe *fa* (122, 124); scapula hoe *fa* (122, 170); root grubber *fa* (124); wood lever, pry roots *A* to prepare plot *fa* (124); wood spile, tap maple tree sap, used with ax (Densmore, 1928, 311)

2 tu: sticks, harvest wild rice (128)

3 tu: ax, tap maple tree, used with spile (break dirt clods; cut branches of fruit-bearing trees) (Densmore, 1928, 311; 122, 127, 169); ice pick, ice fishing, used with lure and leister *AA* (122, 125)

Weapons

Simple

1 tu: bone knife, presumably used to kill wounded game (129, 169); club, kill sturgeon, used with leister at weir (126)

3 tu: leister, used at weir (lure at holes in ice) *AA* (125–6)

Complex

  3 tu: self bow #1 (146); self bow #2, squirrel (146); self bow #3, big game (146)

 18 tu: arrow total: waterfowl, 3 tu; deer A #1, 5 tu; rabbit, 5 tu; deer #2, 5 tu (129, 147)

Tended facilities

Simple

  1 tu: fish weir-trap, tree branches in shallow stream (126)

  2 tu: torch, used with leister at night (125–6); pole snare, partridge (131)

  3 tu: fishhook assembly, 1 tuA (126); doe call, used with bow & arrow (129)

  4 tu: catfish jig (126); blind, ice fishing, used with lure and leister, 1 tuA (126); sturgeon weir, used with fishhook, killed with club, 1 tuA (126)

  5 tu: fish lure, used with leister and ice pick at hole in ice (126); torch, deer hunting, used with bow & arrow (149–50)

Untended facilities

Simple

  3 tu: scarecrow, 1 tuA *fa* (122); rabbit spread net, 2 tuA (131)

  4 tu: otter spread net, 3 tuA (130)

  7 tu: set gill net, shallow water, 2 tuA (125, 154)

  8 tu: floated gill net, deep water, 4 tuA (125, 154)

Complex

  5 tu: small-game "fall trap," 4 tu, 1 tuA, & guide ,1 tu (131); bear deadfall, 2 tuA (131)

  8 tu: small-animal deadfall (131)

	Subsistants	Technounits	Average
Foraging	32	114	3.6
Farming	5	7	1.4
Total	37	121	3.3

28   *Lepcha*

Numbers in parentheses refer to pages in Gorer (1938), Morris (1938), Nebesky-Wojkowitz (1953), or Siiger (1967)

Instruments

Simple

1 tu: cattle-braining stone N *ah* (Gorer, 105); pointed bamboo stick, kill livestock *ah* (Gorer, 105; Siiger, 89); digging stick ♯1, planting *fa* (Gorer, 93; Morris, 180–1); digging stick ♯2, harvest wild plants (Gorer, 91)

2 tu: wood plank, level plowed plot, 1 tu*A fa* (Siiger, 87); ax, clear large trees from plot *fa* (Siiger, 87, 88); hoe, weed (prepare ground) *fa* (Siiger, 86, 87, 88); weeding spud *fa* (Siiger, 88)

3 tu: iron-bladed knife, harvest crop (*A* castrate boars and butcher livestock), 1 tu*A fa* (Gorer, 102; Morris, 191: Siiger, 88, 89); hooked iron-bladed knife, weed plot *fa* (Siiger, 88); iron sickle, harvest millet (clear plot), 1 tu*A fa* (Gorer, 92; Siiger, 83, 88)

5 tu: wood harrow *AA fa* (Siiger, 87)

6 tu: plow, 1 tu*A fa* (Gorer, 91; Siiger, 83, 86, 87, Pl. IV)

Weapons

Simple

1 tu: stone, stun (drive) fish from beneath rocks, taken by hand (net) N (Nebesky-Wojkowitz, 29); wood hammer, stun (drive) fish from beneath rocks, taken by hand (net) (Nebesky-Wojkowitz, 29; Siiger, Pl. XIV, 47)

5 tu: spear (Nebesky-Wojkowitz, 22–3, 24; Siiger, 97)

Complex

3 tu: self bow (Morris, 196; Nebesky-Wojkowitz, 22; Siiger, 96, 97); slingshot, 2 tu, & stone (clay) missile, 1 tu (Siiger, 96)

11 tu: pellet bow, 8 tu, 2 tu*A*, & clay missile, 3 tu *AA*, protect crop from birds *fa* (Morris, 197; Nebesky-Wojkowitz, 23; Siiger, 96)

25 tu: arrow total: bird stunning, 2 tu; game ♯1, poison (kill domestic cattle, no poison, instrument usage), 7 tu; game ♯2, poison, 7 tu; game ♯3, poison, 9 tu (Morris, 196; Nebesky-Wojkowitz, 22–3; Siiger, 96–7)

Tended facilities

Simple

1 tu: beating sticks *A*, drive animals, used with wild pig-impaling sticks (bow & arrow; tended bamboo fish basket & weir) N (Nebesky-Wojkowitz, 27, 30); bamboo torch, clear plot (immobilize tree frog, collected by hand) *fa* (Gorer, 93; Morris, 180; Siiger, 82, 104); wild pig-impaling sticks, rows of bamboo spikes at base of cliff over which pigs were driven (Nebesky-Wojkowitz, 27)

3 tu: fish poison *AA* (Siiger, 99)

4 tu: fish dip basket (Siiger, 99); fishhook assembly (Nebesky-Wojkowitz, 28); fish dam, 3 tu, & poison, 1 tu (Nebesky-Wojkowitz, 30); fish gorge (Nebesky-Wojkowitz, 28)

5 tu: conical fish net, thrown (Nebesky-Wojkowitz, 28)

Complex

6 tu: bird net and stone to drop net (Nebesky-Wojkowitz, 26–7)

Untended facilities

Simple

1 tu: stone *A* terraces, wet rice cultivation (nursery plot) *fa* (Gorer, 90, 91; Siiger, 82, 83, 86, 97); plot fence, thorny branches *fa* (Siiger, 82); stone weir, used with bamboo pocket fish trap (conical fish trap) (Nebesky-Wojkowitz, 28)

2 tu: livestock tether *AA ah* (Gorer, 101); steep plot terrace planks *fa* (Morris, 180)

3 tu: poisoned bait, crop protection *fa* (Nebesky-Wojkowitz, 22–3, 26); pyramidal bamboo fish trap (Siiger, 99); bird snare line #1, 1 tu*A* (Siiger, 97); bird snare line #2 (Nebesky-Wojkowitz, 25)

4 tu: bamboo pocket fish trap, used with stone *A* weir, 3 tu*A* (Nebesky-Wojkowitz, 28); fish chute trap, 2 tu*A* (Nebesky-Wojkowitz, 29); pitfall, 1 tu*A* (Nebesky-Wojkowitz, 27; Siiger, 97); conical bamboo fish trap, used with stone weir, 1 tu*A* (Nebesky-Wojkowitz, 28); plot fence, 1 tu*A fa* (Siiger, 86, 87, Pl. II, IV); pigsty *AA ah* (Siiger, 94)

5 tu: bird lime (Nebesky-Wojkowitz, 25–6); multiple fishhook set (Nebesky-Wojkowitz, 28)

7 tu: bamboo fish basket, may be used with stone weir and tended, 4 tu*A* (Nebesky-Wojkowitz, 29–30)

10 tu: hen coop, 7 tu, 5 tu*A*, & nest, 1 tu, & night cover, 2 tu *AA* basket *ah* (Gorer, 103; Siiger, 94–5)

Complex

2 tu: samson-post deadfall (Nebesky-Wojkowitz, 25)

6 tu: spring-tripped bear deadfall, 2 tu*A* (Morris, 193–4); spring-pole snare, small game (bird, deer) (Nebesky-Wojkowitz, 25)

7 tu: monkey cage trap, crop protection *AA fa* (Nebesky-Wojkowitz, 27)

8 tu: crossbow, 6 tu, 3 tu*A*, & arrow, 2 tu, protect crop from rats *fa* (Nebesky-Wojkowitz, 21, 26); overhung *A* deadfall, birds (Nebesky-Wojkowitz, 25)

9 tu: automatic missile spear trap, deer (Nebesky-Wojkowitz, 22–3, 26)

	Subsistants	Technounits	Average
Foraging	37	145	3.9
Farming	21	67	3.2
Animal husbandry	7	18	2.6
Total	65	230	3.5

29 *Caribou Eskimos*

Numbers in parentheses refer to pages in Birket-Smith (1929).

Instruments

Simple

4 tu: caribou-killing dagger (108); fish-killing bodkin, used with weapon or facility (118–9); ice pick, fishing (122)

Weapons

Simple

1 tu: missile stone, ptarmigan (ermine) N (113, 114)

6 tu: 2-pronged leister, used with fish lure (weir) (119–20)

7 tu: caribou lance, used in water from kayak (109–10)

Complex

2 tu: throwing-board, used in water with bird dart, 1 tu*A* (115)

3 tu: bird dart, used in water with throwing-board, 1 tu*A* (115)

4 tu: bird sling, 3 tu, & missile, 1 tu (116)

5 tu: composite sinew-backed bow, birds (103); arrow, general purpose, 1 tu*A* (104–5)

6 tu: composite sinew-backed bow, general purpose, 2 tu*A* (103)

Tended facilities

Simple

1 tu: antlers held over hunter's head, lure caribou during mating season (107); wolfskin disguise, guide caribou (110)

2 tu: dam, 1 tu, & weir, 1 tu, used with leister (119); caribou guide (110–11)

3 tu: caribou guide poles with gull skins attached, 1 tuA (111); fishskin lure, used with leister, 2 tuA (123)

4 tu: caribou pitfall (108); caribou cairn lure, 1 tu snow, & pitfall, 3 tu (108)

5 tu: fish-shaped lure, used with leister (123)

6 tu: fish trap, used at weir (120–1); fishhook assembly (124)

Untended facilities

Simple

3 tu: fox pitfall, 2 tuA (114); bird snare (116); hare snare line (114)

4 tu: gull (fish) gorge (115–6, 121); wolf pitfall, 2 tuA (108, 113); blood knife, wolf (113)

Complex

4 tu: fox cage trap ♯1 (113–4)

5 tu: fox cage trap ♯2, 1 tuA (113)

	Subsistants	Technounits	Average
Foraging total	34	118	3.5

30 *Nabesna, Upper Tanana group*

Numbers in parentheses refer to pages in McKennan (1959) unless noted otherwise.

Instruments

Simple

1 tu: digging stick A (36; Osgood, 1937, 41)

Weapons

Simple

2 tu: bear spear (club) (49, 60)

3 tu: multipronged leister, 1 tuA (63–4)

4 tu: bear spear made from knife (58, 60)

Complex

6 tu: self bow (51–2)
21 tu: arrow total: lanceolate, 5 tu; narrow (broad), blunt, 5 tu: cone-
shaped (rounded) head, 5 tu; compound foreshaft, 6 tu (52–5)

Tended facilities

Simple

1 tu: felled trees as straight (V-shaped) caribou (moose) guide, used with
snares (48)
2 tu: bear-holding poles, used with club (spear) (49); caribou (moose)
snare, used with guide fence (48, 49); hare snare (60–1); mountain
sheep snare (49)
3 tu: adz, A open muskrat house, used with spear (50, 65)
5 tu: muskrat pole net, used on land, 3 tuA (50)
6 tu: dip net, used with weir, 3 tuA (62)

Untended facilities

Simple

2 tu: grouse snare (61)
4 tu: weir, used with trap (dip net), 1 tuA (62)
5 tu: fish trap, used with weir, 2 tuA (62)

Complex

3 tu: caribou drag snare, 1 tuA (48)
4 tu: spring-pole snare (60–1)
6 tu: tossing-pole snare, 2 tuA (60)
7 tu: samson-post deadfall (61)
14 tu: overhung deadfall (62)

	Subsistants	Technounits	Average
Foraging total	25	105	4.2

31   *Ingalik, Anvik-Shageluk group*
Numbers in parentheses refer to pages in Osgood (1940) unless noted otherwise.

Instruments

Simple

 1 tu: wood club, fish (small animal) N (207, 216, 217, 224; Osgood, 1958,
        245, 246); digging stick (177; Osgood, 1958, 248, 249)

 2 tu: fish impaler, remove burbot from fish trap: wood handle + bone
        impaler fitted into hole at right angles to handle (224–5)

 3 tu: ice pick, fishing in winter: bone point + wood shaft + babiche,
        point-shaft binder (221–2)
        impaler, kill fish in traps: bone point + wood handle + babiche,
        point-handle binder (225)

 4 tu: animal-killing club: prepared bone + wood plug + babiche, bone-
        plug binder and wrist loop + oil in bone for weight (207–8)

Weapons

Simple

 3 tu: spear: bone point + wood shaft + babiche, point-shaft binder (200–
        201); 2-pronged leister: bone points + wood shaft + babiche, point-
        shaft binder (196–7); hunting knife: antler blade + composite wood
        handle + babiche, blade-handle binder (93)

Complex

 3 tu: self bow: wood shaft + sinew bowstring + waterproofing oil on
        bowstring (201–2); throwing-board, used with bird dart: wood body
        + shaft-receiving peg + wood finger holds (201)

 4 tu: bird dart, used with throwing-board: points + wood shaft + inter-
        point binder + point-shaft binder (201)

 5 tu: fish harpoon dart: detachable bone point + wood shaft + babiche,
        shaft end binder + point line tied to shaft + babiche binders to hold
        line against shaft (199)

 7 tu: toggle-headed harpoon, salmon: stone blade + antler, toggle head
        + fixed bone foreshaft + wood shaft + babiche, foreshaft-shaft
        binder + babiche, toggle head line tied to shaft + babiche binders
        to hold line against shaft (197–8)

33 tu: arrow total (203–6)
        duck, 6 tu: bone points + wood shaft + point-shaft binder +
        feather vanes + gum, shaft-vane binder + sinew, shaft-vane binder;

hare, 6 tu: antler point + wood shaft + point-shaft binder + feather vanes + gum, shaft-vane binder + sinew, shaft-vane binder; arrow dart, aquatic mammal, 6 tu: detachable bone point + wood shaft + point-shaft line + feather vanes + gum, shaft-vane binder + sinew, shaft-vane binder; small bird, 7 tu: bone point + wood shaft + gum, point-shaft binder + sinew, point-shaft binder + feather vanes + gum, shaft-vane binder + sinew, shaft-vane binder; big game, 8 tu: stone point + bone arrowhead + point-head peg + wood shaft + head-shaft binder + feather vanes + glue, shaft-vane binder + sinew, shaft-vane binder

Tended facilities

Simple

1 tu: lure sticks, simulate call of rutting moose N (Osgood, 1958, 243); beaver dam-breaking log, used with beaver net (216); forked stick, hold trapped lynx to kill (195); burbot trap-checking poles, placed between trap and ice (230)

2 tu: pole, set gill net beneath ice: pole + line (215, 223)

3 tu: bear lure, used with spear: willow stick bundle + rawhide line, bundle binder + tree support (Osgood, 1958, 41); lamprey snag: notched crosspieces + pole handle + spruce root, crosspiece-handle binder (173–4)

4 tu: beaver spread net: babiche netting + backing lines + vertical support posts + willow bark, post-netting binder (215–6)

5 tu: caribou snare, used with guide and surround (bow & arrow): vertical post set inside surround + horizontal snare support pole from the vertical post to guide (surround) fencing + babiche noose line + upright snare-spreading poles + willow bark line, noose-spreading pole binder (237–8, 251); fishhook-lure: bird claw hook + antler, fish-shaped lure + wood peg, claw-lure binder + sinew line + wood pole (220–1)

7 tu: blackfish dip net: crossed stick frame + crossed stick binder A + splint "netting" + stick, rim frame + frame-netting binder A + wood handle + frame-handle binder (218–9); caribou guide & surround, used with snares (bow & arrow): guide posts + guide post binders + guide poles in post crotches; + pairs of surround posts driven upright in ground + ends of horizontal posts placed between pairs of upright posts + babiche lines tied to tops of upright post pairs + support stakes against upright posts (237–8, 251)

9 tu: salmon (whitefish) dip net: pole handle + wood hoop frame + babiche, handle-hoop binder + wood, hoop crosspiece + crosspiece hoop-pole binder + handle extension piece + handle extension binder + willow bast netting + frame-netting binder A (216–8)

12 tu: king salmon drag gill net: willow bast netting + backing lines + bark floats + backing line-float binder + bone sinkers + backing line-sinker binder + sealskin float + thread to stitch holes in skin A + float nozzle A + nozzle-skin binder A + nozzle plug A + netting-sealskin float line (212–4)

Untended facilities

Simple

3 tu: screen, used with whitefish (chum salmon, burbot) trap: vertical splints + splint crosspieces + vertical-crosspiece binder (227–33)

4 tu: blackfish trap weir: vertical poles + horizontal poles + grass between poles + vertical pole lashings (234–5)

5 tu: squirrel snare ♯1: tree + pole leaned against tree + nettle, noose line + forked willow stick noose tie + noose-forked stick binder (244)

6 tu: squirrel snare ♯2: willow pole, snare suspension + stake to hold pole + willow line, pole-stake binder + gate sticks + sinew noose line + grass, gate-noose binder (241)

7 tu: ptarmigan (grouse) snare & fence: willow pole, snare suspension + stake to hold pole + willow line, pole-stake binder + gate sticks + fishskin noose line + grass, gate-noose binder; + brush guide fence (240–1)

8 tu: waterfowl snare & fence: willow pole, snare suspension + stake to hold pole + willow line, pole-stake binder + gate sticks + fishskin noose line + grass, gate-noose binder + sticks above and below noose opening; + willow guide fence (240–1); standard weir, used with chum salmon (burbot, whitefish) trap (leister): crossed poles with lower ends stuck in riverbed + willow, crotch binders + horizontal poles in crotches + vertical poles between crossed poles + vertical-horizontal pole binder + vertical weir splints + horizontal weir splints + spruce root splint binders (236, 237); blackfish trap, used with blackfish weir: sets of basket splints [2 trap sections] + sets of enclosing splint binders + sets of spruce root basket binders + mouth framing poles + framing-basket splint binder +

removable rear funnel binder to empty trap + vertical poles to hold trap in place + trap-pole binder *A* (232–3); gill net set, whitefish, used with net-setting pole and ice pick: willow bast netting + backing lines + bark floats + backing line-float binder + stone sinkers + backing line-sinker binder + anchor posts + netting-anchor line (214–5)

12 tu: whitefish (pike, used with blackfish weir; salmon or trout, used with standard weir) trap, used with standard weir and screen: sets of basket splints [3 trap sections] + sets of encircling splint binders + sets of spruce root basket binders + mouth framing poles + framing-basket splint binders + rear-middle section removable binder + rear funnel end binder + vertical poles to hold trap mouth in place + crossed poles to hold trap end in place + vertical pole, trap end holder + horizontal pole, trap end holder + trap end holder binders (227–9, 230–1, 233–4); chum salmon trap, used with standard weir and screen: sets of basket splints [3 trap sections] + sets of encircling splint binders + sets of spruce root basket binders + mouth support poles + support pole-basket splint binders + rear funnel door splints + rear funnel door-splint binders + door-funnel binders + rear funnel splint closure + rear funnel splint closure binder + vertical poles to hold trap mouth in place + trap-pole binder *A* (226–7); burbot trap, used with standard weir, ice pick, fish rake, screen, and checking poles: sets of basket splints [2 trap sections] + sets of encircling splint binders + sets of spruce root basket binders + mouth support poles + support poles-basket splint binders + door splints at end + door splint frame + door splint-frame binder + trap-door opening binder + willow poles to hold trap in place + willow poles to remove trap + removal pole-trap binders (229–30)

Complex

10 tu: bear snare: partially toppled cottonwood tree + crossed stakes beneath section of tree + crossed stake binder *A* + stake suspension stick + willow bark, crossed stick-suspension stick binders + babiche noose line tied to tree + willow bark, cross stick-noose binder + bait beyond snare + basket bait container + container-tree binder (243–4); hare tossing-pole snare & fence: vertical snare-spreading poles on each side of trail + diagonal snare foundation pole + willow line, vertical pole-foundation pole binder + crossed

poles as tossing pole mount + crossed pole binder A + tossing pole +snare line + grass, snare line and snare-separating pole binder + trigger stick; + willow guide fence (238–40); beaver deadfall: vertical poles + horizontal pole on verticals + poles as weights + dirt on pole weights + pole weight support poles + vertical trigger support + willow line, support pole-trigger support binder + trigger stick as bait + small vertical pole + willow line, trigger-small pole and trigger support binder (248–50)

11 tu: lynx tether snare: vertical post (tree) + diagonal snare support pole + babiche, post-pole binder + sinew snare line tied to diagonal pole + vertical snare-spreading poles + babiche, diagonal pole-vertical pole binder + grass, snare line-vertical post binder + house backing tree + willow house + horizontal barrier poles + bait (241–2); samson-post deadfall, bears (etc.): horizontal barrier logs + sets of vertical posts + fall log support post + fall log + fall log weight posts + samson post + trigger (bait) stick + bait + bait-bait stick binder + backing logs + cover on backing (244–6)

12 tu: friction trigger overhung deadfall, marten (mink, river otter, etc.): guide stakes + fall log + fall log rest post + fall log weight poles + step over pole on ground + stick house backing + branch house roof + trip support pole + willow bark, fall log-trip pole binder + trigger stick catch + trigger stick + bait (246–8)

	Subsistants	Technounits	Average
Foraging total	55	296	5.4

32 Tanaina, Kachemak Bay group

Numbers in parentheses refer to pages in Osgood (1937) unless otherwise noted.

Instruments

Simple

1 tu: stick as club N (35, 40, 92); seal club (37, 85, 91–2); sharpened stick, bullheads (30); crab-impaling pole (31); porcupine spear, barbed, pointed stick (35)

3 tu: beaver hook, used with club, 2 tu$A$ (35)

5 tu: porcupine hook, 3 tu$A$ (35)

Weapons

Simple

1 tu: missile stone, ptarmigan N (40)
3 tu: sea mammal lance (85–6); bear spear (86)

Complex

2 tu: skin sling, 1 tu, & missile, 1 tu (92); throwing-board, used in water with arrowlike lance (86)
5 tu: "arrowlike lance," used in water with throwing-board AA (86)
6 tu: salmon harpoon dart (83)
7 tu: sinew-backed bow (86–9)
10 tu: harpoon bladder dart, sea otter (seal, porpoise) (84–5)
11 tu: toggle-headed beluga harpoon ♯1 (85); toggle-headed beluga (sea lion) harpoon ♯ 2 (83–5)
22 tu: arrow total: bird (small game), 4 tu, 1 tu$A$; seal (duck), used in water, 5 tu, 1 tu$A$; big game, 6 tu, 1 tu$A$; arrow dart, used in water, 7 tu (88–9)

Tended facilities

Simple

2 tu: fish sweep (100)
5 tu: dip net, 3 tu$A$ (100–1)
10 tu: burbot fishhook assembly (29, 101)

Untended facilities

Simple

1 tu: octopus trench dug in sand (30)
4 tu: bird snare (94)
5 tu: salmon pen trap, used with weir (99)
8 tu: salmon weir, used with pen trap (basket trap) (71, 99)
12 tu: halibut hook set (29, 101)
15 tu: salmon pole trap, used with weir, 1 tu$A$ (99–100)

Complex

6 tu: bear snare (94); tossing-pole hare snare (92)
7 tu: common deadfall (96)
8 tu: grouse deadfall (98); tossing-pole snare, lynx (river otter) (92)

9 tu: bear deadfall (96–8)
10 tu: marmot deadfall (95)
12 tu: fox torque trap (98; Nelson, 1899, 122–3)

	Subsistants	Technounits	Average
Foraging total	40	224	5.6

33 *Copper Eskimos*

Numbers in parentheses refer to pages in Jenness (1946) unless otherwise noted.

Instruments

Simple

1 tu: stone, kill fish, used with leisters N (Jenness, 1922, 156)
4 tu: seal-killing ice scoop (seal stabbed in eye with pointed scoop handle) (119)
5 tu: ice pick, fishing (113–4)
6 tu: char snag (112–3)

Weapons

Simple

1 tu: missile stone, birds N (Jenness, 1922, 124)
4 tu: multibarbed leister, char at weir (111); caribou spear (135)
9 tu: 2-pronged leister, char (trout) at weir (111)

Complex

9 tu: composite sinew-backed bow (also held above head with stick as caribou lure) (122–5)
11 tu: arrow total: antler point, 4 tu; copper point, 7 tu (125–6)
15 tu: toggle-headed sealing harpoon (115–6)

Tended facilities

Simple

1 tu: walking stick held above head with bow to look like caribou antlers, lure caribou, killed with bow & arrow (Jenness, 1922, 146); pit blind for caribou, used with bow & arrow (Jenness, 1922, 124, 148; 105); hand-held snare, squirrel (Jenness, 1922, 124, 152)

  2 tu: caribou guide (Jenness, 1922, 149)

  4 tu: caribou frightening board, 3 tu, & beating sticks, 1 tu (Jenness, 1922, 149; 128); fish weirs, 2 tu, & dam, 2 tu, used with leister (Jenness, 1922, 155–6); fish lure, used with leister for tomcod (107–10)

  7 tu: tomcod fishhook assembly (105–7)

12 tu: trout (char) fishhook assembly, 1 tu*A* (105–7)

Untended facilities

  Simple

    2 tu: bird (squirrel) snare (Jenness, 1922, 152)

    3 tu: gorgelike form, trout (char) (Jenness, 1922, 155; 110)

    6 tu: caribou pitfall (Jenness, 1922, 151)

  Complex

    6 tu: fox deadfall (Jenness, 1922, 151)

	Subsistants	Technounits	Average
Foraging total	27	122	4.5

34 *Iglulik*

Numbers in parentheses refer to pages in Mathiassen (1928) unless noted otherwise.

Instruments

  Simple

    1 tu: one-piece *A* wood seal club (45, 46)

    3 tu: ice pick, fishing (sealing): iron point + wood shaft + point-shaft binder *A* (68)

    4 tu: snag hook, young seal, used with ice pick: iron hook + wood shaft + sinew, hook-shaft binder + sealskin handle (42, 44, 45)

Weapons

  Simple

    1 tu: stick, kill geese at stone enclosure N (66); stone missile, small animals (birds) N (64)

    3 tu: char snag: iron hook + wood shaft + brass, hook-shaft mounting (70–1)

4 tu: bear-killing knife: iron blade + wood handle + iron, blade-handle reinforcement strip + iron, blade-handle rivets (62, 154)

5 tu: caribou (bear) spear: iron blade + antler foreshaft + iron, blade-foreshaft rivets + wood shaft + sinew, foreshaft-shaft binder (59, 62)

10 tu: 2-pronged leister, char: antler side prongs + iron barbs inserted in prongs + sinew, prong-barb binders + center prong + wood shaft segments + pegs *A* to join shaft segments + shaft segment lashings + iron, side prong-shaft rivets + sinew, center prong-shaft binder + sinew, side prong-shaft binder (67, 70)

Complex

2 tu: bird dart throwing-board: wood body + iron, dart receiving peg (65)

3 tu: bird sling & missile: skin pocket + sling thongs; + missile (65)

7 tu: bird dart, used with throwing-board: bone end points + wood shaft segments + baleen, shaft segment binders + point-shaft binder + ivory, midshaft side prongs + prong-shaft binders + ivory, throwing-board receiving ferrule (64–5)

8 tu: composite sinew-backed bow: antler shaft segments + antler, shaft joint reinforcement pieces + sinew, shaft segment-reinforcement piece binders + sinew backing + sinew, backing binder + sealskin wedged beneath sinew backing + copper plate, shaft joint reinforcement piece + sinew bowstring (55); walrus lance: iron blade + ivory foreshaft + blade-foreshaft rivet + ivory socketpiece + wood shaft + thong, foreshaft-shaft binder + finger rest + rest-shaft binder (47–8; Boas, 1888, 494–6)

12 tu: toggle-headed bladder harpoon, seals hunted from kayak: iron blade + ivory head + ivory foreshaft + head-foreshaft-shaft line + wood peg to hold line on shaft + wood shaft + baleen, shaft reinforcement strip + bone, bladder inflation nozzle + nozzle-shaft binder + bone nozzle plug + bladder + bladder-nozzle binder *A* (46)

13 tu: toggle-headed ice hunting harpoon, walrus: iron blade + antler head + iron, blade-head rivet *A* + thong, head-hand line + ivory foreshaft $\sharp$ 1 + ivory foreshaft $\sharp$2 + wood shaft + thong binder of foreshafts to shaft + sinew, foreshaft $\sharp$2-shaft binder + finger rest + rest-shaft binder + bone ice pick + shaft-ice pick binder (47)

17 tu: toggle-headed ice hunting harpoon, seals: metal, blade-head combination + sealskin line + sealskin line tension strap + ivory, line buckle + ivory, coiled line buckle + ivory stop to hold line to

shaft when seal is harpooned + long iron foreshaft + antler hand-grip at shaft butt + wood shaft lashed to side of foreshaft + ivory finger rest + rest-shaft binder + sinew, shaft-foreshaft binders + wood wedges to tighten shaft-foreshaft binders + sealskin thong loop for harpoon line + sinew, thong loop-shaft binder + iron peg to receive tension strap + brass band to hold peg to foreshaft (37–40)

22 tu: arrow total (56–7, 61): caribou ♯1, 3 tu: iron point + wood shaft + sinew, point-shaft binder A; caribou ♯2, 5 tu: antler point + wood shaft + sinew, point-shaft binder + feather vanes + sinew, shaft-vane binder; caribou ♯3, 7 tu: iron point + antler foreshaft + iron, point-foreshaft rivet + wood shaft + sinew, foreshaft-shaft binder + feather vanes + sinew, shaft-vane binder; musk-ox, 7 tu: stone point + antler foreshaft + skin, foreshaft wrap + wood shaft + sinew, foreshaft-skin-shaft binder + feather vanes + sinew, vane-shaft binder A

26 tu: toggle-headed narwhal harpoon, sealskin float and drag anchor, used from kayak: iron blade + antler head + iron, blade-head rivet A + ivory foreshaft + ivory socketpiece + wood shaft + socketpiece-shaft rivets + thong, foreshaft-shaft binder + thong, harpoon line + ivory finger rest + rest-shaft binder + copper, line-tension peg + harpoon line swivel body + swivel stem + sealskin float + sinew, skin hole stitching A + line attachment toggle + sinew, toggle-float binder + bone inflation nozzle + nozzle-float binder + wood nozzle plug + wood drag anchor frame + frame binders + sealskin anchor cover + thong, frame-skin binder + thong, drag-harpoon line (50–2)

Tended facilities

Simple

1 tu: caribou guide, rows of piled-up stones, used with spears (59–60); goose enclosure of stones, used with sticks as clubs (66); fish weir of stones, used with leisters (70)

2 tu: fish snare: baleen noose + stick handle (70)

3 tu: baited gull snowhouse blind: snow walls + snow roof with opening at top + meat as bait placed on roof (66)

6 tu: char lure, used with leister: wood rod + sinew line + brass sinker + ivory, fish-shaped lure + caribou teeth + sinew, lure-tooth attachment line (67–8); bird pole net: wood net frame + frame binder A

+ netting + net-frame binder + handle + handle-net frame binder *A* (65)

7 tu: fishhook assembly: iron hook + ivory shank + wood, hook-shank peg binder + sinew, hook-shank binder + sinew line + wood reel + salmon skin bait (68–9)

Untended facilities

Simple

2 tu: hare snare: baleen noose + anchor *A* (64)

3 tu: bird snare line: noose attachment line + baleen nooses tied to line + stone, noose line anchor (65); blood glass, wolf: broken bottle + snow cover + blood as bait (63)

4 tu: wolf pitfall: hole in top of snowbank + thin snow slab cover + bait on cover + snow wall surrounding pit (63)

5 tu: gull hook: wood shank + bone barb set in shank + blubber bait over hook + hook line + stone anchor (65–6)

6 tu: blood knife, wolf: iron blade + wood handle + musk-ox horn handle reinforcement + iron, blade-handle-reinforcement rivets + snow over blade + blood bait (63, 120); fox ice slip pit trap: stone, cone-shaped chamber + stone slab side opening + stone slab roof + diagonal stone on roof with opening to interior + ice as slippery cover on diagonal stone + bait inside chamber (62)

7 tu: baited snowhouse wolf trap with impaling knife: snowhouse walls + snow roof + bait on roof + 4 tu*A* knife as impaler (63)

Complex

3 tu: spring bait, wolf: baleen strip rolled up + sinew, baleen binder + blubber bait cover (63)

4 tu: fox deadfall: ice fall slab + stick, slab support + bait + slab-bait trigger cord (62)

5 tu: fox (wolf) fall trap: stone passage + flat fall stone + bait + fall stone-bait cord + stone trigger mechanism on trap top (62–3)

	Subsistants	Technounits	Average
Foraging total	42	225	5.4

35   *Tareumiut*

Numbers in parentheses refer to pages in Murdoch (1892) unless otherwise noted.

Instrument

Simple

3 tu: ice pick, set seal net (fish through ice) (307–8; Ray, 1885, 79)

Weapons

Simple

3 tu: caribou spear (whale lance) (240–4); hunting knife (152–3)
4 tu: bear spear (242)
7 tu: 2-pronged leister (286)

Complex

2 tu: sealing dart (bird dart) throwing-board (217–8)
4 tu: bird bolas, used with pit blind and guide posts (244–5)
5 tu: bird dart, used with throwing-board (211); small seal harpoon dart, used with throwing-board (214–6)
6 tu: sinew-backed bow (196–7)
12 tu: toggle-headed ice hunting harpoon, used at seal breathing holes (at cracks in ice) (233–4)
16 tu: toggle-headed ice hunting sealing harpoon, used at edge of ice (231)
17 tu: toggle-headed whaling harpoon and floats (211, 235–6, 246–7)
21 tu: toggle-headed harpoon and float, bearded seals (walrus) from kayak (218–35, 246–7)
28 tu: arrow total: bear #1, 8 tu; bear #2, 5 tu; caribou, 5 tu; large bird, 5 tu; small bird, 5 tu (201–7)

Tended facilities

Simple

1 tu: caribou guide stakes, used with weapons (265); pit blind for ducks, used with duck guide posts (277–8); duck guide posts, used with pit blind and weapons (277–8)
4 tu: caribou pitfall (266, 268); scratcher, lure seal (253–4, 270); seal rattle lure (254)
6 tu: salmon (whitefish) fishhook assembly (280); tomcod fishhook

assembly (278–9); seal net, set beneath ice, used with scratcher and rattle seal lures, 2 tu*A* (250–2, 270–1; Ray, 1885, 40)

8 tu: burbot fishhook assembly (281–2)

Untended facilities

Simple

2 tu: bird snare (260)
4 tu: funnel-shaped net, fish trap, 2 tu*A* (285); gull gorge (260)
8 tu: gill net, 6 tu*A* (284–5; Ray, 1885, 40)

Complex

3 tu: spring bait, wolf (259)
7 tu: fox deadfall, 2 tu*A* (260)

	Subsistants	Technounits	Average
Foraging total	35	205	5.9

36 *Angmagsalik*

Numbers in parentheses refer to pages in Thalbitzer (1914).

Instruments

Simple

2 tu: stiletto, kill wounded seals (453)
3 tu: stiletto, kill wounded narwhal (47, 453)
6 tu: mussel scoop (467)
7 tu: capelin scoop (54, Fig. 37)

Weapons

Simple

1 tu: missile stone, ptarmigan N (407)
3 tu: multibarbed leister, sea-scorpion (salmon, seaweed) (439)
5 tu: 2-pronged leister, salmon at weirs (54, 439)

Complex

3 tu: sling, 2 tu, & stone missile, 1 tu (470)
5 tu: 2-headed toggle salmon harpoon #1, used with lure at hole in ice (438–9)

7 tu: toggle-headed sealing harpoon, used at breathing hole (419–20); lance, used from kayak with throwing-board (418–9); bird dart, used from kayak with throwing-board (436–7)

8 tu: 2-headed toggle salmon harpoon ♯2, used with lure at hole in ice (54, 438–9)

9 tu: lance, bears on ice (418–9)

10 tu: toggle-headed sealing harpoon, used at breathing holes in the spring (422–3)

11 tu: harpoon bladder dart for seals (birds, fish), used with throwing-board from kayak (434-6); throwing-board total: toggle-headed "knob" harpoon (lance) form, 3 tu; toggle-headed "feather" harpoon (bladder dart, bird dart) form, 8 tu (439–45)

14 tu: toggle-headed harpoon, "peep" sealing on ice (50–1, 400–1, 422–3)

25 tu: sealing ("knob") harpoon and sealskin float, used with throwing-board from kayak (46–8, 409–17, 454–7); sealing ("feather") harpoon and sealskin float, used with throwing-board from kayak, 1 tuA (46–8, 409–17; 454–7)

Tended facilities

Simple

1 tu: bloody meat, shark lure (53); stone weir, salmon (54, 407); wood whistle, decoy ptarmigan (470); oil poured on water to prevent swans from flying, killed with harpoons (56)

2 tu: ptarmigan pole snare (55)

3 tu: baited gull (raven) snowhouse blind (406–7); blubber, shark lure, 1 tuA (53)

4 tu: fish lure, used with leisters (464–5); gull gorge, used in water (55–6, 407, 469)

Untended facilities

Simple

6 tu: gull snare, used in water (56, 469)

Complex

7 tu: fall door trap, fox (55, 406)

	Subsistants	Technounits	Average
Foraging total	33	202	6.1

BIBLIOGRAPHY

Albrecht, F. W. *The Natural Food Supply of the Australian Aborigines.* Aborigines' Friends' Association.

Amber, John T., ed. *Gun Digest,* 20th ed. Chicago: Gun Digest, 1965.

———., ed. *Gun Digest Treasury,* 4th ed. Chicago: Follett, 1972.

Balfour, Henry. *The Natural History of the Musical Bow.* Oxford: Clarendon, 1899.

Barnett, H. G. *Innovation.* New York: McGraw-Hill, 1953.

Barrett, S. A. "The Material Culture of the Klamath Lake and Modoc Indians of Northeastern California and Southern Oregon." *University of California Publications in American Archaeology and Ethnology,* Vol. 5, no. 4, 1910.

Basedow, Herbert. "Notes on the Natives of Bathurst Island, North Australia." *Journal of the Royal Anthropological Institute of Great Britain and Ireland,* **43**, 291–323 (1913).

Beaglehole, Ernest. "Hopi Hunting and Hunting Ritual." *Yale University Publications in Anthropology,* No. 4, 1936.

———, and Pearl Beaglehole. "Ethnology of Pukapuka." *Bernice P. Bishop Museum Bulletin,* 150, 1938.

Beatty, Harry. "A Note on the Behavior of the Chimpanzee." *Journal of Mammalogy,* **32**, 118 (1951).

Binford, Lewis R. "Archeological Perspectives." In Sally R. Binford and Lewis R. Binford, eds., *New Perspectives in Archeology.* Chicago: Aldine, 1968. Pp. 5–32.

Birdsell, J. B. *Human Evolution.* Chicago: Rand McNally, 1972.

Birket-Smith, Kaj. "The Caribou Eskimos." *Report of the Fifth Thule Expedition 1921–4,* Vol. 5, no. 1, 1929.

Bleek, Dorothea F. *The Naron*. Cambridge: Cambridge University Press, 1928.

Boas, Franz. "The Central Eskimo." *Bureau of Ethnology Sixth Annual Report*, 1888. Pp. 399–669.

———. "The Limitations of the Comparative Method of Anthropology." *Science*, n.s., **4**, 901–908 (1896).

Bock, Philip K. *Modern Cultural Anthropology*. New York: Knopf, 1969.

Bordes, François. *The Old Stone Age*. New York: McGraw-Hill, 1968.

Boswell, James. *Boswell's Life of Johnson*. George B. Hill, ed. Oxford: Clarendon, 1887.

Brendler, R. A., and Robert C. Rock. *Cost and Practices for Row Crops in Ventura County*. Ventura, California: Agricultural Extension, University of California, 1973.

Brinton, Daniel G. *Races and Peoples*. New York: N. D. C. Hodges, 1890.

Burchfield, R. W., ed. *A Supplement to the Oxford English Dictionary*. Oxford: Clarendon, 1972.

Campbell, Bernard G. *Human Evolution*. Chicago: Aldine, 1966.

Carneiro, Robert L. "Classical Evolution." In Raoul and Frada Naroll, eds., *Main Currents in Cultural Anthropology*. Englewood Cliffs, New Jersey: Prentice-Hall, 1973. Pp. 57–121.

Carpenter, C. R. "Behavior of Red Spider Monkeys in Panama." *Journal of Mammalogy*, **16**, 171–180 (1935).

Champlain, Samuel de. *The Works of Samuel de Champlain*. Vol. 3. H. H. Langton and W. F. Ganong, trans. Toronto: Champlain Society, 1929.

Chard, Chester S. *Man in Prehistory*, 2nd ed. New York: McGraw-Hill, 1975.

Chewings, Charles. *Back in the Stone Age*. Sydney: Angus & Robertson, 1936.

Chisholm, A. H. "The Use by Birds of 'Tools' or 'Instruments'." *Ibis*, **96**, 380–383 (1954).

Clark, Grahame. *The Stone Age Hunters*. New York: McGraw-Hill, 1971.

———, and Stuart Piggott. *Prehistoric Societies*. London: Penguin, 1970.

Clark, J. G. D. "The Development of Fishing in Prehistoric Europe." *Antiquaries Journal*, **28**, 46–85 (1948).

Clark, J. Desmond. *The Prehistory of Africa*. New York: Praeger, 1970.

Clarke, David L. *Analytical Archaeology*. London: Methuen, 1968.

Coleridge, Henry N., ed. *The Literary Remains of Samuel Taylor Coleridge*. Vol. 3. London: William Pickering, 1838.

Coleridge, Samuel T. "Selection from Mr Coleridge's Literary Correspondence." *Blackwood's Edinburgh Magazine*, **10**, 243–262 (1821).

Damas, David, ed. "Contributions to Anthropology: Ecological Essays." *National Museums of Canada Bulletin*, 230, 1969.

Daniel, Glyn E. *A Hundred Years of Archaeology*. London: Gerald Duckworth, 1950.

Deetz, James. *Invitation to Archaeology*. Garden City, New York: Natural History Press, 1967.

Densmore, Frances. "Chippewa Customs." *Bureau of American Ethnology Bulletin*, 86, 1929.

———. "Uses of Plants by the Chippewa Indians." *Forty-fourth Annual Report of the Bureau of American Ethnology*, 1928. Pp. 275–397.

Dixon, Roland B. "The Northern Maidu." *Bulletin American Museum of Natural History*, Vol. 17, pt. 3, 1905.

Dolhinow, Phyllis Jay, and Naomi Bishop. "The Development of Motor Skills and Social Relationships among Primates through Play." In Phyllis Dolhinow, ed., *Primate Patterns*. New York: Holt, Rinehart & Winston, 1972. Pp. 312–337.

Dolukhanov, P. M., et al. "Radiocarbon Dates of the Institute of Archaeology II." *Radiocarbon*, **12**, 130–155 (1970).

Driver, Harold E. "The Contribution of A. L. Kroeber to Culture Area Theory and Practice." *Indiana University Publications in Anthropology and Linguistics Memoir*, No. 18, 1962.

——. "Statistical Studies of Continuous Geographical Distributions." In Raoul Naroll and Ronald Cohen, eds., *A Handbook of Method in Cultural Anthropology*. Garden City, New York: Natural History Press, 1970. Pp. 620–639.

Dunnell, Robert C. *Systematics in Prehistory*. New York: Free Press, 1971.

Elmendorf, W. W. "The Structure of Twana Culture." *Research Studies, Washington State University*, Vol. 28, no. 3, 1960.

Ember, Carol R., and Melvin Ember. *Anthropology*. New York: Appleton-Century-Crofts, 1973.

Fejos, Paul. "Ethnography of the Yagua." *Viking Fund Publications in Anthropology*, No. 1, 1943.

Fisher, Edna M. "Habits of the Southern Sea Otter." *Journal of Mammalogy*, **20**, 21–36 (1939).

Forbes, David. "On the Aymara Indians of Bolivia and Peru." *Journal of the Ethnological Society of London*, n.s., **2**, 193–305 (1870).

Ford, Clellan S. "A Sample Comparative Analysis of Material Culture." In George P. Murdock, ed., *Studies in the Science of Society*. Freeport, New York: Books for Libraries Press, 1937. Pp. 225–246.

Forde, C. Daryll. "Ethnography of the Yuma Indians." *University of California Publications in American Archaeology and Ethnology*, Vol. 28, no. 4, 1931a.

——. *Habitat, Economy and Society*. London, Methuen, 1934.

——. "Hopi Agriculture and Land Ownership." *Journal of the Royal Anthropological Institute of Great Britain and Ireland*, **61**, 357–405 (1931b).

Fürer-Haimendorf, Christoph von. "The Chenchus." In *The Aboriginal Tribes of Hyderabad*, Vol. 1. London: Macmillan London and Basingstoke, 1943.

Goodale, Jane C. " 'Alonga Bush' A Tiwi Hunt." *University Museum Bulletin*, Vol. 21, no. 3, 1957. Pp. 3–35.

——. Correspondence. 1975.

——. *Tiwi Wives*. Seattle: University of Washington Press, 1971.

Goodall, Jane. "Chimpanzees of the Gombe Stream Reserve." In Irven DeVore, ed., *Primate Behavior*. New York: Holt, Rinehart & Winston, 1965. Pp. 425–473.

Gorer, Geoffrey. *Himalayan Village*. London: Michael Joseph, 1938.

Gould, Richard A. *Yiwara*. New York: Charles Scribner's Sons, 1969.

Gouldner, Alvin W., and Richard A. Peterson. *Notes on Technology and the Moral Order*. Indianapolis: Bobbs-Merrill, 1962.

Gusinde, Martin. *The Yamana*. 5 vols. New Haven, Conn.: Human Relations Area Files, 1961.

Haddon, Alfred C. *Evolution in Art*. London: Walter Scott, 1895.

——. *History of Anthropology*. London: Watts, 1910.

Hall, K. R. L., and George B. Schaller. "Tool-Using Behavior of the California Sea Otter." *Journal of Mammalogy*, **45**, 287–298 (1964).

Harner, Michael J. *The Jivaro*. Garden City, New York: Anchor Press, 1972.

Harris, Marvin. *Culture, People, Nature*. New York: Thomas Y. Crowell, 1975.

Harrison, H. S. "Opportunism and the Factors of Invention." *American Anthropologist*, n.s., **32**, 106–125 (1930).

Hart, C. W. M., and Arnold R. Pilling. *The Tiwi of North Australia*. New York: Henry Holt, 1960.

Heidenreich, Conrad. *Huronia*. Ottawa: McClelland and Stewart, 1971.

Hermansen, Victor. "C. J. Thomsen and the Founding of the Ethnographical Museum." Ethnographical Studies, *Nationalmuseets Skrifter, Etnografisk Raekke*, **1**, 11–27 (1941).

Hindwood, K. A. "The Use of Flower Petals in Courtship Display." *Emu*, **47**, 389–391 (1948).

Hobhouse, L. T., G. C. Wheeler, and M. Ginsberg. *The Material Culture and Social Institutions of the Simpler Peoples*. London: Routledge & Kegan Paul, 1965 (original edition, 1915).

Hobley, C. W. *Ethnology of A-Kamba and other East African Tribes*. Cambridge: Cambridge University Press, 1910.

Holmberg, Allan R. "Nomads of the Long Bow." *Smithsonian Institution Institute of Social Anthropology Publication*, No. 10, 1950.

Honigmann, John J. *The World of Man*. New York: Harper & Row, 1959.

Hough, Water. "Environmental Interrelations in Arizona." *American Anthropologist*, **11**, 133–155 (1898).

———. "The Hopi Indian Collection in the United States National Museum." *Proceedings of the United States National Museum*, Vol. 54, 1919. Pp. 235–296.

Hutton, J. H. "The Place of Material Culture in the Study of Anthropology." *Journal of the Royal Anthropological Institute of Great Britain and Ireland*, **74**, 1–6 (1944).

———. *The Sema Nagas*. Bombay: Oxford University Press, 1968.

Isaac, Glynn L., et al. "Archeological Traces of Early Hominid Activities, East of Lake Rudolf, Kenya." *Science*, **173**, 1129–1134 (1971).

Jenness, Diamond. "The Life of the Copper Eskimos." *Report of the Canadian Arctic Expedition, 1913–18*, Vol. 12, 1922.

———. "Material Culture of the Copper Eskimo." *Report of the Canadian Arctic Expedition, 1913–18*, Vol. 16, 1946.

Jolly, Clifford J. "The Seed-Eaters: A New Model of Hominid Differentiation Based on a Baboon Analogy." *Man*, n.s., **5**, 5–26 (1970).

Jones, Rhys. "The Demography of Hunters and Farmers in Tasmania." In D. J. Mulvaney and J. Golson, eds., *Aboriginal Man and Environment in Australia*. Canberra: Australian National University Press, 1971. Pp. 271–287.

Karsten, Rafael. "The Head-Hunters of Western Amazonas." *Commentationes Humanarum Litterarum*, Vol. 7, 1935.

Kaston, B. J. "Some Little Known Aspects of Spider Behavior." *American Midland Naturalist*, **73**, 336–356 (1965).

Kelly, Isabel T. "Ethnography of the Surprise Valley Paiute." *University of California Publications in American Archaeology and Ethnology*, Vol. 31, no. 3, 1932.

Kluckhohn, Clyde, and William H. Kelly. "The Concept of Culture." In Ralph Linton, ed., *The Science of Man in the World Crisis*. New York: Columbia University Press, 1945, Pp. 78–106.

Kortlandt, Adriaan. "Experimentation with Chimpanzees in the Wild." In D. Starck et al., eds., *Progress in Primatology*. Stuttgart: Gustav Fischer Verlag, 1967. Pp. 208–224.

———, and M. Kooij. "Protohominid Behaviour in Primates." In *The Primates, Symposia of the Zoological Society of London*, No. 10, 1963. Pp. 61–88.

Krantz, Grover S. "Brain Size and Hunting Ability in Earliest Man." In Ashley Montagu, ed., *The Origin & Evolution of Man*. New York: Thomas Y. Crowell, 1973. Pp. 161–164.

Kroeber, Alfred L. "Culture Element Distributions: XI, Tribes Surveyed." *Anthropological Records*, **1** (7), 435–440 (1939).

———. "Handbook of the Indians of California." *Bureau of American Ethnology Bulletin*, 78, 1925.

———, ed. "Walapai Ethnography." *American Anthropological Association Memoir*, No. 42, 1935.

———, and Clyde Kluckhohn. *Culture*. New York: Random House, 1963.

La Barre, Weston. "The Aymara Indians of the Lake Titicaca Plateau, Bolivia." *American Anthropological Association Memoir*, No. 68, 1948.

Lack, David. *Darwin's Finches*. New York: Harper, 1961.

Laguna, Frederica de. "Under Mount Saint Elias." *Smithsonian Contributions to Anthropology*, Vol. 7, 1972.

Lane Fox, Augustus H. *The Evolution of Culture*. J. L. Myres, ed. Oxford: Clarendon, 1906.

———. "On the Improvement of the Rifle, as a Weapon for General Use." *Journal of the Royal United Service Institution*, **2**, 453–493 (1858).

———. "On the Principles of Classification Adopted in the Arrangement of His Anthropological Collection." *Journal of the Anthropological Institute of Great Britain and Ireland*, **4**, 293–308 (1875).

Leakey, R. E. F. "Fauna and Artefacts from a New Plio-Pleistocene Locality near Lake Rudolf in Kenya." *Nature*, **226**, 223–224 (1970).

LeBar, Frank M. "The Material Culture of Truk." *Yale University Publications in Anthropology*, No. 68, 1964.

Lee, Richard B. "Subsistence Ecology of !Kung Bushmen." Unpublished dissertation. Berkeley: University of California, 1966.

———. "What Hunters Do for a Living." In Richard B. Lee and Irven DeVore, eds., *Man the Hunter*. Chicago: Aldine, 1968. Pp. 30–48.

Lindblom, Gerhard. "The Akamba." *Archives D'Études Orientales*, Vol. 17, 1920,

Linton, Ralph. "The Tanala." *Field Museum of Natural History, Anthropological Series*, Vol. 22, 1933.

Lumley, Henry de. "A Paleolithic Camp at Nice." *Scientific American*, **220**, 42–50 (1969).

Lustig-Arecco, Vera. *Technology: Strategies for Survival*. New York: Holt, Rinehart & Winston, 1975.

Man, Edward H. "On the Aboriginal Inhabitants of the Andaman Islands." *Journal of the Anthropological Institute of Great Britain and Ireland*, **12**, 69–116, 117–175, 327–434 (1883).

Mason, Otis T. *The Origins of Invention*. London: Walter Scott, 1895.

Mathiassen, Therkel. "Material Culture of the Iglulik Eskimos." *Report of the Fifth Thule Expedition 1921–4*, Vol. 6, no. 1, 1928.

McGee, W J. 'The Seri Indians." *Seventeenth Annual Report of the Bureau of American Ethnology*, Part 1, 1898. Pp. 1–344.

McGuire, E. Patrick. "The High Cost of Recalls." In *The New York Times*, "Business and Finance," March 30, 1975.

McKennan, Robert A. "The Upper Tanana Indians." *Yale University Publications in Anthropology*, No. 55, 1959.

Means, Philip A. *Ancient Civilizations of the Andes*. New York: Charles Scribner's Sons, 1931.

Merfield, Fred G., and Harry Miller. *Gorillas Were My Neighbours*. London: Longmans, Green, 1956.

Michael, Henry N. "The Neolithic Age in Eastern Siberia." *Transactions of the American Philosophical Society*, n.s. Vol. 48, pt. 2, 1958.

Morgan, Lewis H. *Ancient Society*. New York: Henry Holt, 1877.

Morris, John. *Living with Lepchas*. London: William Heinemann, 1938.

Murdoch, John. "Ethnological Results of the Point Barrow Expedition." *Ninth Annual Report of the Bureau of Ethnology*, 1892. Pp. 3–441.

Murdock, George P. *Ethnographic Atlas*. Pittsburgh: University of Pittsburgh Press, 1967.

Naroll, Raoul, and Frada Naroll, eds. *Main Currents in Cultural Anthropology*. Englewood Cliffs, New Jersey: Prentice-Hall, 1973.

———, and Ronald Cohen, eds. *A Handbook of Method in Cultural Anthropology*. Garden City. New York: Natural History Press, 1970.

Nebesky-Wojkowitz, Rene de. "Hunting and Fishing among the Lepchas." *Ethnos*, **18**, 21–31 (1953).

Nelson, Edward W. "The Eskimo about Bering Strait." *Eighteenth Annual Report of the Bureau of American Ethnology*, Part 1, 1899.

Nelson, N. C. "The Origin and Development of Material Culture." *Sigma XI Quarterly*, **20**, 102–123 (1932).

Notes and Queries on Anthropology. London: Routledge and Kegan Paul, 1951.

Oakley, Kenneth P. "Skill as a Human Possession." In Charles Singer et al., eds., *A History of Technology*, Vol. 1. London: Oxford University Press, 1954. Pp. 1–37.

Okladnikov, A. P. *Yakutia*. Henry N. Michael, ed. Montreal: McGill–Queen's University Press, 1970.

Osgood, Cornelius. "Culture: Its Empirical and Non-empirical Character." *Southwestern Journal of Anthropology*, **7**, 202–214 (1951).

———. "The Ethnography of the Tanaina." *Yale University Publications in Anthropology*, No. 16, 1937 (reprint, New Haven: HRAF Press, 1966).

———. "Ingalik Material Culture." *Yale University Publications in Anthropology*, No. 22, 1940 (reprint, New Haven: HRAF Press, 1970).

———. "Ingalik Mental Culture." *Yale University Publications in Anthropology*, No. 56, 1959.

———. "Ingalik Social Culture." *Yale University Publications in Anthropology*, No. 53, 1958.

Oswalt, Wendell H. *Habitat and Technology*. New York: Holt, Rinehart & Winston, 1973.

Parts Catalog, John Deere, Planter, Vegetable-33. 1969.

Parts Catalog, John Deere, 7700 Combine. 1973.

Penniman, T. K. *A Hundred Years of Anthropology.* London: Gerald Duckworth, 1965.

Pitt-Rivers, Augustus H. Lane-Fox. *See* Lane Fox, Augustus H.

Pospisil, Leopold. Correspondence. 1974, 1975.

———. "Kapauku Papuan Economy." *Yale University Publications in Anthropology,* No. 67, 1963 (reprint, New Haven: HRAF Press, 1972).

Radcliffe-Brown, Alfred R. *The Andaman Islanders.* Glencoe, Ill.: Free Press, 1948 (reprint from Cambridge: Cambridge University Press, 1933).

Rasmussen, Knud. "Intellectual Culture of the Iglulik Eskimos." *Report of the Fifth Thule Expedition 1921–4,* Vol. 7, no. 1, 1929.

Ratzel, Friedrich. *The History of Mankind.* 3 vols. New York: Macmillan, 1896.

Ray, P. H. "Ethnographic Sketch of the Natives of Point Barrow." *Report of the International Polar Expedition to Point Barrow, Alaska,* 1885. Pp. 35–87.

Ray, Verne F. *Primitive Pragmatists.* Seattle: University of Washington Press, 1963.

Reynolds, Barrie. *The Material Culture of the Peoples of the Gwembe Valley.* Manchester, England: Manchester University Press, 1968.

Richardson, Miles, ed. *The Human Mirror.* Baton Rouge: Louisiana State University Press, 1974.

Robinson, George A. *Friendly Mission.* N. J. B. Plomley, ed. Kingsgrove, New South Wales: Tasmanian Historical Research Association, 1966.

Robinson, J. T. "Australopithecines, Culture and Phylogeny." *American Journal of Physical Anthropology,* **21**, 595–605 (1963).

Roth, Henry L. *The Aborigines of Tasmania.* London: Kegan Paul, Trench, Trübner, 1890.

Roth, Walter E. "Domestic Implements, Arts, and Manufactures." *North Queensland Ethnography Bulletin,* 7, 1904.

———. *Ethnological Studies among the North-West-Central Queensland Aborigines.* London: Queensland Agent-General's Office, 1897.

———. "Food: Its Search, Capture, and Preparation." *North Queensland Ethnography Bulletin,* 3, 1901.

Rowe, John H. "Inca Culture at the Time of the Spanish Conquest." *Handbook of South American Indians,* Vol. 2, *Bureau of American Ethnology Bulletin,* 143, 1946, Pp. 183–330.

Russell, Frank. "The Pima Indians." *Twenty-Sixth Annual Report of the Bureau of American Ethnology,* 1908. Pp. 3–389.

Ryden, Stig. *A Study of the Siriono Indians.* Göteborg, Sweden: The Humanistic Foundation of Sweden, 1941.

Sagard, Gabriel. *The Long Journey to the Country of the Hurons.* H. H. Langton, trans. Toronto: The Champlain Society, 1939.

Salpukas, Agis. "Wankel Engine." In *The New York Times,* "The Week in Review," September 3, 1972.

Sayce, R. U. *Primitive Arts and Crafts.* New York: Biblo and Tannen, 1965.

Schaller, George B. *The Mountain Gorilla.* Chicago: University of Chicago Press, 1963.

———. "The Orang-utan in Sarawak." *Zoologica,* **46**, 73–82 (1961).

Schapera, I. *The Khoisan Peoples of South Africa.* London: Routledge & Kegan Paul, 1951.

Scudder, Thayer. Correspondence, 1975.

———. *The Ecology of the Gwembe Tonga.* Manchester, England: Manchester University Press, 1962.

———. "Fishermen of the Zambezi." *Rhodes-Livingston Institute Journal,* **27**, 41–49 (1960).

Service Instruction Manual, TR 2, 3rd ed. Coventry, England: Service Division, Standard Motor Co., n.d.

Siiger, Halfdan. "The Lepchas." *Publications of the National Museum, Ethnographical Series,* Vol. 11, pt. 1, 1967.

Simons, Elwyn L. *Primate Evolution.* New York: Macmillan, 1972.

Simpson, John. "Observations on the Western Eskimo." In *Arctic Geography and Ethnology.* London: John Murray, 1875. Pp. 233–275.

Spencer, Baldwin. *Native Tribes of the Northern Territory of Australia.* London: Macmillan, 1914.

———, and Frank J. Gillen. *The Arunta.* 2 vols. London: Macmillan London and Basingstoke, 1927.

Spier, Leslie. "Havasupai Ethnography." *Anthropological Papers, American Museum of Natural History,* Vol. 29, 1928, Pp. 83–392.

———. "Klamath Ethnography." *University of California Publications in American Archaeology and Ethnology,* Vol. 30, 1930.

Spier, Robert F. G. *From the Hand of Man.* Boston: Houghton Mifflin, 1970.

———. *Material Culture and Technology.* Minneapolis: Burgess Publishing, 1973.

Stanhay (Ashford) *Ltd. S766. Spare Parts List and Illustrations.* n.d.

———. *S870. Spare Parts List and Illustrations.* n.d.

Starr, Chauncey, and Richard Rudman. "Parameters of Technological Growth." *Science,* **182**, 358–364 (1973).

Stephen, Alexander M. "Hopi Journal." *Columbia University Contributions to Anthropology,* Vol. 23, 2 pts., 1936.

Steward, Julian H. "Ethnography of the Owens Valley Paiute." *University of California Publications in American Archaeology and Ethnology,* Vol. 33, no. 3, 1933.

———. *Theory of Culture Change.* Urbana, Illinois: University of Illinois Press, 1955.

Stirling, E. C. "Anthropology." *Report on the Work of the Horn Scientific Expedition to Central Australia,* pt 4, 1896. Pp. 1–157.

Stirling, M. W. "Historical and Ethnographical Material on the Jivaro Indians." *Bureau of American Ethnology Bulletin,* 117, 1938.

Taylor, Walter W. "A Study of Archeology." *American Anthropological Association Memoir,* No. 69, 1948.

Thalbitzer, William, ed., "The Ammassalik Eskimo." Part 1. *Meddelelser om Grønland,* Vol. 39, 1914.

Tindale, Norman B. "Natives of Groote Eylandt and of the West Coast of the Gulf of Carpentaria." *Records of the South Australian Museum,* Vol. 3, 1925–1928. Pp. 61–132.

Titiev, Mischa. "Old Oraibi." *Papers of the Peabody Museum of American Archaeology and Ethnology,* Vol. 22, no. 1, 1944.

———. *The Science of Man.* New York: Holt, Rinehart & Winston, 1963.

Tooker, Elisabeth. "An Ethnography of the Huron Indians, 1615–1649." *Bureau of American Ethnology Bulletin,* 190, 1964.

Treistman, Judith M. *The Prehistory of China*. Garden City, New York: Doubleday, 1972.

Trigger, Bruce G. *The Huron*. New York: Holt, Rinehart & Winston, 1969.

Tschopik, Harry. "The Aymara." *Handbook of South American Indians*, Vol. 2, *Bureau of American Ethnology Bulletin*, 143, 1946. Pp. 501–573.

Tylor, Edward B. "On the Tasmanians as Representatives of Palaeolithic Man." *Journal of the Anthropological Institute of Great Britain and Ireland*, **23**, 141–152 (1894).

———. *Primitive Culture*. 2 vols. London: John Murray, 1871.

———. *Researches into the Early History of Mankind and the Development of Civilization*. London: John Murray, 1865.

van Lawick-Goodall, Jane. "The Behavior of Free-living Chimpanzees in the Gombe Stream Reserve." *Animal Behaviour Monographs*, Vol. 1, pt. 3, 1968a.

———. "Tool-using Bird: The Egyptian Vulture." *National Geographic*, **133**, 630–641 (1968b).

van Rippen, Bene. "Note on Some Bushman Implements." *American Anthropological Association Memoir*, 5, no. 3, 1918.

Ventura Planter, Model 'E.' J. L. Mitchell, Oxnard, California, n.d.

Voegelin, Erminie W. "Culture Element Distributions: XX, Northeast California." *Anthropological Records*, **7** (2), 47–251 (1942).

Wagner, Roy. *The Invention of Culture*. Englewood Cliffs, New Jersey: Prentice-Hall, 1975.

Washburn, Sherwood L., and C. S. Lancaster. "The Evolution of Hunting." In Sherwood L. Washburn and Phyllis C. Jay, eds., *Perspectives on Human Evolution*, 1. New York: Holt, Rinehart & Winston. 1968. Pp. 213–229.

Webster's Third New International Dictionary. Philip B. Gove, ed. Springfield, Mass.: G. & C. Merriam, 1961.

Wissler, Clark. "Psychological and Historical Interpretations for Culture." *Science*, n.s., **43**, 193–201 (1916).

Zierhut, Norman W. "Bone Breaking Activities of the Calling Lake Cree." *Alberta Anthropologist*, **1** (3), 33–36 (1967).

▲▲▲▲▲▲▲▲

AN
ANTHROPOLOGICAL
ANALYSIS
OF FOOD-GETTING
TECHNOLOGY

Augustus Henry Lane Fox Pitt-Rivers

(1827–1900)